BIRTHRIGHTS

Birthrights

WHAT EVERY PARENT SHOULD KNOW

ABOUT CHILDBIRTH

IN HOSPITALS

SALLY INCH

Foreword by the Boston Women's Health Book Collective

PANTHEON BOOKS
NEW YORK

First American Edition

Foreword copyright © 1984 by Random House, Inc.
Copyright © 1982, 1984 by Sally Inch.

All rights reserved under International and Pan-American Copyright Conventions. Published in the United States by Pantheon Books, a division of Random House, Inc., New York. Originally published in Great Britain in 1982 by Hutchinson & Co., Ltd.

Library of Congress Cataloging in Publication Data

Inch, Sally
  Birthrights: what every parent should know about
childbirth in hospitals.

  Includes bibliographical references and index.

  1. Childbirth   2. Labor (Obstetrics)   3. Hospitals,
Gynecologic and obstetric.   I. Title.
RG525.I45 1985   618.4   84-42667
ISBN 0-394-53685-1
ISBN 0-394-72568-9 (pbk.)

Manufactured in the United States of America

CONTENTS

For Jenny

FOREWORD

Ninety-eight percent of women in the United States give birth in hospitals, where they are faced with a bewildering array of procedures, technologies, and drugs, all of which have become a routine part of obstetrical practice. There are amniotomies and episiotomies, intravenous drips and fetal monitors. Believing these interventions to be a necessary part of childbirth, most parents-to-be not only lack information about them but often find it difficult even to ask questions about what is going on. Women, especially, have been made to feel both fearful and inadequate when confronted with modern technology.

Over the course of the past one hundred years, there has been a systematic substitution of surgical, chemical, and electronic techniques for every one of the natural processes of labor. As modern childbirth has moved from the home to the hospital and become increasingly "medicalized," many researchers have questioned the increasingly routine use of such interventions, many of which were originally intended only for emergency situations. Their studies have cast doubt on the safety of some procedures and challenged whether their routine use benefits the mother, the baby, and the whole process of labor. Yet the practitioners who might have been expected to make use of the results of this research have often ignored or denied them. At present, the rate of routine intervention continues to rise.

The strength and originality of *Birthrights* lie in the fact that Sally Inch brings together past and present research on this subject as no one else has yet done—and makes it accessible to us all. She has a knack for presenting the kind of information offered in medical journals and texts simply and clearly, combining it with commonsense observations about the actions and attitudes that enable women to feel most at ease during childbirth. Her tone is objective throughout, but her underlying passion for the truth and her respect for women are evident in her systematic presentation of medical and sociological findings and in her assurance that it is possible—indeed, necessary—to make hard facts about childbirth in hospitals available to everyone concerned.

We wish that *Birthrights* had been around when we were pregnant, for it is the best childbirth preparation one could have. Inch accurately reveals the current state of obstetrics and confirms what many women already know about obstetrical abuses, a knowledge often gained through their own difficult experiences with the medical establishment. Carefully describing each phase of labor, Inch presents the facts, figures, and studies that demonstrate how all interventions interfere with the delicate balance of natural labor; she notes the few instances when medical intervention may really be necessary—and the many when it can in fact be hazardous. Inch does not deny that some interventions may be necessary some of the time, but she shows that, most often, simply because the mother is in the hospital, they become inevitable. She exposes the prevailing medical ideology that is partly responsible: the "if it's there, use it" attitude, the view of childbirth as pathology, the general replacement of midwifery skills with manipulation and even coercion on the part of doctors, and the lack of respect for women and their babies. Moreover, as *Birthrights* shows, once interventions become routine, they set off complications like exploding firecrackers, each one incurring another intervention followed by another complication. Thus, after giving birth, a woman may be utterly convinced that "in my case" a certain drug or procedure was necessary or even indispensable to saving the baby's or her own life, when in fact the reason for its use was the practitioner's attitude, hospital routine, or just the existence of the intervention.

With this book as background, laypeople—and professionals
—can go on to seek additional information, update what they
already know, and work to change existing obstetrical practice
in their communities. Parents-to-be in particular must have access both to the facts about technology and the attitudes that
accompany its use in order to understand the exact nature of the
assembly-line situation almost every pregnant woman faces from
the moment she enters the obstetrical system. The hospitalization process, down to its most innocuous-seeming routines—
riding in a wheelchair from the lobby to the labor room, lying
only on her back, or getting hooked up to a monitor "just for
twenty minutes to see how you're doing," for example—moves
the pregnant woman inexorably toward more and more intervention. If she doesn't understand this in advance, it will be
difficult for her to express any doubts or refuse certain forms of
care once labor has begun.

The proliferation of drugs and technologies has certainly had
the effect of keeping us all passive and dependent, "in our
place." The majority of women watch their self-confidence being
eroded by contact with the medical system. In the past, women
were anxious about the danger of childbirth: they feared their
own or their babies' deaths; they dreaded the debilitating illnesses that sometimes followed labor and birth. But today, we
have less reason to fear than ever before: women in general are
much healthier than they used to be; maternal and infant mortality rates have greatly diminished; and we know so much about
what makes labor go well naturally. We also know that interventions are unnecessary for most of us most of the time. Yet,
ironically, obstetrics, the branch of medicine that deals with
childbirth, is a surgical specialty, oriented toward crises. Most
obstetricians depend profoundly on drugs and interventions
and have a great deal of authority; when they tell prospective
mothers directly and indirectly that some form of childbirth
technology will be necessary when the time comes, women often
have no other recourse than to "choose" it or submit to it.
Doctors succeed in tapping into a powerful combination of our

oldest fears—"What if something goes wrong?," "What if I can't stand the pain?"—and our particularly modern beliefs that technology equals progress and that the magic of obstetrical technology will guarantee a "better" or "perfect" baby. Too easily we become trapped in a contradiction from which there seems no comfortable escape: failure to use the available tools makes us feel that we are tempting fate, yet these drugs and technologies may be dangerous and can also make us feel defective, or incomplete, our bodies at fault. Whether or not anything has actually gone wrong, childbirth technology forces gratitude from us because we and everyone around us must believe that without our dependency on these tools, the birth could never have proceeded as well as it did. Everything conspires to make it difficult for us to feel justified in refusing interventions, to voice doubts about literally surrendering our bodies to current medical practice. We are effectively silenced.

Sally Inch won't allow this silence to continue. She does all she can to prepare parents for what they may encounter in the course of trying to wrest from the hospital situation a birth that is both personally satisfying and safe. She also describes a range of birthing alternatives. In addition, she shows us what we must do about a world in which we are increasingly dominated by rapid and uncontrolled technological developments: first understand, then evaluate, and finally speak out critically. By giving us the facts, *Birthrights* enables us to combat the charge that our opposition to many routine procedures is mere superstition, paranoia, or emotionalism. It helps us to define the limits of childbirth technology so that it can work for us without harming us. Above all, *Birthrights* confirms our conviction that once again it is we, ourselves who must do this work of warning and explaining, for neither those who have the power to introduce and use these tools nor those who stand to profit most from their use will do it for us.

Use this book in many ways. Treat it as a reference and learn about a specific procedure or drug. Read it straight through, a massive dose of demystification. Give it to your pregnant sisters, daughters, and friends. Send it to your obstetrician. Put copies in your local library. Take it as the basis for a self-help study group. This is a book for everyone involved in childbirth, parents and practitioners, lawyers and students, childbirth educators and health activists.

Jane Pincus and Norma Swenson,
for the Boston Women's Health Book Collective

INTRODUCTION

This book is written primarily for the expectant mother. It is intended to take her step by step through common obstetrical practices applicable to each stage of labor and delivery and to examine them critically in the light of available scientific research.

If changes are going to take place in the way in which women (and their babies) are treated before, during, and after delivery, the driving force must come from the "consumers." Attempts to change any system from within are often stifled at the outset, especially when vested interests are at stake; and the people most likely to be critical are also those who are most vulnerable in terms of their position in the hierarchy. Even when criticism comes from people at a higher level—for instance, from eminent professors—they are still able to affect the policy only of those directly below in the chain of command and can only point out to their colleagues what they are doing and why. They have no authority to make their peers change their practices.

When any procedure becomes part of an established routine, it becomes almost sacrilegious to ask why it is done, and junior staff run the risk of generating great ill-feeling by their inquiries, even when the practice may be totally mechanical and performed without thought for the needs of the individual mother. Even pinpointing the time when the procedure was first advocated may be quite difficult. Furthermore, not only are the findings of fellow obstetricians and pediatricians questioned when they do not suit the practice of individual doctors, but in some cases even research that is actually requested to support a course of action is ignored if the data happen to end up proving the opposite of what was intended.

The people who could make the most effective use of the results of such research are expectant parents. In a sense, they have far more power at their disposal than health workers, for if a particular course of action is unacceptable to them, they can simply refuse to subject themselves to it. Few people, however, are sufficiently convinced solely by their own instincts or feelings about what is right for them to be prepared to oppose the "we know better" attitude of many doctors. Lack of concrete facts to support their intuition in the face of such opposition has reduced many women in prenatal clinics to impotent fury or tears. The major function of this volume is to back up their arguments with the carefully considered and published work of obstetricians, sociologists, statisticians, pediatricians, and other researchers around the world.

This book begins by examining the assumptions behind the common view that all women should give birth in a hospital. It then goes on to look at how hospital routine alters the physiological patterns of all three stages of labor, and finally it considers the treatment of the newborn baby. One of the reasons that the thinking of the (still largely male) medical profession has had such a profound influence on the childbearing woman in America is that it has, for the most part, not been subject to the restraining and moderating influence of the midwife as she is perceived in Western Europe. The midwife as an independent practitioner is at least as important for what she does *not* do as for what she does during the course of a normal birth, and may be equally valuable by virtue of what she prevents others from doing. The more the midwife has been pushed out of her role as primary caretaker of the parturient woman, the more physiology has become pathology and the higher are the perinatal mortality statistics. While absolute proof of causality may be lacking, these associations are hard to refute. Norway, Denmark, Holland, and Sweden all rely on midwives to conduct normal labors, and these countries have the lowest perinatal mortality rates in the world. Until the midwife is reinstated in the United States, there will be few alternatives to conventional hospital delivery available to the majority of childbearing women, and American parents, even more than European ones, will be unsupported in the front line of any efforts to create the conditions for the sort of birth they want.

Concrete and specific information will provide some of that support. But having said this, it is important to remember that expectant parents, however well informed, still must use tact in questioning their birth attendants; in the final analysis, they also need to be able to trust them.

It is my hope in writing this book that such trust will spring increasingly from mutual understanding and respect for the views of all concerned, and from a continuing ability to share responsibility and to communicate throughout the whole of the pregnancy, the birth, and the postnatal period.

I am grateful to Annie Cowie, formerly of the Cairns Library, Oxford, for her efforts in obtaining much useful research material, and to Chloe Fisher both for the drawer in her filing cabinet and for her efforts as "runner."

In addition to the research work actually reported (and therefore listed in the References), I gratefully acknowledge the information, guidance, and encouragement given to me by Dr. Alistair MacLennan, Dr. Murray Enkin, Nicky Lean, and Sheila Kitzinger. My thanks are also due to my friends Helen and Keith Rose, who were patient sounding boards; to Eileen Frazer, Kate Newson, Jane Harrison, Alison Gee, Jerrilyn Meyer, Dorothea Lang, Katy Dawley, and Jeanne Warren for their help and advice; to Caradoc King for his enthusiasm and professional assistance; and to Alison Harris, who introduced him to me.

I am greatly indebted to my mother, Nora Cade, for her help and encouragement and for painstakingly deciphering, correcting, and typing the original manuscript; and to Kay Willbery for typing additional material. Thanks go, too, to Dr. Iain Chalmers, who gave most generously of his time and expertise in reading and criticizing the whole of the original manuscript, and to Dr. Martin Richards, who read and commented on the drugs section.

Special thanks are due (again) to Chloe Fisher. This book began as a result of a meeting which I went (in great trepidation) to address as her last-minute stand-in. That the seeds sown there have germinated and flowered has been due primarily to her support. This has taken many forms, including the loan of books, magazines, tapes, and clippings, reading and correcting parts of the manuscript, many hours of her time, the benefit of her considerable experience, and her unfailing enthusiasm for what I have tried to do.

Finally, this book could not have been written without the help of my husband, Steve. It was through his endeavors that most of my writing time was created and our children instructed in the delights of the Oxfordshire (and Derbyshire!) country-side.

BIRTHRIGHTS

First follow Nature, and your judgement frame
By her just standard.

Alexander Pope, 1688–1744

CHAPTER ONE

Birth As Pathology

Until the last two centuries in Western Europe and America, birth was seen by and large as a normal, natural process. Most women expected to receive physical or moral support during childbirth, but the basic assumption was that women's bodies were physically equipped to cope with birth (although some worked better than others). The usual practice was for women in labor to be attended by female relatives or neighbors who had attended numerous births and thus had gained experience of the wide variations in childbirth. Such women became known as midwives. The fact that the subject of childbirth was largely ignored by the European medical profession until the sixteenth century may well be a measure of how uneventful, and therefore uninteresting, birth was thought to be by the medical mind.

The Reformation in Europe brought changes in the field of obstetrics. A few books were printed on the subject, and several maternity hospitals were founded, notably the Hôtel-Dieu in Paris. The early seventeenth century gradually saw more men entering the field, spurred on by the new advances in operative midwifery that had begun in France (for example, the introduction of forceps by the Chamberlen family). As midwifery became more "interesting" to the medical profession, however, attempts were made to curtail the practice of midwives by making it illegal unless the midwife possessed a certificate of competence—issued by a board of doctors. At the same time, the study of midwifery became compulsory for medical students. By the end of the nineteenth century, any treatment for the variations of normal labor, including the use of forceps, was firmly in medical hands. And the more equipment doctors amassed with which to treat problems associated with childbirth, the less mobile they were. It now became a logical step to bring the woman to the hospital rather than to try to "take the hospital to her" when difficulties arose or were anticipated.

The definition and redefinition of what constitutes an actual or potential obstetrical problem—together with the development of such resources as large, high-technology teaching hospitals to deal with the problems—has to a great extent been responsible for the present medical position in both America and Britain, which strongly advocates birth in hospitals. In these countries, where the physician's view of labor and delivery prevails, birth is no longer seen as a physiological process that occasionally needs assistance, but as a pathological event that is normal only in retrospect. It is on this assumption that it becomes reasonable to insist that childbirth take place in a hospital, on the grounds that it will automatically be safer in the presence of expertise and technology.

This unsubstantiated assumption of the greater safety of hospital birth has determined official British and American policy in the recent past. Moreover, it is now justified retrospectively by those who draw attention to the decline in the perinatal mortality rate during the period hospital births were increasing. This argument, however, does not stand up to scrutiny. First, there are no statistical grounds for assuming a *causal* relationship between the fact that the hospital births rose and perinatal deaths fell over a given period. If it were sufficient simply to point to two trends occurring within the same time span in order to assert such a connection between them, the fall in perinatal mortality could be correlated with, say, the increase in air traffic across the Atlantic. Second, there *are* grounds for suggesting that not only *should* the perinatal mortality rate have fallen in the last ten to fifteen years, but it should have fallen more than it did—suggesting that rising hospital confinement rates have actually been counterproductive in reducing perinatal mortality rates.[1] Furthermore, researchers in Britain found that from 1963 to 1973 the places with above-average hospitalization rates in England and Wales also had above-average perinatal mortality rates.[2]

In the face of this, the argument put forward by the advocates of 100 percent hospital confinement is that hospital perinatal mortality rates are higher than elsewhere because a relatively greater proportion of the mothers who give birth there are at high predelivery risk. But this argument also crumbles when the available data are analyzed statistically. When Marjorie Tew, a research statistician at the University of Nottingham, examined both the published and unpublished data from the 1970 survey of British births, she found that an "excess of predelivery risk in hospital is not nearly sufficient to explain the excess of perinatal deaths there." Moreover, when she looked at the death rates for each category of risk and compared hospital births with those that took place in birth centers or at home, she concluded that her results completely discredited the claims that delivery in a hospital is safer for all births and that the greater the predelivery risk, the greater the advantage of hospital care.[3]

A third argument raised in favor of 100 percent hospital confinement is that occasionally there are unanticipated complications during labor and/or delivery. But the issue is really whether, in a given case, a complication is less likely to occur in a hospital than elsewhere, and also what the outcome is. If a complication can be coped with adequately at home, then the fact of its occurrence is not relevant.[4] Further, the risks associated with transferring to a hospital those women who develop problems at home are balanced, in statistical terms, by the very small proportion who will need it.

Finally, it may be argued that 100 percent hospital confinement would automatically include those women who had not been identified as being at increased predelivery risk, but who nevertheless make up 10 percent of perinatal deaths; this would ensure a greater chance of successful outcome. But if increasing the hospital confinement rate has had no effect on the overall mortality rate, then however valid the claim may be in individual cases, the available statistical evidence does not support the general assertion.[5]

It is misleading to suggest that a death that occurred at home could necessarily have been prevented if the birth had taken place in a hospital. A study of 5,000 home births in Holland showed that, of the few deaths that occurred, not one could have been prevented by hospitalization.[6] Indeed, Holland, which still has the highest home confinement rate in the developed world, also has one of the lowest perinatal mortality rates.

At this point it may be useful to consider what constitutes a "risk factor."[7] The indications for a hospital confinement have grown considerably in the last fourteen years, and in Britain and the United States, as in Holland, the absence of the following indications is now a precondition for home confinement.

Risk Factors

1. A woman expecting her first child (a primigravida) who is over 35 years of age.

2. A woman who is expecting her second or subsequent child and who is over 40 years of age.

3. A woman who is expecting her fourth or subsequent child. This is commonly held to be a risk factor, although, unpublished observations from the 1958 British Perinatal Mortality Survey show that, provided the preceding pregnancies have been uneventful, this group is not at risk if the woman is not over 35 years of age.

4. A woman who is (or has recently been) employed as a semi-skilled or unskilled worker.

5. Disorders of maternal growth—in particular, women who are small or grossly overweight. A height of less than 5 feet 2 inches is associated with a higher perinatal mortality rate. This is probably because women from lower-income groups are less likely to reach full height, due to unsatisfactory diet or a poor environment. The fact that the majority of perinatal deaths of women in this category are not due solely to mechanical causes

(that is, disproportion: the maternal pelvis being too small to allow the baby's head to pass through) supports this explanation.

6. A woman who has Rh problems or other forms of isoimmunization. (This does not mean all women who are Rh negative, only those who have circulating antibodies present.)

7. A woman who has had an operation on her uterus, such as a previous cesarean section, removal of fibroids (myomectomy), or a previous hysterotomy to terminate a pregnancy. Again, this does not mean that such as woman cannot have a perfectly normal delivery, but simply that a scar on the uterus requires careful watching during labor; if it were to give way, an immediate cesarean would be necessary.

8. Previous third-stage problems. Either a history of a retained placenta or a postpartum hemorrhage (bleeding after the birth of a baby resulting in the loss of a pint or more of blood) indicates the need for a hospital delivery, as recurrence is likely even if intervening third stages have been normal.

9. A woman with a problematic obstetrical history: previous forcep deliveries or premature labors, for example.

10. Previous low-birth-weight babies—not only premature babies, but also those who failed to grow properly in the uterus. Such babies account for 66 percent of all perinatal deaths.

11. Coexisting maternal illnesses: for example, high blood pressure, renal disease, or diabetes.

12. Any woman who has not received any prenatal care. Women in this category are automatically considered to be at risk, since none of the potential risk elements have been ruled out.

13. Any condition that has developed during the course of the pregnancy that may move the mother into a higher-risk category:

(a) Pre-eclampsia (toxemia of pregnancy): normally considered to be present when two of the three possible symptoms are present—a rise in diastolic blood pressure of more than 20 mmHg pressure above the woman's initial blood pressure, or a rise above 100 mmHg; protein in the urine (proteinuria); fluid retention (edema).

(b) Prenatal hemorrhage (bleeding during pregnancy from the placental site).

(c) Malpresentation: any position of the baby other than head first—breech, shoulder, or transverse lie; or head first with the face or the forehead, instead of the back or the top of the head, lying over the cervix.

(d) Retardated fetal growth: when the uterus does not expand at the expected rate or the baby is smaller than expected for its stage of pregnancy. This condition may prompt further investigation of placental function.

(e) Poor maternal weight gain. A weight gain of 20 to 35 pounds is the range within which there is the lowest rate of perinatal mortality and delivery of low-birth-weight babies.[8]

It follows from the above listing that a woman over 5 feet 2 inches, under 35 years of age, having her first baby, (or under 40 and having her second or third baby), who is in a professional, managerial, or skilled occupation, and who shows no medical or obstetrical problems, is in a category of low risk and could, if she so desired, be confined at home or in a birth center rather than a hospital.

There are strong arguments to be made for not confining women in this low-risk group in a large teaching hospital. First, there is the economic argument. The total cost to the parents of delivery in a birth center or at home is anywhere from a third to a quarter of the price of hospital childbirth,[9] which in 1984 was about $4,000.

Second, where there is no medical reason for the mother to be delivered in a hospital, exposing her to the hospital system may in itself put her at greater risk than if she delivered at home or in a birth center. Tew's analysis led her to propose that the place of delivery itself should be recognized as a risk factor.[10] Her conclusion has been supported by two studies, published in 1976 and 1983 respectively. The first, conducted in California, compared two groups of women matched on a case-by-case basis, one of which delivered in the hospital and the other at home. It found that the mothers in the hospital had more forceps deliveries, cesarean sections, episiotomies and tears; greater use of anesthetics, analgesics, and oxytocin (Pitocin); and more heavy bleeding after the birth than the mothers who delivered at home. In addition, the newborns had more problems—birth injuries, infections, and breathing difficulties—if they were born in a hospital. (Explaining these results, the study noted one key difference: both the first and the second stages of labor lasted longer if the mother delivered at home. In the hospital group, the majority of mothers were delivered by forceps if the second stage lasted more than one hour, whereas the home-delivered group were allowed unlimited time in the second stage so long as progress was being made and the baby showed no signs of distress.)[11]

The second study, conducted in England, compared the outcomes of two low-risk groups of women, using two different systems of care in the same hospital. Community midwives familiar to the women supervised labor and delivery for one group; the other women were cared for by midwives they had not met before, from the hospital's maternity unit. (These hospital midwives are just as well trained and qualified as the community midwives, but they work more like obstetrical nurses, that is, under the control of the obstetrician and are accustomed to working in an environment geared to technological treatment of high-risk situations.) Immediate access to obstetrical, anesthetic, and pediatric assistance was provided for every woman and every procedure was equally available to both groups. All deliveries took place within the labor rooms of the hospital, so the environment and facilities were the same—only the caretakers were different.

This study found that the mothers who delivered in the more technologically oriented system, with the obstetrician in control, received more oxytocin to augment labor, more analgesics and anesthetics, and had their labors monitored electronically much more frequently. The babies delivered by the hospital midwives developed fetal distress in labor more often, were in poorer condition at birth, and needed more help with breathing than the babies delivered by the community midwives.[12]

Both these investigations suggest that some risk is *acquired* as a direct consequence of the place chosen for birth. The fact is that a mother is more likely to be exposed to unnecessary intervention in a hospital than she is at home;[13] or, in the case of the British study when her care is controlled by doctors rather than midwives.

In spite of their claim to greater safety, then, the evidence suggests that hospitals contribute to the risk. Most women in America, however, still give birth in hospitals. It therefore becomes particularly important for women to understand why unnecessary interference is more likely in the hospital setting and what the consequences of such procedures are, so that they will be better placed to avoid them.

There are several reasons for the increased incidence of intervention in hospitals. One of the features of modern medicine that can be demonstrated in several aspects of maternity care is that

> the techniques which are developed to provide benefits for specific groups of people gradually tend to be used for more and more people, on wider and vaguer indications (on the grounds that what is beneficial for some must be beneficial for all), to the point where people who do not require any treatment at all are being given it. As this latter group will have nothing to gain from the technique, they will be worse off if it carries any risk than they would be if left alone.[14]

An example of this "if it's there, use it" philosophy is the use of X-rays in late pregnancy. Despite evidence produced in the late 1950s suggesting that X-ray exposure increased the incidence of cancer in childhood, in many hospitals X-rays are still being used just as extensively, even though the dosage may be lower; in some areas, 35 percent of the pregnant population are exposed.[15] "There is very little reason to think that exposure rates as high as this can be justified in terms of medical benefits."[16] In one hospital where the X-ray facilities were withdrawn, necessitating the transfer of patients to a nearby hospital if the technique was required, this small barrier to the full use of X-rays resulted in a drop in the number of pregnant women exposed.[17] With the tendency for prenatal care to be increasingly based in hospitals, wider use is being made of a broad range of diagnostic techniques in pregnancy, including the routine use of ultrasound scans, and there is little reason to believe that the more general use of such techniques offers substantial benefits to mothers or children.[18]

Another aspect of the problem is that, in the eyes of some doctors, "more" necessarily equals "better." The director-general of the World Health Organization stated in in 1975:

> It might appear that . . . some doctors . . . consider that the best health care is one where everything known to medicine is applied to every individual by the highest-trained medical scientist in the most specialized institution. . . . It is frightening but expected that when a specialized group is formed to perform certain actions, it is evaluated, and continues to be supported, because of the *number* of such actions which it does rather than whether a problem is solved.[19]

Doctors who "overtreat" expectant or parturient mothers might be forgiven, however, if their motives for so doing were those of genuine concern for the mothers in their care. Unfortunately, in some cases there is a strong element of self-interest or self-protection in their clinical management. As one physician has remarked:

> There is a subtle influence in obstetrics that operates to absolve a doctor who intervenes in the course of a normal pregnancy, and that, by implication, exposes his conservative colleague to censure for inactivity when an infant is born dead. This places a premium on intervention as a form of personal insurance for

the doctor, although the consequences are detrimental for some patients.[20]

This is the philosophy behind current debate in America over the routine use of electronic fetal monitoring. Many doctors are now concerned that they may be sued for malpractice in the event of complications if they do not routinely attach a monitor to every mother in labor, irrespective of whether or not it is actually indicated at the time. This anxiety has prompted new research into the effectiveness of electronic monitors, but the vast majority of medical interventions have never been evaluated by randomized, controlled trials, which in the final analysis would be far more ethical in protecting the interests of patients than uncontrolled innovation and experiment.[21]

Possibly the worst aspect of institutionalized care during labor is that there are many professionals who have yet to master the art of inactivity in situations where their "help" is unnecessary. This may well be a result of a training that is geared to the treatment of the pathological. A study of one American hospital maternity unit observed that

> a modulated kind of crisis seemed always to exist. . . . In cases where no complications were . . . present . . . an atmosphere of general apprehension pervaded the team—particularly during delivery. In cases with possible imminent complications, the members of the team seemed considerably more at ease; tension lessened and they appeared able to set about their tasks in a more relaxed and workmanlike manner. To the students, the latter situations were those in which they were actually "learning something."[22]

Suzanne Arms, in *Immaculate Deception*, quotes the noted Dutch obstetrician G. L. Kloosterman in his emphatic belief that 80 to 90 percent of women are perfectly capable of delivering normally, without any help. Kloosterman asserts, "Spontaneous labor in a healthy woman is an event marked by a number of processes which are so complex, so perfectly attuned to each other that any interference will only detract from their optimum character." He feels that the doctor or midwife who is "always on the lookout for pathology and eager to interfere" will much too often change physiology into pathology, "either out of jealousy ['because women can make new life,' as Margaret Mead said] or idleness, or because it is so easy to take over." As one British pediatrician has remarked, "We must never forget that it takes more experience, more judgement, and more courage, often, to stand back and do nothing."[23]

Since all aspects of the active management of labor carry a potential risk to the mother and/or child, it is totally indefensible to apply them in the absence of medical, obstetric, or pressing social indications. Because, moreover, the induction, acceleration, and monitoring of labor are seldom, if ever, carried out at home, the hazards of unnecessary interference are more or less confined to hospital practice. The situation is further complicated by the fact that it is often difficult to use any technique in isolation: very often, further intervention is required to counteract the effects of the initial action—the "cascade of intervention" (see chart and Appendix).[24]

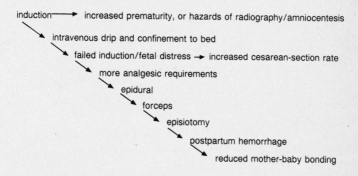

induction ——▶ increased prematurity, or hazards of radiography/amniocentesis
↘ intravenous drip and confinement to bed
↘ failed induction/fetal distress ➔ increased cesarean-section rate
↘ more analgesic requirements
↘ epidural
↘ forceps
↘ episiotomy
↘ postpartum hemorrhage
↘ reduced mother-baby bonding

Unless there is a basic change in the traditional attitude of doctors, the future is likely to bring further outbreaks of doctor-produced (iatrogenic) illness in hospitals. One way of bypassing the problem, at least for a certain proportion of the community, is to deliver low-risk mothers at home or in birth centers. Unnecessary interference is much less of a problem in these settings, partly because doctors and midwives who undertake such deliveries are likely to have a noninterventionist attitude, and partly because of the technological limitations (any act that interferes with the natural process of labor will be much more carefully considered if the machinery to correct unwanted side effects is not available). Another alternative is for women to become aware of and knowledgeable about procedures and practices in hospitals so that they are less vulnerable to unnecessary interference.

The separation of the mother from familial support is another troubling aspect of hospitalization. The birth of a new baby does not take place in a vacuum; it is an event that impinges greatly on other lives, in particular those of the mother, father, and existing brothers and/or sisters, and it originally took place in a home setting as part of the flow of those lives. Women who leave their homes to give birth in a hospital are, wittingly or unwittingly, sacrificing a great deal of their control over this important moment. In *some* cases, when intervention and help are necessary, this loss of control is certainly in exchange for the security and safety of the hospital; but in other cases it is not in exchange for anything.

In her own home a woman is not considered a patient but an individual fulfilling a natural and highly personal task. She is the center around which everything and everybody revolve. The midwife and doctor are guests in her house and are there to assist her; anything they do is in relation to her individual needs. This setting reinforces her self-respect and self-confidence, and she retains her sense of responsibility both for herself and, when born, for her baby.

In a hospital, the reverse is true. The mother is on the doctors' and nurses' territory and under strong pressure (direct and indirect) to accept their routines and submit to their procedures. In many instances she is unknown personally to the people caring for her, and rapidly loses her individual identity. She is likely to find that hospital rules bend very little to accommodate her individual wishes, and if she does not readily conform she runs the risk of being branded as a difficult patient—in some cases even to the extent of having it printed on her chart!

It is not surprising, therefore, that the majority of women who have had experience of both settings and have some genuine choice elect to have their babies at home.[25] In an extensive review of current research carried out in 1964, it was concluded that the factors that affect or control uterine activity are basically the same in all mammals.[26] One of these factors is the environment in which the labor and birth take place. Ideally this should be in peaceful, undisturbed surroundings. Experiments with mice have shown that disturbances in the environment at this critical time significantly lengthen labor and produce much higher perinatal mortality.[27] The effect on the human uterus of disturbance during labor is frequently seen in the admission section of maternity units, as contractions seem to decrease or disappear temporarily when the mother moves from her home to the hospital setting, even if she is unafraid and recognizes her need to be in the hospital. If she is not only disturbed but also frightened by her new environment, the effect is more profound; as one obstetrician has remarked, "there are certain conditions that predispose to normal uterine action. Almost everyone is convinced that peace of mind is important."[28] It has been shown that fear adversely affects uterine activity and blood flow,[29] and more recent investigations have linked this to changes in the baby's heart-rate patterns. When the mother was exposed to a "controlled psychic stress," her heart rate increased, and this was followed by an increase in her baby's heart rate, a condition that persisted for about 10 minutes after the cessation of the stress. The researchers announced that "in susceptible women, the entry of four or more white-coated physicians into the room is sufficient to produce changes in the heart-rate patterns of the baby."[30]

In many hospitals, the first thing that happens to a woman admitted in labor to a new, possibly threatening environment is that she is separated from her husband while she is admitted or "prepped." This process often includes vaginal examinations, administration of enemas or suppositories, and perineal shaving, all of which may well be alarming or unpleasant for her, so that she might be expected to need more, rather than less, emotional support. It seems to be a feature of many hospitals that the times when the husband is likely to be asked to wait outside are precisely those times when he is most needed by his wife—when examinations or obstetrical maneuvers are being carried out, progress is being assessed, and future plans are being made, among which may be the administration of intravenous drugs or drips. The main reason for this seems to be to spare the staff the need to explain their actions before the event or the embarrassment of carrying out procedures (such as vaginal examinations) in front of the husband! It is not uncommon for the husband to reenter the labor room to find that his wife has consented to the administration of drugs or procedures that he knows she did not want and might have refused even in labor had he been there to back her up. In other cases the husband, once excluded from the room, is not readmitted—either because his presence is not thought desirable by the staff or because they simply forget that he is there. Many obstetricians will not permit husbands to be present for forceps deliveries, and even fewer will allow a husband to be present for a cesarean section. But as one doctor points out:

> The mother should have the right to have her partner with her at this important time in her life. It is true that [these are] surgical procedures, and that rigid aseptic technique in the operating room is required. But there is no reason why any intelligent man cannot be shown how to put on proper operating room attire, wear a cap and mask, and stay away from the sterile field.[31]

Once the birth is completed, the couple, now a family (or a larger family), are still at the mercy of hospital routine that may allow little time for them to be alone together and to get to know their new child. The baby may be routinely placed in the nursery for a specified period of time and the husband sent out again if stitches are required. Even in the most permissive hospitals there comes a time when the husband is expected to go home; husband and wife are thus separated when they most need each other to talk to in order to assimilate what has happened to them. Very often the wife is then given sleeping pills and the baby removed from her room, while the husband, having spread the good news, may be lonely and depressed as a result of spending his first night as a father in an empty house.

For as long as the mother remains in the hospital, she will continue to have dictated to her by the hospital the times she is expected to sleep, wake, eat, and feed her baby. Her husband may be allowed to visit her only at certain times, and in some hospitals other children of the family may not be allowed at all —hardly likely to make for untroubled acceptance of the new baby.

The hospital continues to be "responsible" for the baby until the mother takes the baby home—in some hospitals she may not carry her baby in her arms in case she drops him or her— and the mother is sometimes sheltered from the implications of her childbirth to the extent that, when she gets home, she feels incompetent and panic-stricken to find herself with a helpless, dependent human being to care for. Many women describe a curious feeling of having been in limbo while in the hospital— a feeling that may take many weeks to overcome and that interferes with their ability to feel confident as mothers.

The degree to which the mother is regimented seems to bear little relation to the size of the hospital or the maternity ward. It might be thought that in hospitals that have large wards some degree of routine is essential, but there is little difference between these and hospitals with private rooms for mothers, suggesting that the routines stem from the social organization of the whole hospital rather than from the individual requirements of the maternity ward staff or the mothers.[32]

Very little thought is given to the effect of the hospital itself on the emotional or psychological state of the mother or the harm that may be done to intrafamilial relationships. One reason put forward is that parents are always assumed to be normal and capable of adjusting to their circumstances. But as one authority on child abuse points out, "Little attempt is made to identify those families which are vulnerable and in which the probable benefit [of routine hospital procedures] may be outweighed by the emotional and psychological damage." He continues, "The care of the newborn baby and the mother should be recognized as at least as much a matter of human relationships as it is of scientific method and apparatus."[33]

It is a fact that in a hospital setting where there is a large group of professional people with varying degrees of skill and experience, there is the need for a certain amount of central direction to ensure the physical health and safety of mother and baby. If an accident occurs, moreover, and the routines have been followed, the responsibility of the individual is lessened—and to some extent the mother is protected by this policy. But the price of following routines is the neglect of the need to think about the mother as an individual; indeed, one purpose of a routine procedure is precisely to spare any need to think. Yet periodic rethinking of the necessity for some of these routines is essential for the comfort as well as, in some cases, the safety of mother and child. Professionals need to ask themselves from time to time, "Why am I doing this? Is it really necessary?" and mothers need to ask questions whenever the reason for a proposed procedure or line of action is not clear to them, rather than simply submitting to authority. If they do not feel able to do so at the time for their own benefit, then they should be encouraged to set down their complaints and questions in a letter once they have left the hospital, for the benefit of future mothers. Similarly, if they were pleased by the treatment and consideration they received, they should again say so in some form. Staff are often misled about the acceptability of hospital practices because mothers tend to tone down their criticisms while in the hospital for fear of making life more difficult for themselves; once home, they often complain to relations or friends rather than to the hospital authorities. Unfortunately, in the worst of these situations—where there is the most need to bring to the staff's attention the feelings of the mother for whom they are caring—the mother herself is most likely to try simply to blot out the experience.

There will always be mothers who need the expertise of the obstetricians and pediatricians and the machinery at their disposal; for their sake, every effort must be made to make the hospital as comfortable and as welcoming as possible, given the limitations of design, staffing, and organization. Mothers who do not need the help given in hospitals nevertheless often have no alternative but to give birth there. Every pregnant woman thus has important vested interests in understanding the risks and benefits associated with standard modern hospital practices for labor and childbirth. Only when fully informed can she put obstetrical procedures into perspective in her individual situation, as she prepares for her own safe and satisfying birth experience.

CHAPTER TWO

The Process of Labor

It is useful at this point to outline the three stages of normal labor, before proceeding to a detailed examination of each and of the obstetrical procedures associated with it.

Countdown to Labor

The countdown begins with low backache, general feelings of heaviness in the vagina and pelvic floor, menstrual-like discomfort with strong painless (Braxton Hicks) contractions. There may be a burst of "nesting" activity—washing floors, clearing out cupboards, and so forth. Very often the lower bowel is completely emptied, by either loose or small, frequent bowel movements.

The Beginnings of Labor

The first sign is a "show" maybe—thick, jellylike mucus, possibly light-brownish, purply-red, or streaked with bright red. It is usually an indication that the cervix has started to dilate and detach itself partly from the membranes. It may precede the onset of labor by a few days or a few hours, and sometimes it is passed after regular contractions have started. Occasionally it may be dislodged by a vigorous vaginal examination, and in this situation the fresh blood streaking may be slightly heavier; there should, however, be no real bleeding—if there is, seek medical attention immediately.

A show is not always reliable as an indication that labor is about to start; however, many birth attendants feel that it is an event that needs to be reported to the midwife, doctor, or hospital.

Before labor starts, the baby's chin is in most cases tucked into his or her chest, so that the top or back of the head fits snugly into the cervix. When this happens, the fluid in front of the head is cut off from the remainder of the amniotic fluid and becomes known as the forewaters, the remainder being known as the hindwaters. This system reduces the pressure that is applied to the forewaters by the contracting uterus and helps to

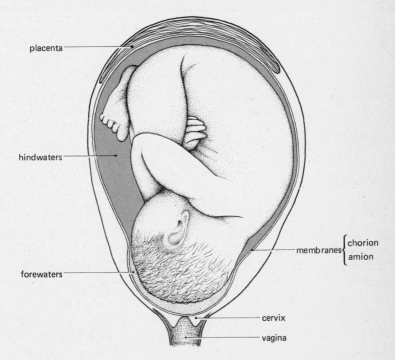

keep them intact despite strong contractions. Thus, the closed system of amniotic fluid can continue to perform its physiological function in labor—that of equalizing the pressure applied to all parts of the baby, the cord, and the placenta—in most cases throughout the greater part of the first stage.

The membranes may rupture, however, before the contractions start. This is more common when the baby is lying in a posterior position. The break in the bag of waters may be behind the baby's head and therefore the amniotic fluid trickles out slowly: a "hindwater leak." The easiest way for the mother to decide whether she is leaking urine or amniotic fluid is to empty her bladder deliberately, put on a sanitary napkin, and see whether or not she continues to get wet. If in doubt, she should call the doctor or midwife. The birth attendant may test the fluid with litmus paper (amniotic fluid is alkaline and will turn red litmus paper blue, while urine is commonly acid and will turn blue litmus paper red). A new alternative is nitrazine sticks, which turn from yellow to black in the presence of amniotic fluid. Sometimes the membranes in front of the baby's head rupture. In this case, the waters will gush out more obviously (anything from ½ to 1½ cupfuls—just that which is "trapped" in front of the baby's head). This is more likely to occur after contractions have started, but may be early on in labor. If it happens as the first event, contractions usually start fairly quickly afterward, unlike those in the case of the hindwater leak.

In both instances, the midwife or doctor should be informed. The main reason for this is that the longer the interval between membrane rupture and delivery, the greater the risk of infection of the amniotic fluid. Doctors vary in their views of how long it is safe to wait for contractions to start after the membranes rupture before giving Pitocin in an intravenous drip, but most will give prophylactic antibiotics after 12 to 24 hours. The other reason for reporting a rupture of the membranes is so that a vaginal examination can be carried out to exclude cord prolapse if an abdominal examination shows that the baby's head is not engaged.

The First Stage: Labor

Contractions rarely start out of the blue; there is usually some warning that things are about to happen. Of course, the woman may miss the very beginning of labor, in the sense of knowing the precise time that contractions begin. The unseen physiological preparation for labor which takes place in the woman's body is a gradual process. Over the weeks and months, the Braxton Hicks contractions slowly become more noticeable and stronger and may begin the process of thinning out and shortening the cervix before labor starts in earnest. Quite often this beginning of labor is discounted as just another bout of Braxton Hicks contractions until the realization that these are occurring at regular intervals. It is, however, not uncommon for a woman to have one or more episodes of regular contractions toward the end of pregnancy which are fairly weak and do not become progressively longer and stronger, and which then cease altogether, after having lasted as long as 4 hours.

True labor contractions, therefore, may be recognized by the fact that they not only occur at regular intervals, but as time goes by the intervals become shorter and the contractions feel stronger (and are in fact dilating the cervix). They may begin at intervals of 20 to 30 minutes and last 30 seconds or so, but gradually increase to 5- to 10-minute intervals with about a 45- to 50-second duration; toward the end of the first stage, they may be between 2 to 4 minutes apart, lasting 50 to 60 seconds. As the second stage approaches, the contractions may in some cases occur every 1½ to 2 minutes and last 60 to 90 seconds, so that the woman may feel that they are continuous.

The Second Stage: Delivery

Sometimes the contractions may die down for a short period before the second stage starts; when they resume, they are different in quality as the expulsive urge builds up. In other instances the first and second stages seem to overlap, and the urge to push may begin before the cervix is fully dilated. This transitional phase of labor may be characterized by irritability, disorientation, nausea, vomiting, backache, a trancelike state in which the woman feels rooted to the spot and any movement requires enormous effort (onlookers may think she is asleep), shaking of the legs and/or the whole body, cold feet, and a gradual building up of rectal pressure as the baby's head follows the sacral curve down, around, and forward. She may also find that she is catching her breath or grunting with contractions.

In most cases, second-stage contractions build up gradually both in quality and efficiency: the expulsive urge usually comes at the height of the contraction, not at the beginning (it may recur in a wavelike fashion within one contraction). In some women the expulsive sensation is mild or absent, in others totally overwhelming, and in the majority it is experienced as a powerful surge of energy. As the baby's head starts to stretch the vagina and perineum, the mother may feel a hot, stretching, burning sensation around the entrance to the vagina, which reaches its peak as the widest part of the baby's head is born (crowning).

Often there is a pause (1 to 2 minutes) after the head is born while the final contraction is awaited—the contraction that will deliver the baby's body. As the newborn emerges, the baby will follow the continuation of the pelvic curve onto the mother's abdomen with her help or the help of the birth attendant.

The Third Stage: After Delivery

The final contraction of the second stage, the one that delivers the baby's body, initiates the third stage. As the baby is being born, the uterus reduces its size enough for the process of placental separation to begin. To some extent, the placenta becomes compact: as the uterus grows smaller, the placenta at first shrinks with it. Once, however, the placental site is reduced by more than half, the placenta can shrink no more; it peels off the inside of the uterus, in much the same way as a postage stamp stuck on the side of an inflated balloon would peel off as the balloon deflated.

The separated placenta then folds in on itself, peeling off the membranes as it descends into the lower part of the uterus. It is expelled without resistance through the cervix and into the vagina, with very little effort from the mother. If she is upright, the placenta will fall out of the vagina due to gravity, or another, slight expulsive effort may be needed.

CHAPTER THREE

The First Stage:

ALTERING THE PHYSIOLOGICAL PATTERN

Shaving the Perineum

Removal of the pubic hair before delivery is a medical custom that began at the turn of the century. A 1904 volume called *Obstetrics for Nurses* gives a meticulous account of perineal shaving and states that "many cases of puerperal fever are due to lack of surgical preparation of the patient." Modern textbooks on obstetrics and midwifery also describe shaving in great detail and invariably seem to accept the need without question. The theoretical advantages of the procedure are that surgical cleanliness is improved, that episiotomy may be performed and repaired without hair interference, and that the fastidious birth attendant is not affronted. One current textbook for midwives places shaving as the first item in its list for preparation of the woman in labor. It states, "The pubic hair is usually shaved . . . because otherwise it is difficult to keep the vulva clean throughout labor." Moreover, "The majority of midwives prefer shaving to be done, and many think patients' objections to this have been exaggerated." Yet a study carried out at a British hospital that conducts over 3,000 deliveries a year found that 98 percent of mothers, when asked, objected to shaving.[1]

There is no physiological basis for removing pubic hair. Early obstetrical authorities omit it: Denman (1821), Churchill (1848), and Bedford (1868) do not mention the subject, and all the illustrations in their books show pubic hair present. Warren (1902) appears to be the first to recommend clipping the hair as well as washing, but even he does not deem shaving necessary.

Williams, in the first three editions of his textbook (1903, 1908, 1915), suggests that "if the pubic hairs are very long they should be cut short with scissors, or shaved." In the fourth edition (1919) he deletes the word "very."[2]

Williams was, however, rather puzzled by the low infection rate observed in precipitate deliveries of unprepared patients. He therefore suggested a study, which was undertaken by Johnston and Sidall, who published their results in 1922. In 1921, Lankford had described how the use of soap and water tended to wash contaminating material into the vagina, especially in women who had already borne a child; it seemed plausible to Johnston and Sidall to assume that the routine preparation employed in their clinic might be harmful rather than beneficial. In an effort to substantiate this assumption, the routine preparation was purposely omitted in forty-four consecutive cases, and it was found that only four of them (9.1 percent) had a raised temperature following delivery, compared with the usual finding of 19 percent.[3]

In view of this, Johnston and Sidall decided to extend their study. In every alternate patient in a total of 389 women, the routine preparation was omitted, with only clipping of the pubic hairs permitted. Of the prepared group, 16.3 percent (compared with 12.4 percent of the unprepared group) had raised temperatures in the days following delivery. They considered this a statistically significant difference, due probably to iatrogenic contamination. Although an additional series of observations gave identical results, Williams stated that he was not yet prepared to abandon the time-honored method of preparation, and his fifth edition (1924) read, "The patient should be placed on a douche pan and the pubic hair cut short with scissors or shaved."[4]

Forty years later, it was observed that indigent obstetrical patients who entered the hospital late in labor and had no vulval preparation usually had an uneventful postdelivery period. As a result of these observations, a simplified method of preparation was instigated in certain British hospitals in 1960. The pubic hair of women in labor was neither cut nor shaved; the vulva was simply wiped with gauze to remove mucus or blood and the area sprayed with an antiseptic. Between 1960 and 1964 more than 7,600 women were prepared in this way, and the infection rate dropped.[5]

Further work confirmed that "shaving of the perineum in preparation for delivery does *not* permit more effective perineal sterilization." In addition, it established that "clipping or cutting the hair round the episiotomy area is satisfactory and will avoid the irritation caused by (shaving and) the regrowth of perineal and pudendal hair."[6]

In spite of the weight of this evidence, perineal shaving is still an integral part of the delivery preparations in many hospitals. Lomas suggests that "there is a formality (in this and other practices) which has something of the character of a public ritual." He continues, "We do not regard the practices surrounding childbirth in our society as ceremonial or ritualistic, but may it be that the ritual is hidden from us only because we are so hypnotized by the apparently rational assumptions behind them that we do not even begin to seek a further explanation."[7]

In view of all this, it does not seem unreasonable for women to voice their objections to the practice of shaving. The procedure, even in skilled hands, often results in multiple scratches and abrasions that are painful and sting when antiseptics are applied, and the urge to scratch the irritating, regrowing stubble may prove acutely distressing. Above all, there is no longer any basis for the assumption that it has any value on therapeutic or hygienic grounds.

Administering Enemas and Suppositories

In many hospitals, part of the admission procedure for a woman in early labor is the administration of two suppositories or an enema. A suppository is a small, bullet-shaped cone of a readily meltable jelly or waxlike substance, which is inserted into the rectum. Enemas come in a variety of forms, but the small disposable enema commonly used in childbirth is a quarter-pint of a clear, watery solution of salts in a plastic bag to which is attached a small nozzle (3 to 4 inches long) with a sealing cap. When the nozzle has been lubricated and the cap removed, the nozzle is inserted into the rectum and the contents of the bag squeezed into the lower bowel. Having the lower bowel evacuated in this manner is not particularly pleasant even for a woman not in labor. If she is coping with contractions at the same time, it may be very uncomfortable.

There are advantages to having the lower bowel empty from early on in labor: it is more comfortable for the mother, as there is more room for the baby's head to descend and rotate as labor progresses, and it ensures a "clean field" for the actual delivery. Anything in the way of the descending head will be expelled immediately before and during the birth, which may disturb the unprepared mother.

Another effect of bowel evacuation or stimulation is that it may stimulate the uterus. The nerve supply to bowel and uterus is apparently connected, and this feature may be made use of at the end of a pregnancy as a nonsurgical form of induction. In some instances, a woman may be given a quantity of castor oil to drink, an enema, and a hot bath—all in an effort to initiate labor. This procedure is only likely to be effective if labor is imminent and if a vaginal examination has revealed a soft, "ripe" cervix. The reflex stimulation of the uterus is also a reason why an enema should not be given to a woman in strong labor, particularly if she has had a previous child, for the augmented contractions may speed labor to the extent that the baby is expelled along with the enema. For this reason also, the enema or suppository should always be preceded by a vaginal or rectal examination.

The most cogent argument against the use of *routine* enemas or suppositories is, however, that in a great number of women the physiological overture to labor is spontaneous emptying of the bowel—either as small, frequent movements or as a mild attack of diarrhea—often initially attributed to what the prospective mother ate the night before! In this case, there is reflex stimulation of the bowel by the uterus as contractions gently begin. Nothing is gained in this common situation by the additional administration of an enema. Even if the midwife is reluctant to take the mother's word that the bowel is empty, this can be easily confirmed when the vaginal or rectal examination is made to assess the state of the cervix, and it would be unkind to insist that the mother be subjected to the discomfort of an enema in such a case. If there is a need for evacuants and the mother understands the need, she is less likely to feel assaulted; if there is no need—and often there is not—the mother should not be afraid to make the fact known and thus spare herself unnecessary discomfort.

Confining the Laboring Woman to Bed

The practice of restricting the position and movement of a woman in labor seems to have been introduced in the first half of the eighteenth century. Until then, most women adopted some variation of an upright and relatively mobile theme. They might stand, sit, kneel, or squat, but always the lower half of the trunk was more vertical than horizontal. In Europe, the birth stool—a low-backed chair with the center of the seat missing, so that it was roughly horseshoe-shaped—was a common sight at labor and delivery. It supported the laboring woman in an upright position without impeding the actual birth. In 1668, François Mauriceau, in his treatise on midwifery, proposed that the recumbent position be adopted in preference to the use of the birth stool—a position that he advocated not because it might benefit the mother or the baby, but in order to make forceps deliveries, vaginal examinations, and other obstetrical maneuvers easier for the physician.[8] As it became fashionable to have male accoucheurs and forceps deliveries, the recumbent position became widespread in Europe and across the Atlantic. By 1824, a book by a Philadelphian obstetrician was insisting that delivery was best achieved when the mother was lying flat on her back with her knees drawn up. The lying-in bed continued as the major determinant of posture during labor in the nineteenth and early twentieth centuries. As hospital deliveries increased, it was superseded by the delivery table, where the woman lay in the lithotomy position (flat on her back with her feet in stirrups) for the birth. This is now the most common position in hospitals of the Western world.

There were, however, some obstetricians who were not in favor of this departure. In 1816, another Philadelphia doctor wrote, "The patient may be allowed to sit, stand, kneel, or walk out as her inclinations prompt her; if fatigued she should repose occasionally on a bed or couch, but it is not expedient during the first stage . . . that she should remain for very long at a time in a recumbent posture."9

Half a century later, Professor G. J. Engelmann asserted in his book *Labor among Primitive Peoples*:

> A vast and important fund of knowledge may be derived from a study of the various positions occupied by women of different peoples in their labors. . . . The recumbent position is rarely assumed among those people who live naturally . . . and have escaped the influence of civilization and modern obstetrics. . . . According to their build, to the shape of their pelvis, they stand, squat, kneel or lie on their belly; so also they vary their position in various stages of labor according to the position of the child's head in the pelvis. . . . I deem it a great mistake that we should follow custom or fashion so completely, to the exclusion of reason and instinct, in a mechanical act which so nearly concerns our animal nature . . . instinct will guide the woman more correctly than the varying custom of the times.10

In 1894 another obstetric text warned that "the patient should be encouraged not to take to bed at the onset of labor. In the upright or sitting posture gravity aids in the fixation of the head and promotes passive hyperaemia [increased blood flow] and dilation of the cervix."[11]

In Britain, William Smellie had pointed out over a century earlier that the uterus contracted less efficiently in the dorsal position, and his work was still being quoted in 1876.[12] Yet despite all this, the practice of confining the laboring woman to bed has continued to be the accepted procedure for the advantages it gives the midwife or doctor.

A 1963 study demonstrated that when a heavily pregnant woman lies flat on her back, the enlarged uterus partially or totally blocks the venous blood supply returning to the heart through one of the major vessels (the inferior vena cava). This has serious side effects in a minority of women (15 percent) who are unable to develop an adequate alternative system for returning the blood to the heart during the period when the uterus is enlarging. These women suffer from supine hypotension: if they lie flat, they sustain a marked drop in blood pressure, which in turn reduces the blood supply to the uterus and placenta and hence the oxygen supply to the baby. In extreme cases this may result in the death of the mother, the baby, or both. The remaining 85 percent are able to compensate for the obstruction by returning the blood through an alternative network of veins. If these women, however, receive epidural anesthesia during labor and are then allowed to lie flat, they will also develop supine hypotension.[13] Apart from this consideration, the weight of evidence is not that lying down is directly harmful, but that a vertical position has overwhelming advantages.

It was established in 1976 that an increase of 30 to 40 mmHg pressure is exerted by the fetal head on the cervix as a result of the effects of gravity, that is, standing instead of lying down. This means that, although the frequency of the contractions is the same, the effectiveness of the contractions is much greater, and hence the efficiency and rate of the dilatation of the cervix is improved. If the woman lies on her side, the efficiency of the contractions is improved somewhat but the frequency decreases, so that the net improvement is not nearly as great as while standing, sitting, squatting, or kneeling. In order to prove the superiority of the upright position in practice, the 1976 study alternated the posture of women volunteers every half-hour from the dorsal to the standing position. There was an abrupt fall in the intensity of the contractions when the women lay down, and the effectiveness of contractions in dilating the cervix was doubled when they stood up. The mothers also found the standing half-hour much less uncomfortable or painful; it was often difficult to persuade them to lie down again. The mean length of labor in this study group (all first labors) was 4 hours, and none of the mothers required drugs to relieve pain.[14]

These findings were confirmed and elaborated in a Latin American collaborative study that represented the coordinated efforts of eleven maternity hospitals in seven countries. All the mothers included in the study were in the lowest possible risk category; all started labor spontaneously at term, with intact membranes and the babies in anterior positions. At each hospital, 50 percent of the randomly selected volunteers remained lying down in bed for the first stage; the other 50 percent chose their own position. Of all the mothers in the study, only 5 percent elected to lie down. All the rest (95 percent) preferred to stand, walk, or sit. Nothing was done or given to those mothers that would affect labor—the membranes were left intact and no drugs of any kind were administered. (Less than 3 percent of the mothers in the study had required pain-relieving drugs, and these women were then excluded from the study.)

The investigation showed that:

1. In 85 percent of the labors, the membranes did not rupture spontaneously until the cervix was dilated 9 centimeters or more, and none ruptured spontaneously before 4 centimeters.

2. When only the first-time mothers were considered, the median length of labor was 36 percent shorter in the vertical group than in the horizontal group. When all the mothers were considered, the vertical group were 25 percent faster in producing their babies than the horizontal group.

3. The fact that 95 percent of mothers preferred to be upright when given the choice indicates that they were probably more comfortable when upright. This is confirmed by another study, which found that when mothers spent their time in different positions in labor, they reported less or equal pain and greater comfort in lateral, sitting, and standing positions than when lying down.

4. Provided that the membranes were intact, there was no difference between the vertical and horizontal groups with regard to "molding" of the baby's head, caput (swelling of the tissue over the presenting part of the baby's head caused by pressure against the cervix during labor), or changes in the baby's heart rate, despite the increase in pressure on the baby's head brought about by gravity in the vertical group.

The study concluded that in normal, spontaneous labors the vertical position facilitates the progress of labor, shortens its duration, and reduces maternal discomfort and pain.[15]

It would seem wholly unreasonable, in the light of this evidence, to deny women in normal labor the right to choose the positions they find most comfortable during the first and second stages of labor, since these are also likely to be the most advantageous positions for them in terms of individual pelvic shape and the position of the baby.[16] It is no argument at all to say that it is more convenient for the midwife or doctor if the woman lies flat, particularly if by doing so she is likely to prolong labor and possibly necessitate pain-relieving drugs, with all their attendant hazards. In the words of a nineteenth-century obstetrician, "The physician should accustom himself to conduct labor with equal facility, no matter where the woman lies."[17]

Withholding Food and Drink

Withholding food and drink from the normal, undrugged woman in labor is a relatively new practice. In many cultures the laboring woman is refreshed from time to time with beverages of one kind or another, particularly herbal teas. Hottentots, for example, feed soup to women in labor to "strengthen" them, while the Manus give their laboring women a hot coconut soup to prevent bleeding.[18] A British obstetrics text of 1816 advocates the use of nutritional supplements in labor: "She [the prospective mother] should be supplied from time to time with mild, bland nourishment in moderate quantities. Tea, coffee, gruel, barley water, milk and water, broths, etc., may safely be allowed."[19] Relatively recent European texts have continued to advocate oral sustenance. "The laboring woman requires a certain amount of nourishment . . . her own appetite should be a certain guide to what she wishes to eat or drink." "Oral fluids, rich in glucose, such as sweetened tea or fruit juices should be given; one to two liters should be taken over twenty-four hours."[20]

When a woman is pregnant, the carbohydrates (starches and sugars) that she eats are converted as usual into glucose. But instead of being rapidly converted to glycogen and stored in the liver for future use, the glucose remains for longer periods in her bloodstream so that her developing baby has an easily available source of energy that can be used both for growth and storage as fat (+ glycogen). This is one of the reasons why pregnant women may have sugar in their urine, as the greater quantity of sugar in the blood means that some will spill over into the urine via the kidneys. The mother, however, does need to store some energy against her future needs, and this she does mainly by converting some of her blood sugar into fat. A sudden demand for energy, as occurs in labor, rapidly depletes her low stores of glycogen (which can be converted straight back into glucose); she then has to start using her fat stores as a form of energy. This is a rather inefficient process, however, and there are by-products in addition to the release of energy. These by-products, called ketones, can be detected in the mother's urine. (If they are present in large quantities, they can be smelled on the breath as "pear drops.") If ketones are allowed to build up in the

bloodstream unchecked (ketosis), they will cause alterations in
the blood chemistry and weakening of the muscle cells. The
uterus then contracts less effectively and labor slows down. A
study of 3,500 pregnant women, for instance, found a significant
relationship between ketosis and abnormal labor. There was an
increased need to augment spontaneous labor with Pitocin and
greater use of forceps delivery—suggesting uterine malfunction
in the presence of ketosis.[21]

If all mothers are starved during labor, as is the practice in
many hospitals, many are likely to develop ketosis. Once detected, ketosis means that intravenous feeding has to be instigated, which adds to the pathological environment of the hospital birth. It also severely restricts the mobility of the mother and
limits the positions she can adopt, as the needle in her arm is
attached via a plastic tube to a bottle, which is suspended from
a metal stand. In order to correct ketosis, this bottle need con-
tain only glucose and water, but in many cases a chemical stimu-
lant (to increase the frequency and intensity of the contractions)
is introduced, rather than simply waiting for the ketosis to be
corrected.

The practice of administering intravenous glucose to a
woman in labor is not without potential hazard. Large quantities
of intravenous salt-free fluids, especially when used in conjunction with Pitocin and/or opiates, may result in water intoxication with consequent convulsions. If large quantities of sugar
(glucose/dextrose) are given intravenously to the mother, they
will rapidly cross the placenta and cause high blood sugar levels
in the baby. The baby's pancreas responds by increasing its
output of insulin (to lower the blood sugar). When the baby is
born, he or she is rapidly cut off from the previous high supply
of glucose, and the now excessive amount of insulin still present
in the baby's circulation may cause a rebound fall in his or her
blood sugar level (hypoglycemia). Severe hypoglycemia is a cause
of convulsions and subsequent brain damage in newborns. In
addition, both 5 and 10 percent glucose or dextrose infusions
have been implicated as possible causes of neonatal jaundice.[22]

The rationale behind the practice of starving women in labor is that, should they need a general anesthetic, the danger of inhaling stomach contents if they vomit while being anesthetized is greatly reduced. The effects on the baby of depriving the mother of food and drink for many hours have not yet been sufficiently researched. Obviously, when the condition of the mother or baby in pregnancy or early labor is such that a general anesthetic for cesarean section seems likely, it seems prudent to prepare her like any other preoperative patient by withholding food and drink. The problem arises when the practice is extended to all women, irrespective of their condition. The normal woman is more likely to be at risk from ketosis than from gastric inhalation. It would seem logical, therefore, to prevent ketosis rather than waiting for it to occur and then correcting it by intravenous means (it is difficult to correct by oral means once it has developed).

In some British hospitals, a low-residue diet is prescribed for women in labor. Its aim is to provide foods that are easily absorbed, do not have long fibers (that is, are low in roughage), do not form a ball or clot in the stomach (as do milk or soft bread), and do not remain in the stomach for long periods (as do fats). The diet includes tea, sugar, fruit juice, toast, honey, plain cookies, applesauce, and canned peaches, pears, and mandarin oranges. This kind of diet provides the carbohydrates necessary for a fairly rapid conversion to glucose and appears to be compatible with an emergency anesthetic.

Another alternative is oral glucose. Pure glucose is rapidly absorbed from the stomach (despite the slowing of absorption from the gut that occurs at the end of pregnancy) and is then readily available as an energy source. Glucose tablets taken by mouth have the added benefit of cooling the mouth slightly as they dissolve and also avoid the problem of solids in the stomach.

It is likely that the majority of women in labor will not want to eat, although most require fluids of some sort, particularly as labor advances; the mouth dries rapidly when breathing is speeded up in the late first stage. Those who do eat large quantities, or who have had a heavy meal before labor begins, run the risk of becoming sick when the rising and contracting uterus begins to push on the stomach—but this alone is not an indication to withhold food should the mother desire it. It seems illogical to pay so much attention to the mother's diet during pregnancy, in part to maintain her "physical strength and vitality for labor," and then to deprive her of any source of energy when she needs it most.[23]

Moving the Laboring Woman to a Delivery Room

It is still a fairly widespread practice to require women giving birth in a hospital to move from the labor room to another room —or worse, to another bed in another room—for normal delivery. Yet the point has already been made that labor should ideally take place in peaceful, undisturbed surroundings, and that fear and disruption may adversely affect the course of labor. During the hours when a woman is in the first stage of labor, it is to be hoped that she has had time to acclimate herself to the room she is in and to allow her body to settle into the work of dilating the cervix. The end of the first stage, the transition period, is often the most difficult and stressful part of labor. It is at this point, or shortly thereafter, that in institutions that use a separate delivery room, the woman will be moved. Alternatively, she may be moved when she is established in the second stage, and delivery is imminent. In both cases, this process will involve great physical upheaval if the woman has to get off the labor bed and onto a stretcher or the delivery table; it will also frequently bring about a change (usually a drop) in temperature as she is wheeled from one room to another. She will have to deal with the intrusion of staff and the conduct of a difficult part of her labor under a more public gaze, if she has to cross hospital corridors. The delivery room is often colder than the room from which she has come and is a new and possibly frightening environment with which she is expected to cope while being greatly involved with the changing sensations inside her body. In many cases, this sudden assault on the laboring woman's senses has the effect of causing a decrease in or a disappearance of uterine contractions.

There is no reason and certainly no evidence to indicate that it is necessary for a woman in normal labor to give birth in a delivery room (in essence, an operating room) rather than in a labor room equipped with good lighting, suction, and oxygen in some form. The fact that this practice continues seems to suggest a lack of trust in the woman's ability to give birth normally and an unimaginative use of available facilities.

CHAPTER FOUR

The First Stage:

THE ACTIVE MANAGEMENT OF LABOR

Inducing Labor

Induction is the initiation of labor before it begins spontaneously, but it is in no sense a replication of the events that would naturally occur given the passage of time. The actual mechanisms involved in the initiation of spontaneous labor are complex and at present poorly understood, but it seems likely that they involve factors in both the mother (uterus, placenta, pituitary gland) and the baby (adrenal and pituitary glands), and that these factors in the two are interrelated. Induction of labor is a pharmacological process, which "reflects only very distantly the natural process."[1] It is therefore likely that there is a price to pay for the disruption of normal physiology.

The most common methods employed to induce labor are amniotomy (breaking the waters), cervical stimulation (stretch and sweep), Pitocin infusion (intravenous drip), and prostaglandin administration. (A more conservative method of induction is discussed in the section on enemas in Chapter Three.)

1. *Amniotomy* Either the forewaters or the hindwaters may be ruptured (see the section on amniotomy below). In order to rupture the hindwaters, a Drew Smythe cannula has to be passed through the cervix and behind the baby's head to puncture the bag of waters in the region of the baby's neck. Either amniotomy forceps (like long, thin scissors with a toothed end) or an amnihook (like a large, blunt plastic crochet hook) is

passed through the cervix in order to rupture the forewaters. Hindwater ruptures may be performed when the baby's head is not engaged or does not fit snugly over the cervix, to avoid the possibility of prolapse of the umbilical cord; a cannula is also easier to push through an unripe (closed) cervix than two fingers, but it is also more likely to cause bleeding, either fetal or maternal, which may be so severe that a cesarean section is required.[2]

Simply removing the amniotic fluid has no effect on the initiation of labor; its effectiveness as a means of induction lies in the fact that in the absence of intact membranes, the baby's head is more likely to fit well onto the cervix and thus stimulate it. The effectiveness of this procedure is in part dependent on the state of the cervix: if the cervix is ripe or "favorable" (soft, effacing, beginning to dilate), then labor is much more likely to occur without any other form of intervention. When the cervix is unripe (long, hard, closed), additional intervention is much more likely to be necessary.[3] This is particularly true for women having their second or subsequent babies. In 70 to 80 percent of cases, amniotomy alone will initiate labor within 24 hours, but the remaining 20 to 30 percent will have a high incidence of intrauterine infection.[4] Opinions vary within the medical profession on how this problem can be avoided. Some advocate antibiotics routinely once the membranes have been ruptured for 24 hours; others prefer not to wait for spontaneous labor, but prescribe a Pitocin infusion after 12 hours, 12 to 16 hours, or simultaneously.[5]

In the majority of hospitals, amniotomy is performed at the same time that a Pitocin infusion is set up, on the grounds that the induction-delivery interval is likely to be shorter, the amniotic fluid can be inspected for meconium staining (sometimes an indication of fetal distress), and a scalp clip (internal fetal monitor) can be attached to the baby's head.[6] (It may be argued, however, that electronic fetal monitoring via a scalp clip is of doubtful benefit [see section on monitoring below] and that the color of the amniotic fluid can be observed, if required, via an amnioscope, which does not necessitate breaking the waters.) The disadvantages of amniotomy during a spontaneous labor are discussed later in this chapter, and they are equally valid— in some cases compounded—when amniotomy is performed in conjunction with Pitocin. In addition to this, breaking the waters before labor has started, particularly when the cervix is unripe, has been shown to be a painful procedure in as many as 20 percent of women.[7] The only consideration that could possibly outweigh these disadvantages is a genuine medical need for induction, and therefore social reasons for induction are not considered in this text.

2. *Cervical Stimulation* This is an integral part of induction in breaking the waters, as the membranes are "swept" off the lower segment of the uterus and the cervix is stretched by the examining fingers. It is sometimes, however, performed when the woman is at term and the cervix is found to be ripe, in order to precipitate contractions when the woman is about to go into labor spontaneously. It is thought to mimic events at the onset of spontaneous labor in a number of ways. It may trigger a reflex in the cervix (although the precise activity is unknown); it can and does lead to a release of oxytocin from the maternal pituitary gland, although this is short-lived and its functional significance is doubtful; and it may lead to a release of prostaglandins in the area of the cervix and lower uterus, which would have a more persistent effect.[8]

3. *Pitocin Infusion* The use of synthetic oxytocin (Pitocin) as a means of inducing labor bears little relation to the part oxytocin plays in initiating spontaneous labor. There is no evidence to suggest that there is an increase in the levels of oxytocin in the woman's bloodstream before the onset of labor. When oxytocin is released from the maternal pituitary gland *during* labor, moreover, it is in very small quantities—2 to 8 microunits per minute

(no greater than the minimum rate of infusion used for induction) and in spurts throughout labor, increasing in frequency as labor progresses, rather than continuously. Oxytocin, in the form of pituitary extract, has been administered in the past through intramuscular injections, tablets to be sucked, or a nasal spray. When given in any of these ways, the dose was difficult to control, and overdosage was not uncommon, producing spasms of the uterus and fetal distress as the major complications. Oxytocin itself was synthesized in 1953 and became commercially available two years later as Pitocin in the United States and Syntocinon in Britain. It was used intravenously in very low doses in the beginning; although there was little risk of over-stimulating the uterus, there was a risk of "water intoxication" because of the large quantities of fluid that had to be transfused in order to obtain the required effect. The failure rate was high (40 to 50 percent), although slightly lower when amniotomy was performed simultaneously.[9]

In response to this situation, the concept of Pitocin titration was developed in the 1960s. Instead of having the dextrose solution containing the Pitocin fed directly to the mother, with the drips per minute counted by the midwife or by a drip-counting machine, the plastic tube from the infusion bottle is passed through a machine called a Cardiff pump, which causes the dose to be doubled every 12½ minutes until the desired contraction rate is reached. The desired contraction rate is pre-set, and information about the strength and frequency of contractions is conveyed by a catheter (a thin plastic tube) that is introduced into the uterus and, having ruptured the membranes, fills with amniotic fluid. When the uterus contracts, the intrauterine pressure rises, and this rise is transmitted by the fluid-filled catheter to the pump. The pump then maintains the dose at the level that produces the desired contraction rate (plateau state). This method of administering Pitocin virtually eliminated failure of induction and reduced both the induction-delivery interval and the incidence of infection. But once obstetricians had an efficient means of induction at their disposal, the induction rate started to rise.

Pitocin administration has subsequently been further refined by the development of the MM2 machine (a Pye prototype in 1979): the Pitocin is still given intravenously, via a pump, and the intrauterine pressure is still measured via a fluid-filled catheter, which necessitates rupture of the membranes (although an air-filled balloon linked to the pressure recorder [transducer] is currently being developed). The MM2 uses Pitocin in a highly concentrated form, so that very small volumes of fluid can be used, and its rate of increase is much slower than that of the Cardiff pump (dose doubled every 30 minutes). It is programmed to respond to any increase in intrauterine pressure above 18 mmHg, which is considered to be the resting or muscle-tone pressure exerted on the amniotic fluid. The machine has a positive-negative feedback system and can respond to the presence or absence of contractions by increasing or decreasing the dose of Pitocin (it does not "plateau" the dose). Once the desired contraction rate has been reached, it goes into reverse and begins gradually to decrease the dose. If the contractions also decrease, the dose rate goes back up again; if they do not, the dose rate continues to decrease. It thus makes use of the fact that the requirements for oxytocin during an induced labor vary. There appears to be a point at which the sensitivity of the uterine muscle increases, probably because of the release of prostaglandins (usually at 5 or more centimeters). This has the effect of maintaining the length, strength, and rate of contractions despite a gradual decrease in the amount of Pitocin administered, and in some cases the MM2 can reduce the dose to the absolute minimum as normal labor supervenes. Many of the hazards of induction, however, are associated with the administration of Pitocin, and these will be discussed separately.

4. *Prostaglandin Administration* The discovery, isolation, and synthesis of the various types of prostaglandin aroused great

interest in the 1970s because of their effect on the pregnant uterus and cervix. Prostaglandins are not hormones; that is, they are not substances produced at one site and conveyed via the bloodstream to their site of action. With one or two exceptions, they are locally produced, locally acting "cell messengers." Thus, oral and intravenous administration cannot in any sense be regarded as physiological. Despite the success that has been obtained in using prostaglandins to initiate labor, there is little evidence that they are primarily responsible for initiating spontaneous labor and their precise function is still not very well understood. They do appear to have a direct effect on the mechanical properties of cervical tissue, and possibly on the lower part of the uterus as well. It is this effect that led to their being used in women for whom induction of labor was considered desirable, but who had unfavorable (unripe) cervices; prostaglandins caused softening of the tissue and lowered the point at which it yielded to stretching, thus making amniotomy—with or without Pitocin—easier and more effective. It may be that this property renders them unsuitable for use as a means of induction in mothers who have previously had a cesarean section, since the connective tissue of the uterine scar may also be softened, leading to uterine rupture in labor.[10]

Prostaglandins have been administered in a variety of ways. Intravenously they are as effective as Pitocin, but have a higher incidence of such side effects as diarrhea and nausea. Given orally, they have similar gastrointestinal side effects and are insufficiently effective in inducing labor in women having their first babies to make them suitable for routine use.[11] They have been found to be moderately effective when given extra-amniotically (that is, when instilled into the uterus outside the bag of waters), but this is an invasive technique and therefore carries a risk of infection; moreover, for this procedure the prostaglandin is contained in a gel that requires sterilization and is unstable (it breaks down rapidly into a simpler form), so frequent preparations of this gel are necessary.

More recently, the use of a vaginal prostaglandin tablet to induce labor has been investigated. It has the advantage of being simple, effective, and noninvasive. It produces results that are superior to those obtained using Pitocin *without* amniotomy, but inferior to those obtained using Pitocin *with* amniotomy. It is preferable to both of these more invasive techniques in that the women treated do not have their mobility restricted, suffer no gastrointestinal side effects, and seem to develop a uterine action similar to that of a normal labor. Following the vaginal administration of 4 milligrams of prostaglandin PGE_2, one study reported, 58.6 percent of first-time mothers and 81.2 percent of mothers having their second or subsequent child went into labor without further action (an average of about 70 percent). Of the 30 percent that remained, 16 percent showed a significant change in the state of the cervix following the use of PGE_2; its use was thus associated with a reduction in the incidence of cesarean section and fetal distress when labor was subsequently induced using synthetic oxytocin and amniotomy.[12]

Disadvantages to the Mother of Induced Labor

The disadvantages of amniotomy have already been discussed, while prostaglandins have not been in use long enough for their disadvantages (other than the obvious gastrointestinal ones) to have come to light. The following section, therefore, is essentially confined to the side effects of Pitocin.

"Not all the complications which follow induction of labor are necessarily due to the induction itself; some are related to the abnormality which indicated the need for induction in the first place."[13] While this may be true when inductions for which there are strong medical indications are considered, the case becomes harder to argue when the "indications" are widened to include those mothers with less well defined needs; it is impossible to sustain when spontaneous labors and their outcomes are compared with a matched induced group in whom there are *no* medical or obstetrical abnormalities (such a study has recently been carried out in Oxford).[14]

In order to induce a labor with Pitocin, an intravenous infusion (IV, or drip) has to be set up. This automatically restricts the mother's movements and mobility, as she cannot put any weight on the arm with the IV; she will therefore have difficulty in changing her position, particularly when labor is advanced, and walking about (assuming that she is allowed to do so) will be harder if she has to push an IV stand around with her (with few exceptions, the wheels on an IV stand are rather like those on a supermarket cart: they lock when subjected to even minor changes of direction).

If the mother has her labor induced, there is an increased chance that she will be monitored (normally by applying a scalp clip to the baby's head and an external pressure gauge to the top of the mother's abdomen by means of a belt), as opposed to simply having the baby's heart rate checked every 15 minutes with a fetal stethoscope. This procedure appears to be a feature of induction itself and not of the indications for induction.[15] Such women are therefore subjected to all the disadvantages associated with internal monitoring (see below), which cannot be offset by even the theoretical advantage that monitoring has been thought to confer. They are, in addition, at increased risk of developing fetal distress in labor as a result of both amniotomy and the restricted positions for labor (see Chapter Three).

The type and pattern of labor contractions produced by Pitocin are very different from those experienced by women in spontaneous labor. In the majority of cases, established labor (strong, rhythmical, regular contractions accompanied by dilation of the cervix) is preceded by intermittent bouts of regular contractions, sometimes for several hours, in the days or weeks beforehand. Thus, when the true labor contractions begin, the woman may mentally dismiss them (or at least not give herself over to them entirely for some time) until she is sure that this is the "real thing." This means that she has a long period in which to adjust psychologically and physically to the stress of labor. Such is not the case when labor is induced. Frequent contractions begin almost immediately at close, regular intervals (3 to 5 minutes), and the infusion rate will be increased quickly (relative to a spontaneous labor) until contractions are at the level desired by the obstetrician—that is, every 2 to 3 minutes. The prospective mother not only has a greatly reduced period in which to acclimate herself to contractions, but also has to cope with them at very frequent intervals virtually from the beginning of her labor. Conversely, in many cases where labor begins spontaneously, by the time the contractions are as frequent as every 2 to 3 minutes, the mother is well into her total duration of labor.

The contractions in an induced labor, moreover, are of a different quality from those of a spontaneous labor (they have been described as "sharp" or "spiteful" by some mothers). This is not surprising when one considers that the pharmaceutical levels of oxytocin in the mother's bloodstream are two to four times as high as those found in spontaneous labor. Since the feeling of these contractions is not a factor that can be measured externally, however, it is therefore either not considered or is dismissed as "subjective" by many professionals. It has been established for some time that there is an increased need for and use of pharmaceutical pain relief (Demerol [meperidine] and epidural anesthesia in particular) associated with induction of labor using oxytocin, particularly when the membranes are ruptured, and this cannot be attributed to the "reasons" for the induction but rather to the procedure of induction itself.[16] This is confirmed by the aforementioned Oxford study, which found that 94 percent of mothers having induced labors required some form of analgesia, while only 68.5 percent of the spontaneous group needed drugs. When these two groups were further subdivided, it was revealed that 49 percent of the induced group had epidural anesthesia, while only 13.5 percent of the spontaneous group did. (It should be pointed out that eighteen mothers [8.5 percent] in the spontaneous-onset group were "augmented" with oxytocin during their labors, and fifty-one mothers [24.4 percent] in this group had their membranes ruptured artificially out of a total of 210.)[17] Induction also had a marked effect on the method of delivery. The increase in forceps deliveries and cesarean sections has been noted by a number of observers. In some cases this is due to the type of analgesia used (forceps rates in women with effective epidurals are much higher than in those without), and in other cases to the increased incidence of fetal distress (as a result of the stronger contractions) and in association with the increased use of narcotics.[18]

In the Oxford study, where there were no preexisting reasons among those induced that might be expected to increase the likelihood of fetal distress, the forceps and cesarean-section rate in the induced group was nevertheless much higher—32.5 percent, compared with 19 percent in the spontaneous onset group. Furthermore, the excess in the number of operative deliveries in the induced group could not be accounted for by the pain relief and monitoring they received. (Forceps deliveries in the induced group were also more difficult than in the spontaneous group—requiring, for instance, rotation or moderate to strong traction. This may be explained in part by the higher incidence of epidural anesthesia.)[19] The study concluded that "membership in the induced group itself appears to carry an added risk of an operative delivery" (construed as anything other than a spontaneous delivery—for example, forceps or vacuum extractor delivery; not necessarily cesarean section).[20]

Another hazard of induction that is not related to the type of delivery is the increased tendency to postpartum hemorrhage (PPH), that is, a blood loss of 500 milliliters (about 1 pint) or more. In 1978, researchers found that the PPH rate among first-time mothers who had induced labors was almost twice that of those with spontaneous labors. This supported earlier work that had shown an "induced" PPH rate of 8.3 percent compared with an overall rate of 3.4 percent for the same period.[21] In the

Oxford study, the PPH rate was 8 percent in the induced group and 3 percent among the spontaneous-onset group (a finding compatible with the figures for that entire hospital in the preceding year, when the PPH rate for induced labors was 10 percent and the PPH rate for all labors was 5 percent).[22] One possible explanation for this increased PPH rate is that the uterus in an induced labor is exposed to high doses of oxytocin for a long period and will therefore respond poorly to an intramuscular or intravenous injection of the same or a similar oxytocic drug in the third stage of labor;[23] it presumably responds equally poorly, in some cases, to the physiological oxytocin produced spontaneously after the baby is born.

Disadvantages to the Baby of Induced Labor

The increase in the number of cesarean sections and forceps deliveries in recent years may in part be due to the increased diagnosis of fetal distress in labor. Between 1967 and 1973, fetal distress increased rapidly, according to a Welsh study: from 8.9 percent to 20 percent; over the same period, the induction rate (using amniotomy and Pitocin) rose from 3.8 percent to 23.2 percent. Although cause and effect cannot automatically be assumed here, other research has shown an association between fetal distress and the use of synthetic oxytocin.[24]

In 1974, Liston and Campbell showed that "those [labors] with oxytocin [Pitocin] clearly have a higher incidence of fetal distress than those with none," although they pointed out that this might be explained in part by the underlying reason for the induction.[25] Other studies cited in this paper also noted an increase in fetal distress in labors where Pitocin was used. One researcher, addressing the March 1974 conference of the American Foundation for Maternal and Child Health, stated in his conclusion that "in oxytocic-induced labors . . . almost 75 percent of the mothers' uterine contractions were shown . . . to result in a reduction of oxygen to the baby's brain."[26] The

Oxford study found a slightly higher incidence of heart-rate changes in babies whose mothers had labor induced than in those whose mothers had begun labor spontaneously (although this was not considered significant in the statistical sense).[27] It is possible to speculate that the increase might have been greater, relative to the spontaneous-onset group, had the latter not included mothers whose membranes were ruptured artificially and/or who were given oxytocin to accelerate labor.

Possibly more important than whether a baby is diagnosed to have fetal distress during labor is the condition of that baby when born. The number of babies suffering from respiratory depression—that is, taking more than 3 minutes before the onset of regular respiration—is three times greater when labor is complicated by the use of Pitocin and amniotomy than when labor is spontaneous. Some babies will respond to the simple administration of oxygen through a face mask; others (when respiratory distress is due to the drugs—for example, Demerol —administered to the mother during labor) will respond to the Demerol antidote. Those who respond to neither, however, have to be intubated (that is, have a small plastic tube put down the windpipe so that oxygen can be introduced directly into the lungs). The Oxford study documented almost four times as many babies requiring intubation in the induced group as in the spontaneous-onset group, and since in this study *no* inductions were performed for medical or obstetrical abnormalities, none of this increase can be attributed to the underlying "indications" for induction.[28]

When a baby is born, his or her condition is rapidly assessed by a doctor, nurse, or midwife according to the Apgar scoring system. In this system, the baby is marked 0, 1, or 2 for each of five characteristics. The maximum possible score for a healthy, vigorous baby is 10/10. (See table on page 50.)

A baby who does not breathe will get 0/2 in Section C; in this case the baby's color will also be poor: either 0/2 or 1/2 in Section A. If this situation persists without treatment, the baby's condition will deteriorate (the heart rate will start to slow, the bluish color will become more pronounced), and the original maximum score of 7/10 will start to drop. The Welsh study showed an "apparent increase [in the number of babies born with an Apgar score of between 4 and 7] from 13.8 in 1967 to 22.2 in 1973, during which time the number of labors induced with amniotomy and oxytocin also rose, from 3.8 per cent in 1967 to 23.2 per cent in 1973."[29] Again, one cannot automatically assume that the two factors are directly related, but it seems reasonable to suggest that the rise in induction may have played some part in the rise in the number of hypoxic (oxygen-deficient) babies.

One of the ways in which induction and hypoxia at birth may be connected is the increased use of drugs in induced labor. Most of these have the effect of depressing the baby's breathing at birth and/or the Apgar score. One study concludes that there

	Sign	0	1 Point	2 Points
A	Skin color	Generalized purply-blue or white	Pink, with purply-blue extremities	Pink all over
B	Muscle tone	Limp or floppy	Moves limbs	Moves vigorously
C	Breathing attempts	Does not breathe at all	Gasps	Breathes well
D	Heartbeat	Absent	Less than 100 beats per minute	More than 100 beats per minute
E	Response to a stimulus — e.g. touch, pinprick, etc.	No response	Little response	Vigorous response

is little doubt that the combination of greater use of analgesic drugs and the more violent contractions of the accelerated labor can produce newborns with respiratory depression.[30]

Another factor that will contribute to the increase in respiratory depression is the relative immaturity of induced babies. If induction of labor is performed before term, the baby's lungs are less likely to be ready for use outside the womb. Normally, the mature newborn's lungs require an initial effort to inflate them, but thereafter the surface tension in the lungs is high enough to prevent them from collapsing again when the baby breathes out. When this is not the case, the infant suffers from respiratory distress, and each breath requires the same effort as the first one. This is still a significant cause of perinatal deaths. Sometimes, the age of the fetus *in utero* is incorrectly assessed, and the infant produced as a result of the induction may actually be so immature as to develop respiratory distress. (One of the newborns in the Oxford study who developed respiratory distress was thought at induction to be of 39 weeks' gestation, but was subsequently assessed at 36 weeks' gestation.)[31]

Jaundice in infants has also become much more common in recent years. The precise reasons for this are uncertain, but it has been shown to be associated with the use of Pitocin for induction and acceleration of labor. A group of scientists in Ireland have also published work highly suggestive of a causal relationship that may even be dose-dependent. The increase in the use of forceps for delivery (as a result of the increased necessity for epidurals) has also been shown to relate to the rise in the incidence of neonatal jaundice, and it may be that one of the factors increasing the jaundice rate is the amount of bruising the baby receives at delivery.[32]

In many cases, jaundice in babies a few days old requires no treatment, but if it is severe and a blood test shows that the levels of bilirubin (the substance that gives jaundiced skin its yellow color) are high, the newborn may need to be admitted to a special care unit for phototherapy (treatment under lights). If the situation is even more serious, exchange blood transfusions may be undertaken.

Many of the factors discussed above, moreover, may result in the newborn's needing treatment in a special care unit. This frequently means that the mother and baby have to be separated. But it is now well established that separating mother and child at birth may have important psychological consequences (see Chapter Seven).

Having considered the means and the possible hazards of induction, one ought to look at the possible benefits. Social considerations apart, an induction is medically justifiable only when the risks inherent in the procedure are less than those that could be expected were the pregnancy allowed to continue—or, to put it another way, only when the danger to the mother and/or baby, if the latter remains *in utero,* is greater than that of induction and delivery.

There are some obstetrical conditions in which it may be hazardous for the pregnancy to continue to term, and in these cases preterm delivery may prove valuable. In a high proportion of these cases, however, an elective cesarean section rather than induction of labor is indicated, as the stress of labor on top of an already compromised fetal blood/oxygen supply may precipitate acute fetal distress. Maternal conditions that may be included in this category are: essential hypertension, renal disease, pre-eclampsia with proteinuria (that is, protein present in the urine), Rh isoimmunization, and diabetes.[33]

1. *Essential Hypertension* (occurs in 1 to 3 percent of pregnancies) This is a sustained rise in blood pressure prior to pregnancy, precipitated by a generalized spasm of the smaller arteries (arterioles), which in turn leads to greater resistance to the flow of blood. The reason for this is unknown, but the effect is to reduce the blood supply to the uterus; as a consequence, the formation of the placenta may be affected and the fetus may fail to grow properly. If the hypertension is severe, the mother's

health may also be affected. In about 30 percent of cases, protein appears in the urine, so that the condition is indistinguishable from severe pre-eclampsia.

2. *Renal Disease* (occurs in 0.2 percent of pregnancies) Adequately treated renal disease (glomerular nephritis) that has occurred before the onset of pregnancy will only complicate a pregnancy if it is accompanied by a significant rise in blood pressure—which happens in about 40 percent of cases. In these circumstances, the situation is similar to that in (1) above, in that reduced placental blood flow may affect fetal growth. If the actual function of the kidneys (the ability of the kidneys to filter off and excrete toxic waste) has been affected by the disease, the fetus is relatively unlikely to survive (60 percent die *in utero*), and the mother's health may be seriously affected.

3. *Pre-eclampsia* (occurs in 6 percent of all pregnancies; 12 percent of first pregnancies) This is considered to be severe when there is more than a trace of protein in the urine and the diastolic blood pressure—the bottom reading—is over 100 mmHg. It does not normally occur before 28 weeks of pregnancy, so the placenta is likely to be normally formed. Severe pre-eclampsia is associated with a reduced blood supply to and reduced function of the placenta. When visual, gastric, or cerebral disturbances are present, the mother's other organs may be affected as well. Pre-eclampsia is usually a slowly progressive disorder, but it may suddenly develop or suddenly become severe, in which case the mother's health will deteriorate precipitately. Termination of pregnancy by cesarean section is then indicated, whatever the duration of pregnancy. About a quarter of mothers with severe pre-eclampsia are suitable for induction rather than cesarean section, but some researchers have suggested that "a conflict of purpose is introduced . . . every time a foetus who is considered to be at risk is subjected to an extended period of stress with oxytocin."[34]

It should be emphasized that these three conditions—essential hypertension, renal disease, and pre-eclampsia—affect only about 8 percent of the pregnant population, and in only a small proportion of these instances is induction preferable to cesarean section in order to produce a live birth.

4. *Rhesus disease or isoimmunization* It is difficult to estimate the precise incidence of the disease as opposed to the mortality, but in 1969 it was estimated to occur in 0.5 percent of pregnancies; this figure is probably much lower now.[35] The problem occurs in an Rh-negative mother who carries an Rh-positive baby. In normal circumstances it is of no consequence in the first pregnancy, unless the mother has received Rh-positive blood from some source prior to the first established pregnancy, as happens in a very few instances. This could occur with a blood transfusion or a miscarriage or abortion for which there was no medical supervision (and therefore no RhoGAM was given). When the first birth takes place, some placental (fetal) blood may escape into the maternal blood as the placenta separates. If nothing is done about it, the mother's body will react over the next 60 hours to the presence of this foreign material and produce antibodies that will destroy it. These antibodies remain present in the mother's bloodstream and are small enough to cross the placenta in a subsequent pregnancy, when they will begin to destroy the fetus's blood cells.

There are several reasons why this condition is not as frequent today as formerly. These include changes in the birth rank (that is, fewer women have large numbers of children): as the effects of the disease are worse in successive pregnancies, reduction in the number of births per woman reduces the overall incidence of the problem and its severity. In addition, there is the general improvement in perinatal and obstetrical care, as well as the introduction of high-potency anti-Rh gamma globulin (RhoGAM), which, when administered within 60 hours of delivery to an Rh-negative mother, will prevent the formation of antibodies. All this means that the use of induction to terminate a pregnancy in which Rh disease is severe after 34 weeks (before that, cesarean section is preferred) will affect only a very small proportion of women.[36]

5. *Diabetes* (present in 0.1 to 0.3 percent of women of childbearing age) The main problems associated with pregnancy in a diabetic woman manifest themselves after the 28th week, when the incidence of pre-eclampsia and polyhydramnios (too much amniotic fluid) increases; the perinatal mortality rises rapidly after 38 weeks. Most of the deaths are *in utero,* but some occur in labor, and some in the newborn period (usually from respiratory distress syndrome). The cause of intrauterine death is unknown, but it is thought to be due to altered exchange mechanisms in the placenta.[37] (Congenital abnormalities are also thought to be higher in diabetic pregnancies.) Because there is a rise in the perinatal mortality after 38 weeks' gestation, the baby is usually delivered during the 37th week. This will necessarily result in a premature baby, and the mortality in premature babies is already higher than normal. (In individual cases, however, where there is excellent control of diabetes, some obstetricians will now deliver the baby at term, that is, at 40 weeks.) Part of the increased perinatal mortality rate associated with diabetes also stems from the premature labor often brought about by both the increased size of the fetus (when diabetes is poorly controlled) and by polyhydramnios, both of which "stretch" the uterus.

Cesarean section is the usual method of delivery (when the baby is alive, and there are no known abnormalities that would be incompatible with life). Induction of labor in selected diabetic women has its advocates, but it is thought to increase the perinatal mortality rate.

Induction and Placental Insufficiency

A pilot study conducted in Ireland came to the conclusion that induction was seldom undertaken in the interests of the mother and that the indications entered in the records could often not be substantiated as being in the interests of the child. It also stated that almost the only fetal indication for induction of labor was "placental insufficiency," and that this could occur as a primary condition without any maternal abnormality.[38] "Placental insufficiency" is a blanket term—usually what is meant is that the placenta is normally formed and functioning in the early stages of pregnancy, but that something then intervenes to impair its functioning. The condition is usually diagnosed in retrospect, when the uterus does not enlarge as quickly as expected or when the delivered baby is smaller than expected for the period of gestation (then the term "intrauterine growth retardation" is used). Sometimes the underlying cause is apparent (see 1–4 above), but often it is not. Intrauterine growth retardation may be detected during pregnancy, clinically, biochemically, or by ultrasound, but often it is not apparent until after the baby is born.

Placental insufficiency also refers to a form of placental failure, as the oxygen need of the fetus exceeds that which can be supplied by the placenta. Since this is a feature of later pregnancy, it does not manifest itself as intrauterine growth retardation. Sometimes the cause is apparent: for example, partial separation of the placenta, which is usually accompanied by a some hemorrhaging but which is not so great as to cause immediate fetal death or to warrant immediate intervention. Very often, however, it is not apparent, and it is deaths in this category that are referred to as "mature—cause unknown." These are deaths that many obstetricians consider preventable and that are given as a reason for introducing high rates of induction.[39] Where perinatal mortality has been reduced, it is often ascribed to the beneficial effect of a liberal induction policy. One of the difficulties in preventing the "unknown-cause" deaths is precisely that their cause is not known; since other factors were changing during the period when the induction rate was rising, it is therefore equally plausible to attribute the fall in such deaths to obstetrical and pediatric influences other than induction.[40] A study conducted in Glasgow in 1977 is often cited by advocates of an aggressive approach to the induction of labor, as it concluded that "the increased use of induction for labor has contributed to an improved perinatal mortality rate."[41] But there have been several objections to this conclusion from other quarters. It was pointed out by one pair of researchers that over the period in question there had been a general falling tendency in perinatal mortality rates for most parts of the country and that in Glasgow the increasing rate of induction actually interrupted this general downward trend during the early years (the induction rate began to increase after 1970, and in 1970, 1971, and 1972, the perinatal mortality was higher than in 1969). Furthermore, these researchers drew attention to the fact that no comparison had been made between the perinatal mortality rate of an induced group and the perinatal mortality rate of a noninduced group over the same period.[42]

Other observers showed surprise that the authors of the Glasgow study had failed to comment on the fact that the "mature unknown" death rate failed to improve as the induction rate rose between 1974 and 1975.[43] In total contradiction to the findings in Glasgow, another large maternity hospital with over 7,500 deliveries per year showed a perinatal mortality rate that decreased from 38.4 to 16.4 (per 1,000 total births) as the induction rate *decreased* from 26.3 percent to 10 percent.[44]

The aforementioned Welsh study (which analyzed the trends in management and outcome of pregnancy in nearly 40,000 deliveries to women living in Cardiff between 1965 and 1973) revealed no striking change in either the total perinatal death rate or the timing and cause of perinatal deaths. Further work in Cardiff compared the work and results of two local obstetrical teams with contrasting liberal and conservative policies over a five-year period. It failed to demonstrate that any significant advantage was conferred by the wider use of induction.[45]

Intrauterine growth retardation is not always easy to pinpoint. Sometimes the tests used to assess, either directly or indirectly, the state of the placenta identify such cases where none exist; out of 289 predicted cases of fetal growth retardation, for instance, reported by one group of researchers, only 83 actual cases materialized. In many cases, conversely, growth retardation is not picked up where it does exist; out of the five perinatal deaths that occurred in the pregnancies followed in another study, four were due to fetal growth retardation (all four infants weighed much less than expected for the gestation time), and the decision to deliver these babies early could have been made only on individual diagnoses of poor intrauterine growth. Even a liberal induction policy, that is, would not have induced these particular cases.[46]

Furthermore, two of the tests currently used to detect either placental insufficiency or the effects of placental insufficiency—namely urinary estrogen assay ("estriol collections") and serial ultrasound cephalometry scans—were not associated with any differences in the perinatal mortality rates in the comparison study in Cardiff or in work published by Beard. Another study has shown that the number of fetal movements felt by the mother in a 12-hour period is a better indication of fetal well-being than 24-hour urinary estrogen assay. A daily fetal movement count (12 hours) of above 10 was generally associated with a good outcome, even in mothers deemed to be at risk. On the other hand, a low fetal movement count was associated with a high incidence of fetal asphyxia and intrauterine death, even when urinary estrogen levels were normal.[47]

The concept of high risk has greatly influenced contemporary obstetrics. Although it may be the case that pre-eclampsia and prolonged pregnancy are associated with an increased perinatal mortality (because of placental insufficiency), it does not follow that placental insufficiency is a feature of all cases of pre-eclampsia or prolonged pregnancy. Perinatal deaths as a result of pre-eclampsia are increased only when the pre-eclampsia is severe, that is, when the diastolic blood pressure is above 100 mmHg and there is protein in the urine. It follows that pre-eclampsia without these two factors is seldom a valid reason for induction. Nevertheless, in many hospitals every case of pre-eclampsia is induced, no matter how slight. (The Glasgow study actually showed a slight rise in the perinatal mortality rate due to pre-eclampsia, despite their aggressive induction policy, and it is tempting to suggest that if the baby is at risk as a result of maternal pre-eclampsia, the risk is increased when the fetus is subjected to "an extended period of stress with oxytocin.")[48]

Prolonged pregnancy (a pregnancy lasting more than 41 weeks, or 42 weeks by some definitions), which was shown in one study to be associated with an increased perinatal mortality, is the most common reason given for induction.[49] In the Oxford study, over half of the inductions were performed for this reason, in the absence of any other medical or obstetrical abnormalities (110 out of 210).[50] Prolonged pregnancy is not normally associated with placental insufficiency, so presumably the increased incidence of fetal death and fetal distress in labor is due either to a decline in placental function or to the oxygen needs of the fetus exceeding the placenta's ability to supply it—but it does not follow that this will be the case in all prolonged pregnancies. Researchers subjected 104 mothers with "prolonged pregnancy" to weekly oxytocin challenge tests and 24-hour urine collections for estriol measurement three times per week. An oxytocin challenge test (OCT) entails monitoring (externally) the baby's heart rate and the mother's uterine activity for 20 minutes, and then giving a very small dose of intravenous oxytocin, increasing the dose until three uterine contractions are observed in two consecutive 10-minute periods; at this point the test is considered complete. The test is termed positive (cause for concern) if the baby's heart rate drops at the end of a contraction on three or more consecutive occasions. Positive OCTs were registered in 7.6 percent of cases; these were delivered immediately and thus eliminated as possible cases of fetal deaths. Prolonged pregnancy managed in this way was not associated with an increased perinatal mortality rate, but the incidence of fetal distress in labor and babies requiring resuscitation after birth increased. (Estriol measurements were not helpful in predicting the state of the baby, either in labor or after delivery.)[51]

In 1979, another study monitored the progress of 180 women whose pregnancies had lasted for 42 weeks and who had been randomly assigned to two management groups. All the women had an amniocentesis performed to see if meconium was present in the amniotic fluid. Then, 90 had weekly OCTs until delivery (unless the tests were positive, in which case they were induced); the other 90 had weekly amniocentesis to detect meconium (again, if meconium was found, or if no amniotic fluid could be obtained, they were induced.)

Since neither of these tests had been evaluated using a randomized control trial, this study could only demonstrate the relative benefits of meconium detection and positive OCTs as indicators of fetuses at increased risk in prolonged pregnancy. It found that nearly three times as many women had labor induced on the strength of positive evidence of meconium as did for positive OCT, with no statistical difference in perinatal outcome. The conclusion was that the presence of meconium is not by itself an indication that the fetus is at increased risk, but that the historical association of meconium and increased perinatal damage probably led to the assumption of a causal relationship and consequently to its use as an indicator of fetal well-being.

The study also found that 48 percent of those mothers followed by OCT and over 50 percent of all the mothers in the trial (that is, in both groups) were at very low risk of developing problems in labor—as low as those in a normal delivery population. Only one baby whose mother had a negative OCT and clear amniotic fluid actually developed fetal distress in labor (i.e., 2 percent). Comments on the study suggest that although a positive OCT is not an accurate predictor of fetal distress in labor, a negative OCT might be a useful guide to fetal well-being.[52]

In the same year, a different research group gave ninety-seven mothers with prolonged pregnancy oxytocin challenge tests and amnioscopy (looking at the color of the amniotic fluid behind the intact membranes by inserting an amnioscope into the vagina just through the cervix) every 48 hours. (Amnioscopy was considered positive if meconium was present in the amniotic fluid.) In the interval, 24-hour urine collections were made and fetal movements were counted. (Fetal-movement counts in this case were made by counting the number of movements in a 1-hour period in the morning and a 1-hour period in the evening and expressing the results as a daily mean; in this study, a count of 15 or fewer movements was considered low.) If *both* amnioscopy and OCT were positive, the mothers were delivered immediately (usually by cesarean section). If *either* was positive, then labor was induced by amniotomy and oxytocin. Estriol levels and fetal movements did not influence the decision to induce labor and were not predictive of fetal distress except when combined with other positive test results.

This method of screening was rapid, reliable, and highly predictive of fetal distress. Of the fifty mothers in the study with all four tests negative, only one developed fetal distress in labor. In twenty-four of the remaining cases, where OCT and amniotomy were negative but either fetal movements or estriols were abnormal, only one developed fetal distress in labor.

The study concluded that the judicious application of tests of placental function may help to reduce perinatal mortality and morbidity (for example, fetal distress or babies needing resuscitation). It also stated that these measures would detect the cases that needed intervention, thus eliminating unnecessary inductions of labor. This statement was in agreement with the conclusion reached by another researcher that induction should not be performed on the basis of the patient being in an epidemiological "at risk" group, but more specifically on the basis of abnormal fetal monitoring tests.[53]

This conclusion was further supported by a 1982 study in which 2,000 women were randomly allocated to two consultants, one of whom favored noninduction for postmaturity, whereas the other routinely admitted mothers at 42 weeks' gestation for induction. Out of this large, consecutively recorded group, 142 were recorded as having a gestation period of 42 weeks or more. Eighty-one of these were designated "certain postmature"; of these, 30 were induced and 51 awaited spontaneous labor. The remaining 61 were designated "uncertain postmature"; of these, 16 were induced and 45 awaited spontaneous labor.

These researchers found that although babies of "postmature mothers" did show a "significantly increased morbidity in terms of low Apgar scores at one minute . . . this was not confirmed by other assessments of neonatal condition" and "neonatal morbidity was no different whether the labor was induced or not." What induction did do was to significantly increase the number of cesarean deliveries. Spontaneous labor in "certain postmature" mothers resulted in delivery by cesarean section in 9.8 percent of mothers, compared with 9.6 percent in the total population (that is, the rest of the 2,000) and 26.7 percent in the induced "certain postmature" group. In the "uncertain postmature" group, the difference is even more striking. Among the induced group, the cesarean rate was 31.2 percent, compared with 2.2 percent for those allowed to go into spontaneous labor. The study concluded that "a pregnancy prolonged beyond 42 weeks . . . may affect neonatal outcome, but induction of labor does not improve this, and uncomplicated postmaturity is not an indication for the induction of labor."[54]

It will be apparent from the above that there is great controversy among obstetricians about what constitutes an indication for induction, and that "the truth of the matter is that [we are all] largely ignorant about the circumstances in which the benefits of induction outweigh its disadvantages."[55] Until more randomized, controlled trials are carried out to assess the validity of some of the present indications for induction, simply advocating high levels of induction in the hope that this will lower perinatal mortality is a highly unscientific way to proceed —and unethical when it exposes large numbers of normal mothers and babies quite unnecessarily to the risks associated with induction. It behooves those who advocate induction to demonstrate its superiority in specific situations by appropriately designed research.

Accelerating Labor

Acceleration differs from induction (which refers to the initiation of labor) in that it involves the use of Pitocin or amniotomy to speed up a labor that has already started spontaneously. Initially it was advocated to improve the efficiency of labors that were progressing slowly, in order to avoid the problems to mother and baby associated with "prolonged labor" (labor lasting more than 24 hours). Statistically speaking, prolonged labor is more likely to be a feature of first labors, particularly if the mothers are over 30 years of age and/or under 61 inches (5 feet 1 inch) tall. Even so, it is likely to affect only 5 to 15 percent of first labors and 2 to 5 percent of subsequent labors.[56]

The longer the duration of prolonged labor, the higher the incidence of maternal mortality due to infection, traumatic delivery, and shock; but these are very rare causes of death in developed countries, where cesarean sections are performed with relative safety. The baby is also at increased risk from infection, hypoxia (from prolonged reduction in placental circulation), and trauma from difficult delivery. The main cause of prolonged labor, as determined by a study in Edinburgh in 1956, was inefficient uterine action (50 percent ascribed to the quality of the uterus, 25 percent ascribed to the position of the baby), and the overall incidence of prolonged labor was 3 percent.[57] This is a lower figure than the 5 to 15 percent cited above because those mothers in whom there was disproportion (a pelvis too small to allow the passage of the baby's head, which would obviously cause prolonged labor) had usually been delivered by cesarean section before they had been in labor for 24 hours. Since the use of Pitocin can affect the labor beneficially only by improving the efficiency of the uterine contractions, it would appear to be of use only for 2.1 percent of the pregnant population.

Predicting those mothers for whom prolonged labor will be a problem if left untreated is obviously important. This may be done by means of a partogram, which is a graph on which cervical dilation is measured against time. The expected rate of progress is indicated by an "alert line" drawn on the graph, and the individual mother's progress is plotted on top of this. In some cases the alert line is straight, assuming a rate of progress of 1 centimeter dilation per hour; in other cases it curves toward the time axis, in recognition of the fact that many labors do not begin at such a fast rate. This is illustrated by the two examples below:

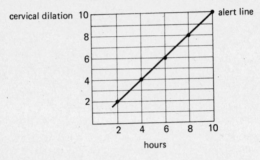

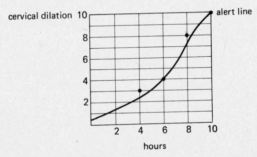

If labor is accelerated whenever it is seen to cross the alert line, not only will all mothers at risk from prolonged labor be "speeded up," but so will all mothers in whom labor would just have taken longer than average, particularly for the first half of labor, but who are not in a category of high risk. The longer-than-average mothers, who can be distinguished from the prolonged mothers only in retrospect, will have nothing to gain from the acceleration and nothing against which to offset the potential hazards associated with the use of Pitocin. In addition, vaginal examinations will have to be made more frequently to check progress and plot an accurate time.

All the hazards associated with the use of Pitocin (with the exception of an unexpected prematurity) that have already been discussed in assessing its administration for induction are also valid when considering acceleration—in particular the increased use of pain-relieving drugs and the associated increase in the rate of operative deliveries and delivery of babies with respiratory depression.

One enthusiastic advocate of acceleration of labor suggests that all mothers should be educated to expect delivery within 8 hours of admission to the hospital, by the early use of Pitocin and amniotomy when progress is deemed to be slow and by cesarean section if labor is not completed within 12 hours. By controlling the duration of labor, he maintains, the allocation of one nurse or midwife to one patient is possible and the need for analgesics will be reduced because the mother's exposure to stress is reduced, partly because the length of labor is potentially shortened and partly because the approximate time of delivery can be predicted in all but a minority of cases. He also asserts that there is an "inverse ratio between the need for analgesia and the quality of care in the delivery unit, which is most likely to reflect the degree of personal involvement of senior medical personnel in the management of labor."[58]

While the aims and motives expressed may be admirable, it could be argued that in the absence of medical indications for intervention or controlled trials to prove the superiority of such a policy, the same ends could be achieved if more consideration were given to the physiological and psychological methods for preventing "long" labors—which would, of course, include the provision of continuous care by one nurse or midwife and the personal involvement of the medical staff.

Breaking the Waters (Amniotomy)

When the fetus is developing inside the uterus during pregnancy, it does so within a double membrane. The outer membrane (called the chorion) is thin, opaque, and easily torn; the inner membrane (called the amnion) is smooth, translucent, and tough. The term "amniotomy" actually refers only to this inner membrane, but in fact both membranes are ruptured. This bag of membranes contains a variable quantity of fluid (the waters), ranging from 500 to 1,500 milliliters (1 to 3 pints). The fluid distends the "bag" and allows the free movement and growth of the unborn baby. It also acts as a barrier to external infection from the vagina and as a shock absorber, protecting the fetus to a large extent from jarring and injury.

When labor starts, the fluid and membranes take on another, equally important hydrostatic function: as the uterus contracts, the pressure inside it rises, and this rise in pressure extends to the unborn baby's circulatory system within the placenta, cord, brain, skull, and scalp. At the same time, the pressure of the amniotic fluid on the outside of the fetus also rises. Thus, while the membranes are intact, the rise in "water" pressure outside compensates for the rise in pressure inside the fetus. It also tends to reduce the downward pressure on the unborn baby's skull bones, particularly when the head is engaged.[59]

In view of the importance of the membranes in the normal physiology of labor and the undesirable consequences to the fetus of amniotomy shown by the research just cited, it would seem appropriate to question the common obstetrical practice of rupturing the membranes artificially as a routine procedure early in labor. This maneuver is unjustified in labors that start spontaneously and where normal progress is being made, especially if the baby is considered to be at low risk. The commonest reason given for breaking the waters in these circumstances is that labor will take a shorter time if this is done; another is that the labor needs to be monitored electronically. But fetal monitoring, if indicated, can be started by methods that do not involve breaking the waters. Either an external fetal electrode and transducer can be used, or else a thin catheter attached to a transducer can be inserted between the intact membranes and the uterine wall.[60]

Amniotomy can be performed later in labor if suspicious signs of fetal distress appear on the monitor tracing, such as a late fall in the unborn baby's heart rate after the contraction has passed its peak, variable rhythms, or a fall in heart rate coinciding with the peak of a contraction.[61] The waters may be broken in these instances to allow a blood sample to be taken from the unborn baby's scalp for a more accurate determination of its condition, and also possibly to insert a small electrode into the scalp.

When Do the Membranes Rupture Spontaneously?

In a recent study, a group of 517 mothers with normal pregnancies were allowed to labor without the membranes being disturbed artifically. Of the group, 66 percent had intact membranes at the end of the first stage. Of these, 34 percent ruptured at 10 centimeters (the end of the first stage and beginning of the second), 20 percent ruptured during the second stage, and 12 percent still had the membranes intact at delivery. The fact that in two-thirds of the group the membranes did not rupture until the end of the first stage suggests that late rupture is a necessary feature of the normal process of labor. Other researchers in the same collaborative study found that in 85 percent of women laboring normally the membranes did not rupture spontaneously until the cervix was dilated 9 centimeters or more, and none ruptured spontaneously before 4 centimeters.[62]

Early versus Late Rupture

1. *Duration of Labor* When two large groups were compared— 464 with membranes ruptured between 4 and 5 centimeters and 380 with membranes ruptured at 10 centimeters—and the re-

sults analyzed, the labors of the early-rupture group were shown to be shorter by an average of 50 minutes. This finding was confirmed by Dr. R. Caldeyro-Barcia, who found an overall reduction of 40 minutes in the labors of the early-rupture group.[63] The probable explanation for these findings is that when the membranes are no longer present between the fetal head and the cervix, the head makes closer contact with the cervix and dilates it more efficiently. This is likely to be at the expense of the greater possibility of mechanical damage to the skull and underlying structures as the protection conferred by intact membranes is removed. Caldeyro-Barcia has gone so far as to say that he considers early rupture, even when it happens spontaneously, to constitute an actual complication.[64]

2. *Formation of Caput Succedaneum* This is an edematous swelling on the newborn's scalp due to the pressure of the cervix. The ring of pressure interferes with the venous blood supply to the scalp and causes the area lying over the cervix to become congested. When caput formation has taken place, it is apparent at birth and usually disappears within 36 hours. There is a very strong association between the time that the membranes rupture relative to delivery and the formation of caput: from a 34 percent incidence with early rupture down to 5 percent with late rupture.[65]

When the membranes are not present, there is no compensatory compression of the scalp, and with each contraction, small amounts of blood and serum are squeezed out of the scalp vessels: this produces the caput. Although no harmful effects can be attributed to the caput itself, it may be an indication of similar circulatory disturbances within the baby's brain tissue.

3. *Disalignment of the Baby's Skull Bones* The pressure on the fetal head, even with a normal labor and intact membranes, is greater on the central skull bones (the parietal bones) than on the others.[66] As a result, these tend to protrude in relation to the bones at the back and front of the skull (the occipital and

frontal bones). This process is called "molding" and can be considered as physiological, provided that it occurs only to a minor degree.[67] The more marked the molding, however, the greater the likelihood of damage to the cerebral membranes and blood vessels in the brain beneath. The bleeding that results when these are damaged is often severe, as the blood vessels are relatively unsupported. According to one study, the incidence of bleeding associated with the tearing of brain tissue increases with the number of hours elapsing between rupture of the membranes and delivery. In agreement with this finding, another researcher reported that the longer this interval, the greater is the incidence of mental retardation.[68] The fact that there is relatively high disalignment of the parietal bones even in infants whose mothers' membranes ruptured late suggests that membrane rupture is not the only factor involved in disalignment. Nevertheless, there is a strong correlation between early rupture of the membranes and the degree of bone disalignment in the newborn's skull, which is borne out by postmortem results that emphasized the role played by rupture of the membranes as a cause of impairment of brain function.[69]

4. *Changes in the Fetal Heart Rate* A transient fall in heart rate that is synchronous with the uterine contraction that produces it (a Type I dip as shown on a fetal monitor) has been shown to have several potential causes: uneven compression and deformation of the fetal head during contractions (resulting in stimulation of the vagus nerve), engagement of the head in the pelvis during labor, and interruption of the blood flow through the umbilical cord.[70] A study carried out to investigate the relationship between the state of the membranes, the engagement of the head, and changes in fetal heart rate concluded that the incidence of such changes (Type I dips) was lower when the membranes were intact, both before and after the head had engaged. There was an even greater difference in the two rates after the head was engaged—the intact group was much lower.[71]

Marked changes in heart rate have also been shown to occur

in a proportion of unborn babies who have a loop of cord around their necks (a feature of 26 percent of all labors) if the membranes are then ruptured. In these cases, the cord is then compressed between the uterine wall and the fetus itself. If the cord compression lasts more than 60 seconds, the fetus becomes seriously short of oxygen and will exhibit signs of distress that require intervention.[72]

In the light of present knowledge, it would seem reasonable for mothers already in labor when they are admitted to the hospital to object to the practice of rupturing their membranes early in labor, if the only reason that can be given for it is that it may speed up the labor. The procedure is almost invariably accompanied by a change in the force and frequency of the contractions (it makes them stronger and closer together) whether or not the labor is speeded up, and it disturbs the rhythm of a labor with which the mother may be coping well until that point. Moreover, painkillers are often required to counteract the effect of this sudden increase in intensity, which may occur after amniotomy long before the end of the first stage or transition. Even if rupturing the membranes in such a case does cause an acceleration in labor (which is in any case a retrospective discovery), there may be a heavy price to pay in terms of iatrogenic damage. Lastly, it should be borne in mind that acceleration of labor is not necessarily beneficial for the baby. A 1972 study demonstrated that perinatal death and neurological damage persisting at least until the first birthday are both increased when the duration of the first stage is shortened below a given optimal range.[73]

Monitoring the Fetus

It has been known for about 150 years that the fetal heart-rate pattern changes during uterine contractions when the mother is in labor, and that while in the majority of cases these changes are a normal response of the fetus, in some cases the changes may be a warning sign that all is not well with the unborn baby. These facts form the basis for careful checking of the fetal heart rate during labor by means of a fetal stethoscope. During the late 1960s, an electronic form of fetal monitoring was introduced as an alternative to listening by ear through a stethoscope. This electronic device takes two forms—external and internal—and in both cases the uterine contractions are monitored simultaneously with the baby's heart rate.

In the external version, two small devices (either flat or doughnut-shaped) are strapped to the mother's abdomen using broad elastic belts: one device is placed over the top or fundus of the uterus to record contractions, the other over the unborn baby's back or shoulder to record its heart rate. The two devices are connected by thin, flexible wires to the monitor itself, which prints out the recordings of contractions and heart rate continuously on graph paper.

The internal version involves the attachment of a spiral needle electrode to the unborn baby's scalp (or whichever part is over the cervix) to record the heart rate; a plastic tube (or catheter) is inserted into the uterus via the cervix to record the actual pressure of the contractions via the amniotic fluid. Again, both devices are attached to the monitor by wires.

In some hospitals the use of electronic monitoring is backed up by fetal-scalp blood sampling—that is, by making a small puncture in the baby's scalp or whichever part is over the cervix and collecting a blood sample, which is then analyzed to determine the oxygen concentration and the acidity or alkalinity of the blood (pH).

Once introduced, the use of electronic monitoring spread rapidly, as it was claimed that it brought about considerable improvements in the infant and perinatal death rates. Most of these claims were based on a comparison of the mortality rates before and after the introduction of electronic fetal monitoring (EFM). Other investigations, however, showed either no difference or a slight rise in death rates after EFM.[74] A Vermont study showed that the decline in perinatal deaths in hospitals that had used EFM extensively and in those that had not was the same.[75] These studies suggest that factors other than EFM were involved in the improvement in perinatal mortality statistics. Nevertheless, a task force meeting at the National Institutes of Health estimated that 60 to 70 percent of all women are monitored electronically in labor, and many obstetricians believe that this figure should be increased to 100 percent.[76]

In the midst of the debate about the benefits of EFM, there has been a growing concern about the risks and inconveniences to the mother and unborn baby from the use of this technique.

1. If the mother is being monitored externally, either for contractions, fetal heart rate, or both, discomfort may be engendered if she has to wear a tight elastic belt throughout labor.

2. Whether internal or external monitoring is used, unless it is being done by radiotelemetry, the mother is confined to bed and her position in bed restricted because she is attached by a few feet of wire, vaginally or abdominally, to the machine. This can result in decreased placental blood flow and consequent fetal distress.[77] Such restriction is likely to make the labor longer than it need be and to increase the mother's need for pain-relieving drugs—with subsequent repercussions for the unborn baby (see Chapter Five).

3. If the mother is being monitored internally, the bag of waters surrounding the fetus has to be broken to allow the introduction of a tube to record changes in pressure and the insertion of an electrode into the unborn baby's scalp. The consequences for both mother and fetus have already been discussed; they include making the contractions sharper and closer together and increasing the degree of molding of the baby's head and the incidence of cord and skull compression (which will, in the last two cases, produce in their own right abnormal heart changes on the monitor).

4. As might be imagined, inserting an electrode into the unborn baby's scalp is not without its hazards. In most cases, the problems are those of scalp abscess and hemorrhage, but there

have been reports of incorrectly positioned electrodes causing lacerations to the arms, cheek, trunk, and thigh (due in one instance to the electrode being partially attached to the mother's cervix); penetration of the eyelid; penetration of the brain tissue causing a leak of cerebrospinal fluid; and even one neonatal death, due to sepsis.[78]

5. Less catastrophic but very much more common is the effect that the monitor may have on the mother's attendants. In many cases, attention that should be given to the laboring woman is given instead to the monitor, and the mother is relegated to the position of a mere generator of electrical impulses. In some instances, this is taken to the point where the monitor is given greater credibility than the mother; if the monitor "says" that she is having weak contractions when the mother maintains that they are strong (this may happen if the base line is incorrectly set), then the monitor is believed and the mother contradicted. This will do nothing to improve her morale or strengthen her trust in her attendants.

6. While there are no doubt mothers who find the presence of monitors at their bedsides reassuring, there are also those who are bothered by the flashing lights, the sound produced with each heartbeat, and by hearing or seeing decelerations in fetal heart rate, even when these are benign.

7. The problem that is most consistently associated with the use of EFM is that of increased cesarean section (with an accompanying increase in postdelivery infection).[79]

In view of these possible side effects and the inadequacy of retrospective studies in deciding the possible benefits, it became apparent that the only scientific way to resolve the question of the effects of EFM was by randomized, controlled clinical trials.[80] In these research projects, women and their babies are randomly assigned to two different types of treatment—in this case, listening to the fetal heart with a stethoscope (auscultation) or through EFM. By 1978, four trials had been carried out: two in Denver, Colorado, from 1973 to 1975 and from 1975 to 1977;

one in Melbourne, Australia, in 1976; and one in Sheffield, England, in 1978.[81] The first three studies all used women who were judged to be at high risk; the fourth used low-risk mothers.

None of the four studies was large enough to demonstrate any difference in perinatal mortality rates; but none of them demonstrated any differences in the Apgar scores between the two groups. The only study to publish enough information about cord blood pH to make any conclusion possible was the second Denver trial, which found no difference between the EFM and the auscultated group of babies. Neurological examination of the newborns was made in all four studies: the first Denver study and the Sheffield study found no difference at all in the two groups. The Melbourne study showed four babies with convulsions in the auscultated group and none in the EFM group, but it was not clear from the published results whether these four were among the five who were delivered by mid-forceps and whether therefore the convulsions should be attributed to the type of delivery, the absence of monitoring, or both. In each of these three trials, the doctors examining the babies knew to which group they belonged. The only study in which the examiners did not know in which group the babies had been was the second Denver study, and this trial reported no significant difference. This was also the only study that provided follow-up assessments at 9 months of age; again, no significant difference was found between the two groups.

Although the results are not conclusive, these trials appear to show no clear-cut advantage for EFM over auscultation with respect to perinatal morbidity.[82] All four studies, however, demonstrated unequivocally that there was a significant increase in the cesarean-section rate (CSR) in the EFM group compared with the auscultated group. In the first Denver study, the EFM group had a CSR of 16.5 percent compared with 6.6 percent for the auscultated group; in the second study, the EFM group had a CSR of 18 percent compared with 6 percent for the auscultated group. In the Melbourne study, the EFM group had a CSR of 22.3 percent compared with 13.7 percent, and in the Sheffield study the EFM group had a CSR of 9 percent compared with 4 percent for the auscultated group. When all the factors except the use of EFM are controlled, there is an approximate doubling of the cesarean-section rate as a result of using EFM.[83] This is a serious finding, for although cesarean sections can be lifesaving for mother and child, they also carry a much higher incidence of intrauterine infection than vaginal deliveries and also entail the increased use of anesthesia, with its own attendant risks. Two American studies have found that the risk of death from cesarean section is ten to twenty-six times that for vaginal delivery, and in England, a large study has shown that in 1972 the estimated mortality from cesarean section was more than eight times greater than from vaginal delivery.[84] As has already been demonstrated, this increase is not offset by any improvement in perinatal mortality rate.

In their careful review of the literature (including the four randomized, controlled clinical trials just cited), Banta and Thacker concluded that there is little, if any, benefit to be derived from the use of EFM compared with auscultation. If EFM is of benefit, that benefit appears to be confined to infants of low birth weight, but as yet there has been no randomized, controlled clinical trial of EFM in this group. The risks of EFM as well as the cost are, they say, substantial; in America, the price was estimated at $411 million per annum in 1979.[85]

Because of these factors, EFM is currently being reevaluated in the United States, and the National Center for Health Care made fetal monitoring one of the first technologies that it discussed. In the meantime, with respect to the problem of malpractice suits in America, the National Institutes of Health task force has concluded that auscultation is an acceptable alternative to EFM in low-risk pregnancies.

If the best that can be said of electronic fetal monitoring is that it is equivalent to auscultation, perhaps we should be looking more closely at its use, both in terms of unwanted side effects and in terms of the enormous cost of the machines. Meanwhile, obstetricians must continue to make clinical decisions about their use, despite the lack of evidence as to their benefits. Since some women will continue to find the presence of a monitor reassuring, while others will not, obtaining the mother's informed consent appears to be the only ethical path to take.

CHAPTER FIVE

The First Stage:

PAIN IN LABOR

The Expectation of Pain

Before examining in detail the drugs that are available for use in labor, it is logical to consider the basic assumption made by a large proportion of the population that labor is necessarily and inevitably painful. When different cultures throughout the world are compared, it is apparent that the extent to which women expect, experience, or express their response to (not necessarily the same thing) pain in labor varies considerably. The Navaho Indians, for example, have two distinct words for labor, one meaning "the pain of labor" and the other, "labor" alone. There is cultural recognition of the fact that childbirth without pain is possible, and one witness of more than 400 Navaho births has reported that though some women definitely experienced pain, there were others who showed no signs of doing so.[1]

Simply comparing the drug-usage rates in different populations is probably a rather crude and inaccurate measure of the perception of pain in labor in these populations. The dramatic difference between the United Kingdom (with a drug-usage rate in labor of 95 percent) and Holland (with a drug-usage rate of 5 percent), however, suggests that social and educational factors are involved in the way in which labor is interpreted, and that pain is not purely a matter of physiology.[2] As Sir Henry Head, one of the great pioneer neurologists, reported, "The mental state of the patient has a notoriously profound influence over the pain initiating in the pelvic viscera."[3] In other words, how the stimulus is interpreted is as relevant as the stimulus itself. Superstition, civilization, and culture have all brought influences to bear on the minds of women, and the more modern the cultures of the earth have become, the more positive they have been (for the most part) in pronouncing childbirth a painful and dangerous ordeal. This may be due in part to the tendency in developed societies to remove childbirth from the family setting, so that it is no longer part of the flow of life, but something separate, unseen, and therefore mysterious and alarming. Another contributing factor may be the posture adopted for labor in Western societies. No other animal species voluntarily assumes such disadvantageous positions during this important and critical event.[4]

There are many fundamental ways in which a woman's expectations of the experience of labor are modified, from early childhood right up to the onset of labor. It is instructive to look more closely at the way in which young girls—and boys—are taught to think about labor. At the moment there seems to be comparatively little material available for children to counteract the disastrous effects of descriptions of childbirth in many works of fiction, and worse still, television, films, and plays where birth is represented (as opposed to recorded); the last three are much more effortlessly and insidiously absorbed. If a child watches a program in which a woman supposedly giving birth lies flat in a bed, hanging onto the sides or the headrail, rigid and screaming, while the attendants act as if this were appropriate behavior, it is likely that this depiction will leave a lasting impression on the child's mind. If this image is not balanced by solid factual information from parents or schools, or if the effects are compounded by half-heard conversations about a neighbor's or relative's "awful time," then it is not surprising that the adult the child grows into views childbirth with extreme trepidation.

The situation may be improved by good prenatal preparation, including information and relaxation and breathing techniques appropriate for dealing with the stresses of labor, received by the now more mature mind of the expectant mother, but even so

the teacher of childbirth classes cannot hope to correct in eight
to ten weeks the impressions and misconceptions that have
accumulated over the years. "What . . . [women] . . . bring to
labor is nothing less than [their] entire socialization as women."[5]
It is therefore worth looking closely at the physiological and
psychological factors that influence the subjective experience of
labor.

There are three layers of muscle fibers in the wall of the uterus
which, while not anatomically separate, have different functions.
The longitudinal fibers run from the cervix, or neck of the
uterus, up to the top (fundus) of the uterus and down the other
side. When these contract, they shorten the uterus and are
therefore mainly used in the expulsive second stage of labor.
The spiral or oblique fibers also start at the cervix and run in
all directions in the body of the uterus; when these contract
during labor, they play a major part in "taking up" or shortening the elongated cervix and then dilating it until eventually it
is wide enough to allow the baby's head to pass down into the
vagina without obstruction—the cervix is then said to be fully
dilated. During and after the separation of the placenta (after-
birth), these fibers, by virtue of being entwined in a figure eight
around the larger blood vessels, help to reduce blood loss after
the baby is born. The circular fibers, as the name implies, pass
horizontally around the uterus, mainly in the lower half and in
the cervix. When these contract, they tend to close the cervix
and inhibit the activity of the lower part of the uterus during
labor.

The precise nerve supply to the uterus is incompletely understood, but the uterus seems to be supplied principally by autonomic nerves from the lumbar and pelvic ganglia; it may also be
that the longitudinal and oblique fibers are supplied by local
ganglia within the uterus, unconnected with the spinal cord or
autonomic system. Certainly the uterus can continue to contract
when the autonomic system is cut off.[6] In practice, in a smoothly
coordinated labor, the longitudinal and spiral muscles contract

and start to open the cervix, while the circular fibers around the cervix stay relaxed to allow this to happen. Simple, unopposed muscle contraction does not in itself produce pain. The only pain receptors in the abdomen are those that detect excessive tension in, or tearing of, the tissues. The intestines and uterus can be burned (cauterized), handled, or moved without any sensation of pain, but if either of these structures is stretched or torn, considerable pain and shock may result. The pain perceived in labor therefore must result from one or both of these specific stimuli.

If a woman in labor has been led to expect pain, then she is likely to be in a state of tension, "waiting for the pain." This diffuse state will increase the intensity of the (new) sensations of labor and thus tend to bring her defense—fight-or-flight—mechanisms into operation; adrenaline will be released. The same chain reaction occurs if she is frightened or alarmed, whether by internal or external events. This release of adrenaline has the same effect as the stimulation of the sympathetic nervous system, and two things happen. First, the circular fibers of the uterus start to contract in direct opposition to the contracting oblique and longitudinal fibers, and a tug-of-war begins. This rapidly produces a state of abnormal tension in the walls of the uterus, which is in turn recorded by the receptors specific for that form of stimulation and is correctly interpreted as pain. Now the prospective mother has involuntarily justified her original apprehension, and the vicious circle of fear-tension-pain described by Grantly Dick-Read is set up.[7]

The other effect of sympathetic stimulation is to reduce the blood flow to organs not needed for defense, diverting it to the heart, lungs, and skeletal muscles. Thus the uterus, not being required for defense, subsequently has its blood supply reduced in spite of the fact that it is actively contracting. The fact that restricting the circulation to an actively contracting muscle produces pain is well known (for example, in angina) and can be simply demonstrated by rapidly opening and closing the fist of one hand while restricting the blood supply at the wrist with the other. The physiological explanation for the pain was put forward by Sir Thomas Lewis, who suggested that in such circumstances the breakdown products of tissue respiration accumulate faster than the bloodstream can remove them, so that they build up in crystalline form, lacerating the walls of the blood sinuses and smaller vessels within the muscle fibers.[8] If a restricted blood supply is allowed to persist for any length of time, the unborn baby within the uterus is also likely to be deprived of oxygen, producing fetal distress, possibly brain damage, and even intrauterine death.

The powerful effect of fear and tension on the physiological process of parturition is well illustrated in the animal kingdom. The laboring female red deer, if frightened during labor, responds with such tension in her muscles and glands that they cease to function, actually causing her contractions to slow down and stop. She can now move away from the source of potential danger. Once she has found another quiet spot, her body relaxes and her contractions begin again unhindered. Other animals cannot as effectively suspend the process of labor and start it again without ill effects. In sheep, for instance, any unnatural disturbance during labor produces a considerable increase in the number of deliveries in which the assistance of the veterinary surgeon is required; in cattle, dogs, and cats, not only do such disturbances prolong labor, but they also result in a much higher perinatal mortality rate.[9]

A frequently observed phenomenon in hospitals is that of the woman who starts experiencing regular contractions at home and is admitted to the hospital in labor, only to discover that her contractions have stopped. Even if the woman has no conscious fear of hospitals and believes that it is necessary for her to give birth in one, the changed surroundings appear to exert a powerful influence on her inner biological rhythm. It is relevant here to quote Grantly Dick-Read's comments on the prolonged labor syndrome. Speaking of course of those cases in

which there is no disproportion or malpresentation of the unborn baby, he says that "a labor . . . is long because it is painful,
not painful because it is long."[10]

Many factors may trigger this unhappy state of affairs, both
in pregnancy and in labor. Prenatal classes that teach relaxation
but stress the availability of drugs for "when it gets too bad" or
for "when the breathing isn't enough" reinforce the inevitabil-
ity of pain. The suggestion of pain is conveyed by the atmosphere of many labor and delivery rooms, which look like operating rooms; it emanates from doctors, midwives, nurses, and
relatives. If they all believe in pain, then consciously or subcon-
sciously they suggest, expect, and even presume pain. To the
sensitive mind of the woman in labor, looks of sympathy, exhortations to "be brave," or even "not to be a martyr" are all
powerful pain producers. Dr. Peter Dunn, a British pediatrician,
has remarked that "it is my belief that the misunderstanding of
this subject [pain in labor] and the use of analgesics as the first
line of defense is one of the saddest developments in obstetrics."[11]

Most of the world's mothers receive few or no drugs in labor
or delivery. The constant emotional support provided by familiar people—relatives, friends, or midwives—is the commonest
cross-cultural resource for dealing with the powerful experience
of labor and appears to improve considerably the mother's toler-
ance of discomfort and to raise her pain threshold. In such
societies, the laboring woman has a greater confidence in her
own ability to give birth unaided than is usually the case in ours:
her attendants keep her morale high and bring no fear to the
normal process. In contrast, the labor-room nurse or midwife in
America and Britain is frequently assigned to look after several
women in labor simultaneously; in this situation, particularly if
the laboring women have received no preparation in coping
with the sensations of labor, drugs are used as a substitute for
emotional support, to relieve the mothers' apprehension, discomfort, and eventually pain—and perhaps to assuage the har-
ried labor attendant's feeling of inadequacy.[12]

It is an indictment of modern obstetric practice that it is possible to look through the case notes for a record of drugs administered in labor and to observe, not what sort of pain the woman had, but which consultant she was under or which midwife was on duty.[13]

Sedating a woman not only makes her quieter and easier to manage, giving the doctor or midwife the feeling that he or she has done something to "improve" the situation, it also subdues the feelings of helplessness and anxiety generated in the professionals themselves by the woman's response to her labor. If the labor attendant is unable to offer emotional support because of personal inadequacy, lack of training, or lack of time, and if the woman is also deprived of those who can offer this—husband, friends, and other labor companions—then analgesics will appear superficially to provide the same effect.

On the other hand, there are those who see no point at all in withholding drugs if they are available and who are unable to entertain the idea that a labor might simply involve hard work rather than pain. "Why should she be allowed to continue to suffer?" they ask themselves, observing a woman in labor. In many cases they totally fail to interpret correctly the signals given out by the woman concentrating hard on the sensations of the late first stage, which are saying, "Support me—tell me this is supposed to happen," and not, as they mistakenly read them, "Stop all this—do it for me."[14] Part of this attitude may be explained by the training received by birth attendants. In the 1950s, it was taught that at a particular stage of labor, a certain quantity of a certain drug was given routinely; the idea that some women might not require an analgesic was never entertained. Even now, very little is included in the training given to birth attendants on the alternatives to drugs.

The purpose of this chapter has been to underline the premise that pain is neither necessary nor inevitable in a normal labor. However, while it may be possible to prevent a woman from perceiving her labor as painful by the understanding and implementation of the principles discussed, it is quite another matter to reverse the situation, nonpharmacologically, when pain exists. When there are underlying physiological causes for that pain, such as disproportion or malpresentation, it may be impossible. It would in any case be cruel to deny the validity of the woman's subjective experience of pain (even in normal labor) on the grounds that it was physiologically "unnecessary." It may well be "all in her mind," but it is nonetheless real. This being so, the next consideration is of the drugs currently used in obstetrics. The argument here is that the potential recipient should be fully aware of the hazards of any drugs, as well as their benefits, and that they should be used highly selectively and with the prospective mother's full knowledge and consent.[15]

Relieving Pain with Drugs

In some instances the use of pain-relieving drugs during labor is indicated on medical grounds: for example, epidural anesthesia is indicated when the mother's blood pressure is very high, or, more rarely, when her response to pain threatens her welfare and that of her baby because of hyperventilation. In the latter instance, when a mother breathes too rapidly and deeply as a result of the pain she is experiencing, she breathes out more carbon dioxide than her body needs to get rid of; as a result, she starts to feel faint, then gets a tingling sensation in her fingers and feet, which may eventually start to curl up involuntarily and go into spasm. The oxygen supply to the unborn baby may thus be reduced, and if the mother cannot correct this condition herself by breathing in and out of cupped hands or a paper bag, it is appropriate to institute pharmacological methods of pain relief as a matter of urgency.

In most cases, drugs are offered to a laboring woman to relieve the pain or discomfort that her attendants assume she is experiencing. Even if they are correct in their assumption, it is vital that the mother's wishes are respected and her consent obtained. "Informed consent sometimes has the effect of alarming a patient, and then taking up the doctor's/midwife's time while her fears are put into perspective—but anything less is not informed consent, it is selling."[16] On the mother's individual refusal or acceptance of the drugs offered may depend the quality of her labor (and her memory of it), the quality and type of her delivery, and more extremely, the condition of her unborn baby and the quality of its future life. It is important that a mother be aware of her right to refuse drugs when they are suggested solely for her comfort and that she realize that this is not an area where anyone else can possibly know better what would be "good" for her, since only she knows what she is feeling. The other important consideration is the range of possible side effects that the proposed drug may have. It is astonishing that so much publicity is given to the dangers of smoking and drug-taking in pregnancy, and so little to the possible dangers of using narcotics and other drugs during labor. Virtually all drugs given during labor tend to cross the placenta rapidly and alter the fetal environment as they enter the circulatory system of the unborn infant within minutes or seconds of being administered to the mother.[17] There is an added problem with drug administration during labor. While the baby is *in utero*, the mother's liver is still involved in detoxifying any circulating drugs. But once a baby is born with any drugs in the bloodstream, the newborn is then dependent on his or her own liver to complete the process of detoxification. As is medically well known, the newborn's liver is one of the last systems to mature, so that the timing of a drug is as important as the type and dose; a drug like Demerol, for instance, which the mother can clear in a matter of hours, may persist in the baby for several days. At best, the drugs given to the mother will have a minimal or negligible effect on her baby; certainly they will have no beneficial effect.[18]

As far as the mother herself is concerned, it would be wrong for her to assume, or for her attendants to assure her, that drugs administered by a doctor or midwife are in any way guaranteed to have the effect that is intended, or that there are no risks involved. In order for her to be able to make a decision about the use of any particular drug during labor, she needs to know as much as possible *prenatally* about the benefits and hazards, both for her and for her baby, of the range of available drugs.

If a mother in labor decides that in her particular circumstances the advantages of accepting a particular drug despite its possible side effects still outweigh the advantages of doing without it, then that is her choice and one that she is perfectly entitled to make. Moreover, the much-repeated exhortations not to "feel like a failure" if drugs are used is unlikely to be relevant, since the mother will be able to justify her decision to herself.

The problems arise when the mother who is ignorant of the possible hazards accepts a particular drug and then discovers later the implications of having done so. It is necessary to keep in mind that it is the mother who must ultimately bear the emotional burden of the decision, particularly if the child is damaged or impaired. "As the public becomes more aware of the possible effects of obstetric practices on infant outcome, failure to disclose or inform the mother of the possible adverse consequences . . . may become the basis of legal liability if or when those adverse consequences occur."[19]

The following is an examination of the drugs commonly used in labor. It cannot be stressed too much that vaginal examination to assess the dilation of the cervix should *precede* the administration of any drug or other form of intervention.

Systemic Drugs Used During Labor

Demerol (meperidine)

This is a synthetic narcotic introduced in 1940 as an alternative to heroin and morphine. Its popularity evolved from the mistaken belief that Demerol was an "antispasmodic" that would both relieve pain and relax the uterus, the latter in contrast to morphine.[20] It can be given in quantities of 50, 100, 150, or 200 milligrams at a time. It is given by intramuscular injection.

Advantages to the Mother Demerol is given with the intention of helping the laboring woman to relax more easily and, by inducing a sensation of distance or separation from reality, helping her to cope better with the contractions; it is not intended to remove pain altogether. It is sometimes used in the belief that it will lower blood pressure.

Disadvantages to the Mother If the above effect is taken a little further, it may make the mother too drowsy to register anything more than the peak of the contractions, making her unable to prepare for them and thus removing what little control she has over her labor. Taken further still, it may make the mother go to sleep, waking only when the drug starts to wear off. It has no direct effect on uterine action, but it has been observed to slow down labor in some cases.[21] In 15 percent of cases it induces nausea or vomiting and is thus frequently combined with an anti-emetic (see below). It is not a good analgesic: in a double-blind trial, only 52 percent of women could distinguish between Demerol and saline administered intramuscularly; in another trial, only 50 to 60 percent of mothers regarded the analgesic effect as satisfactory.[22] If the mother is to be made drowsy without obtaining any analgesic benefit, then the situation is made worse than before as far as she is concerned, even though it may make her "easier" for her attendants to manage. Unfortunately, it is not possible to predict in advance the effect of Demerol on a particular woman: 50 milligrams may send one prospective mother to sleep and have no effect at all on another. For this reason, it would be advisable for any mother not familiar with her own response to Demerol to request that she be given only 50 milligrams to start with (despite the belief that a dose of less than 50 milligrams is indistinguishable from a placebo),[23] on the grounds that she can always have more later if 50 milligrams proves to be ineffective. There is nothing she can do to rid herself of the excess drug if she is given too much for her needs except to wait until it wears off—in 1½ to 2 hours. Some midwives in America start with doses as low as 25 and never expect to use more than 75 milligrams.

Disadvantages to the Baby It has now been well established that Demerol—in common with Nisentil, barbiturates, some tranquilizers, and epidurals—has an effect on the baby's ability to suck, which is not necessarily related to its Apgar score (see Chapter Four). In extreme cases this may actually inhibit lactation. It may also make the baby sleepy and slow to breathe, and the effects on sucking may last for up to two weeks.[24]

It is also well established that Demerol has an effect on infants' ability to habituate, that is, to acclimate themselves to a particular repeated stimulus and then ignore it if it is not relevant. A newborn whose mother has received no drugs during labor may take five to six exposures to the same stimulus—a noise or a shining light—before he or she ignores it. A baby whose mother has received Demerol may need thirteen to fifteen exposures to the same stimulus before he or she can ignore it. Demerol can delay the development of the ability to habituate for at least two months,[25] and the overall effect of Demerol on the newborn may be the unfortunately familiar sight in some maternity hospitals of the baby who is at the same time jumpy and sleepy—and a poor feeder as well. Such babies are difficult to handle and may undermine the mother's confidence, especially if this is her first baby; there may be subsequent deleterious effects on the mother-infant relationship if the mother feels that she can do nothing right. One study of mother-infant interaction states that "meperidine [Demerol] produces outstanding neonatal differences in the ability to process information" and adds that "a major obstetric danger may now be medication itself."[26]

Apart from the dose and the maturity of the infant (narcotics should especially be avoided in preterm deliveries), the effects of Demerol will also depend on the timing of the dose. It is widely held that the drug should be administered 4 hours before the birth in order for it to have the minimal effect on the unborn baby. Measurements of the excretion of Demerol in the urine of newborns, however, indicate that the concentration continues to increase for up to 5 hours.[27] It also appears that the side effects are produced not only by Demerol itself but by one of its breakdown products, so that the drug would need to be given 6 to 8 hours before delivery to have the minimal effect—or 1 to 2 hours before delivery, before the concentration reaches its peak, in which case the mother might well go to sleep immediately after the birth. In the former case, 6 to 8 hours would be somewhat difficult to estimate. Four hours before delivery, however, is probably the worst possible time for administration.[28]

Nisentil (alphaprodine)

The use of this drug is confined largely to America and Canada; it is not used in Britain. It is a narcotic analgesic, chemically related to and with an action resembling that of Demerol, but more rapid in onset and of shorter duration. Unlike Demerol, it is given by subcutaneous injection (that is, it is injected under the skin rather than into the muscle); this may make its absorption a little less predictable. It is given in doses of 20 to 60 milligrams, which may be repeated at 2-hour intervals up to a maximum of 240 milligrams in 24 hours. Often it is given very early in labor, when the cervix has just begun to dilate. As with Demerol, its side effects are of the morphine type, and it may produce respiratory depression in infants and nausea, vomiting, drowsiness, and confusion in the mother.[29]

Tranquilizers

These are given to allay anxiety and reduce tension. The two most commonly used are Valium (diazepam) and Sparine (promazine). Valium is widely used as a tranquilizer and in the treatment of pre-eclampsia in pregnancy, in an attempt to lower blood pressure. Sparine is used for the same reason in labor: to reduce blood pressure by reducing anxiety; it also helps to ameliorate the nauseant side effects of Demerol. Tranquilizers in general and Valium in particular have a direct effect on muscle tone in the newborn (hypotonia) and reduce the ability to breathe at birth and the ability to suck; they may also have the effect of profoundly lowering body temperature (hypothermia).[30] Both these effects may last for days or weeks, and in the view of many pediatricians, these drugs have little place in obstetrics.[31]

Phenothiazine Derivatives

Trilafon (perphenazine) and Phenergan (promethazine) are usually used in labor to counteract the nauseant side effects of Demerol. They both have a sedative side effect and react with Demerol synergistically, that is, the sum total of these drugs' effects is greater than that of simple addition.[32] Phenergan has also been shown in one study to disturb the ability of the baby's blood to clot.[33]

Inhalation Analgesia ("Gas and Air")

The two most common inhalation analgesics used in America and Britain are 0.35 percent methoxyfluorance in air (Penthrane) and nitrous oxide. In America, of the two, Penthrane is used more often; in Britain, 50 percent nitrous oxide with 50 percent oxygen (known as Entonox) is more popular. (Nitrous oxide is more commonly used in America as an anesthetic than as an analgesic; when it is employed as an analgesic, the concentration is more likely to be 40 percent nitrous oxide with 60 percent oxygen.) Both these inhalation analgesics are potentially general anesthetics, but are administered in subanesthetic concentrations through systems that make self-administration possible. If the mother takes too much and falls asleep, the mask slips down from her face: she breathes air and wakes up (one very good reason why the mask should never be forcibly held over the mother's face, unfortunately not an uncommon sight in some institutions). In both cases, successful use depends on the mother's learning how to make the peak concentration of the agent in her blood coincide with the peak of a contraction, and this is best done by prenatal instruction and experimentation under supervision.

The advantages to the mother are that the effects are immediate and short-lived. If she finds it useful—and the majority of those who use it (70 percent for Entonox and 90 percent for Penthrane) finds it is—she can continue to self-administer it; if she dislikes its effect, she can discontinue it and the effects will have worn off within a minute.[34] These two inhalation analgesics may also be useful in reducing the effects of hyperventilation. Penthrane, being a soluble agent, stays in the blood longer, thus making it easier to ensure successful peak pain relief. That is also its disadvantage; over 30 percent of it is metabolized and the breakdown product, a fluoride compound, may damage the kidneys if present in large amounts (though this is unlikely with the low concentration level used). Entonox, being insoluble, is almost totally excreted via the lungs during contractions, but this means that it is more difficult to get the timing right. The fact that the mother can, in both cases, control the gas and air machine herself is, however, of great psychological advantage.

There have been no studies done of the effects of inhalation analgesia alone on the infant, since it is so often used in conjunction with Demerol. Penthrane usage has been shown to result in an increased fluoride concentration in the baby's urine for up to 48 hours, while Entonox appears to have no measurable effect on the newborn.[35] There appear to be no indications to limit the duration of administration; theoretically, Entonox at least could be used throughout labor and is a much undervalued analgesic.

Local Anesthesia Used during Labor

Pudendal-Nerve Block

The pudendal nerves supply most of the perineum, vulva, vagina, and muscles of the pelvic floor. In a pudendal-nerve block,
the nerves in the side walls of the pelvis are injected with local
anesthetic, thus numbing the area completely. This is easy to
perform, usually successful, and is done to provide local anesthesia prior to an instrumental vaginal delivery. The disadvantages
to both the mother and the child are that large quantities of
anesthetic are required to produce the necessary effect, and this
can result in overdose.[36]

Paracervical Block

A paracervical block is an injection of local anesthetic into the
pelvic uterine plexuses that supply the nerves to most of the
cervix and uterus. The advantage to the mother is that this
technique provides satisfactory analgesia for (and shortens) the
first stage of labor for the majority of women. But the disadvantages are so great for the unborn baby that, despite its continued
use in some countries, particularly in Scandinavia and the
United States, at least one authority regards it as "not now
recommended."[37] Several studies have reported severe changes
in heart rate, respiration, and muscle tone in over 30 percent
of newborns whose mothers had this type of anesthesia. According to one study presented at the Internation Symposium on the
Effects of Prolonged Drug Usage on Fetal Development, (1971),
"Fetal depression, even if apparently reversible, might later
affect the motor and intellectual development of the child." The
fact that babies have been known to die as a result of paracervical blocks has also been clearly demonstrated.[38]

Lumbar Epidural Anesthesia

Lumbar epidural anesthesia is an injection of local anesthetic into the epidural or extradural space. (This space is outside the last of the three membranes that cover the spinal cord, just inside the bone and ligament of the vertebral column.) It must only be administered by a skilled practitioner, who should remain on the premises in case complications such as spinal block occur. The process, which is a sterile procedure, takes 10 to 20 minutes to complete and begins with the setting up of an intravenous infusion (drip) of dextrose (sugar) and water; this is in case the fall in blood pressure inevitably caused by the epidural has to be reversed rapidly by intravenous means. The mother then lies on her left side, curled up with her back as close as possible to the edge of the bed. She is asked to inform the anesthetist when she is experiencing a contraction, so that he or she may temporarily halt the procedure; in some cases, she may be given gas and air to breathe. She will then feel the pressure of the anesthetist's thumbs on her back as the anesthetist feels for the necessary bony landmarks. Her back is washed with a cold disinfecting solution, and then a very small central skin area in the lumbar region is injected with local anesthetic, which stings for a few seconds and then produces a feeling of numbness. All the mother should be aware of now is a pushing sensation against her back, until the process is nearly complete. What the anesthetist is doing is making a small hole through the skin and ligaments with a solid needle. This is then removed, and a hollow needle with a syringe half-full of air is inserted in its place. When the syringe gives, indicating that there is no longer any resistance at the point of the needle, it is taken off, and the end of the hollow needle is observed for a few seconds: if the needle has been pushed in too far and the dura punctured (accidental lumbar puncture), this should be apparent at this stage, as spinal fluid would drip out of the needle. If all is well, a fine, soft catheter is then threaded down through the needle. This may cause a slight twinge down one leg. When the catheter has been threaded far enough, the hollow needle is removed, leaving just a long length of catheter protruding from the skin. The point of entry is then sealed, using a sprayed-on plastic film, and a small sponge pad is placed around the area. The external part of the catheter is secured to the skin along the whole of its length, using paper tape; this is continued up the back to the shoulder, or sometimes up to the abdomen. A small filter and a stopper are then attached to the end of the catheter, and a test dose of local anesthetic can then be given by syringe through the catheter via the filter. A full dose follows, and the uterus and cervix are thereby anesthetized (if high concentrations of local anesthetic are used, there may also be some loss of muscle power). The effect usually lasts for 1½ to 2 hours, but the anesthetic can be "topped up" as often as necessary throughout labor. In many major hospitals, dosages are now controlled by machine. The epidural catheter can be inserted before the onset of labor (in the case of induction), if required, with no limitation of the mother's movement, but once the anesthetic has been given, the mother is instructed to lie on her side, because of the potential effect on her blood pressure, which is checked frequently thereafter.

Advantages to the Mother There are numerous advantages of epidural anesthesia:

1. When effective, lumbar epidural anesthesia provides complete pain relief without dulling the mother's mental faculties.
2. It may be of benefit to mothers with serious heart or respiratory disease, as it reduces the work of the lungs during labor.
3. As it reduces muscle activity, it may help in the case of a diabetic mother by reducing her metabolic demands and making it easier to balance her insulin and glucose requirements.
4. As it tends to slow down labor, it may be of value in the management of very rapid (precipitate) labor.[39]
5. Where problems may arise with a very premature pushing

surge—for example, in complete breech—an epidural may be helpful.

6. It is an alternative to a pudendal block, where forceps or vacuum extraction is necessary.

7. It often provides an effective means of lowering the blood pressure where pre-eclamptic toxemia or hypertension is a problem.

8. In some hospitals, nonemergency cesarean section can be performed using epidural instead of general anesthesia. This means that the mother can be conscious for the operation and can see and hold her baby immediately after birth.

Disadvantages to the Mother Epidural anesthesia has its possible drawbacks:

1. Epidurals can be ineffective or only partially effective in removing the sensation of the contractions. This is a serious psychological complication, because if the mother is promised that it will "all be over" for her in terms of dealing with the contractions in 10 to 15 minutes, she may mentally give up her grip on her labor and her responsibility for coping with it. If the promised relief does not then materialize, it may have a devastating effect on her morale.

2. Accidental lumbar puncture occurs in 1 to 2 percent of epidural administrations.[40] Because of the size of the hollow needle, quite a large hole may be made in the dura if the needle is pushed too far. This can result in severe headache, requiring the mother to lie flat in bed for at least 48 hours after delivery. Treatment entails the infusion of fluid into the epidural space to raise the pressure and close the hole. Sometimes 5 to 10 milliliters of the mother's own blood is injected into the epidural space to stop the leak of spinal fluid. Pain may be relieved by taking analgesics (which may have their own complications if the mother is breastfeeding) or by inhaling 5 percent carbon dioxide with 95 percent oxygen for 4 to 5 minutes, although this provides only temporary relief.

3. Accidental subarachnoid injection occurs if the catheter itself punctures the dura when it is being threaded down the hollow needle. It may not be immediately obvious when the test dose is given, but the effect of giving the full dose (five or more times that intended for spinal anesthesia—see below) is that of a widespread block that may paralyze the breathing muscles, so that emergency artificial ventilation becomes necessary.

4. Postdelivery neurological complications are fairly unusual, but mothers do occasionally complain of numbness in the legs or weakness and difficulty in walking. These symptoms do not last more than a few weeks, but may obviously cause the mother considerable concern. The only cases of permanent paralysis as a result of faulty technique that have been recorded occurred twenty years ago, as a result of infection prior to the use of adequate aseptic procedures.[41]

5. Although hypotension (lowering of the blood pressure) is one of the advantages of an epidural if the blood pressure is abnormally high, it is a disadvantage if the laboring woman has normal or low blood pressure. Besides blocking a section of spinal nerves, an effective epidural also blocks off a section of the autonomic ganglia, which control the ability of blood vessels supplied by them to constrict, and thereby to raise the blood pressure. When a woman in late pregnancy or labor lies flat on her back, the weight of her pregnant uterus compresses a major blood vessel returning blood to the heart, which would potentially lead to a lowering of the volume of blood pumped out by the heart and a fall in blood pressure. In 85 percent of the pregnant population, the compensatory constriction of the blood vessels keeps the blood pressure normal. The other 15 percent are unable to compensate effectively, and their blood pressure drops (supine hypotension). By giving the laboring woman an epidural, the anesthetist is depriving her of the ability to counteract the effects of a drop in blood pressure, should it occur; for this reason, no woman with an epidural should ever be allowed to lie flat unsupervised. Maternal deaths have been

recorded when this precaution has been overlooked.[42] Sometimes the blood pressure falls dangerously even when the mother is not lying flat, and large quantities of fluid have to be given intravenously, via the drip system that should already be established.

6. A fully effective epidural in the second stage greatly increases the incidence of forceps delivery. The woman may not be able to feel when her uterus is pushing, and if she is *told* by her attendants and goes through the motions of pushing, she may have no feedback from her vagina and perineum to guide her. There may also be a loss of muscle power, depending on how much anesthetic is used. In addition, there may be a considerable reduction in the strength of the contractions in the second stage, as the normal rapid increase in physiologically produced oxytocin (which is a reflex response to the perceived sensations of vaginal and perineal stretching) is blocked or attenuated by effective uterine and perineal anesthesia.[43] The mother is likely to make much slower progress in the second stage in this situation, and if there is an arbitrary time limit on the second stage, irrespective of the condition of mother and unborn baby, then the incidence of forceps delivery will be higher still.

The incidence of forceps delivery among women having first babies was shown in the 1977 Oxford Epidural Study to be 70 percent; for second and subsequent babies, it was 40 percent. The time of administration (early or late in labor) made no difference. If the epidural was allowed to wear off as the second stage progressed and the mother could feel what she was doing, the forceps rate dropped considerably, but it was still higher than if she had not had an epidural (20 percent). The reason for this is the decrease in tone of the muscles of the pelvic floor. In their normal, unrelaxed state, they form a gutter shape that serves to guide the baby's head as it descends and causes it to rotate toward the front. This process is interfered with when an epidural is given and cannot be reversed by allowing the epidural to wear off. The Oxford study suggests that further research is needed into the possible trauma that might occur to both mothers and newborns if 20 percent of all mothers having epidural anesthesia have to be delivered by Kiellands (rotation) forceps. In some hospitals, all babies delivered by forceps, for whatever reason, spend a period in the intensive care nursery, which results in early separation of mother and child. It has been suggested that in the absence of strong medical indications for regional anesthesia, the mother should be made aware of the increased chance of instrumental delivery, so that she could herself choose between such a method of pain relief and the considerably reduced chance of a spontaneous delivery.[44]

7. Bladder complications do not arise as a result of the epidural itself, but the resultant loss of normal sensation following epidural may necessitate catheterization (passing a soft plastic tube up the urethra and into the bladder to drain the urine) during labor. The more often this is done, the more likely are infection of the bladder and irritation of the urethra, resulting in increased difficulty in passing urine after delivery. This may necessitate a catheter being left in for a day or two while the swelling and irritation subside.

Contraindications The following are strong reasons not to use an epidural block:

1. The mother may not want the procedure. (It removes all sensations of labor and the psychological state that accompanies it.)

2. There may be an area of infection near the proposed site.

3. The mother may be taking anticoagulants or have a bleeding disorder.

4. She may have had substantial bleeding from the uterus prior to labor (prenatal hemorrhage) or be likely to bleed.

5. The mother may have neurological or spinal disease or injury.

6. It has been suggested by certain researchers that the use of epidural anesthesia should be restricted when there is a reason to suspect "fetal compromise," as in severe pre-eclampsia or postmaturity associated with placental insufficiency. These scientists found that even small doses given to mothers in whom low blood pressure was not a problem produced changes in fetal heart pattern (due to the depressant effect of the local anesthetic on heart muscle), which corresponded with those found in fetal hypoxia (oxygen shortage).[45]

Disadvantages to the Baby Epidural anesthesia can endanger the baby:

1. If the mother's blood pressure is allowed to drop as a result of epidural administration and the amount of blood and therefore oxygen supplying the placenta is reduced, fetal bradycardia (a slowing down of the unborn baby's heart rate) may occur, particularly if the mother is lying flat; this is made worse if Pitocin is used.[46] How much the fetus's oxygen supply can be reduced before neurological damage ensues may not be recognized for many years.

2. Since there are blood vessels in the epidural space, the local anesthetic present can be absorbed into the mother's bloodstream and thus transferred to the unborn baby via the placenta. The degree to which this happens depends on the type and quantity of the local anesthetic used. Some types cause slowing of the fetal heart rate, a reduction in the oxygen available to the fetus, and an increase in the acidity of its blood. Others produce poor muscle tone, which has been shown to affect the baby's ability to suck, unrelated to its Apgar score.[47]

3. If the baby has to be delivered by forceps or vacuum extraction purely as a result of the type of analgesia used for the mother (and not for any underlying mechanical difficulties), this can reasonably be regarded as a disadvantage.

Spinal Anesthesia

This is a small quantity of local anesthetic injected into the tissue space immediately surrounding the spinal cord. It is usually given only once, and is used mainly as an alternative to a pudendal block or an epidural to provide anesthesia for forceps or vacuum extraction deliveries. It has the advantage of needing only a small quantity of local anesthetic, so that overdose for the mother and toxicity for the baby are less likely. However, it has the disadvantages of possibly causing a drop in blood pressure and severe headaches after delivery, as the needle must pass through the dura. It is used more commonly in the United States than in Britain, and is sometimes referred to (somewhat inaccurately) as a "saddle block." It may be used to provide anesthesia for cesarean section.

CHAPTER SIX

The Second Stage:

DELIVERY

The Use of the Lithotomy Position for Delivery

The lithotomy position is one in which the woman lies flat on her back on the bed or delivery table with her knees drawn up and spread apart, often with her feet in stirrups. Since it was first advocated in print in 1824, considerable research has been done on the problems it engenders.[1] The recumbent position, as has already been noted in Chapter Three, was advocated to facilitate the use of forceps and to give the birth attendant ready access to the perineum. The arguments used in Chapter Three to demonstrate the ill effects that follow if the laboring woman lies flat on her back in the first stage of labor are equally applicable in the second—namely, the lowering of maternal blood pressure, the reduction in the volume of blood flowing back to the heart, and the potential drop in oxygen supply to the unborn baby.

> The aorta, inferior vena cava, iliac arteries and ureters are all capable of being compressed between the spine and the uterus, causing complete disturbance of the mother's circulation and urine output, which in turn have an unfavorable and distressing effect on the fetus.[2]

Among the other problems that result from the assumption of the lithotomy position are greater pain in the second stage of labor, greater incidence of perineal tears and/or episiotomy, increased need for forceps, need for increased traction when forceps are used, inhibition of spontaneous placental delivery, and greater likelihood of low back strain following delivery.

Greater Pain

One physician, writing in 1894, stated that "during the second stage the patient's posture should be left in general to her own volition."[3] From the subjective point of view, the best position is likely to be the one that results in the minimum of pain and discomfort for the mother. It is also likely to be the most advantageous for delivery from the mechanical point of view.[4] Howard, who in 1954 designed a backrest for the delivery table so that mothers could sit up, claimed that "even now, the majority of humans are born physiologically and for the most part in the squatting position or a variation thereof." He regarded the supine or lithotomy position in general use by modern Western physicians as abnormal and "unphysiologic."[5] This prompted an investigation of the Human Relations Area Files in 1961. (These files are a collection of hundreds of firsthand reports on a large sample of human societies from all over the world. The files are so arranged that the original text of any passage that deals with childbirth in any of the reports can be quickly located and consulted.)[6]

While noting that "primitive peoples display a wider variety of culture patterns than civilized peoples," so that no one position could be singled out as "normal," the investigators found that sixty-two of the seventy-six non-Western cultures that they studied used an upright position: twenty-one used some kind of kneeling position; fifteen, some kind of squatting position; five stood; and nineteen used a sitting position. ("Upright" was defined as a position in which "a line connecting the centers of a woman's third and fifth lumbar vertebrae was more nearly vertical than horizontal," with the third vertebra higher than the fifth.) Since these peoples are not constrained by Western obstetrics, it is reasonable to assume that they adopt these positions because they want to do so—because it is more comfortable. This contention is further supported by a personal communication from M. Newton (professor of obstetrics at the University of Mississippi) to Howard, in which Newton stated that he was looking for a way to achieve more comfort in delivery in a group of underprivileged women who could not afford the expense of analgesia or anesthesia. This was accomplished by allowing them to assume an upright position. In a later study covering 349 mothers, Newton found that those who were upright required less analgesia for delivery than the controls who were lying down—irrespective of the number of children they had already borne.[7]

The Increased Need for Forceps

This is often due in part to the greater need for analgesia if the woman lies flat (see Chapter Five); epidural anesthesia in particular has been shown to result in a dramatic increase in the rate of use of forceps.[8] It may also in part be due to the effect of the supine position on the mechanics of the second stage.

One researcher has estimated that the force of gravity in the upright position alone is equivalent to a continuous uterine contractile force of 30 to 40 mmHg—and that this increased efficiency is achieved without any increase in the incidence of fetal distress.[9] If the mother is lying flat, she is pushing her baby out at right angles to the gravitational force. This results in a greater incidence of tearing (see page 115), as the resultant force is directed at the perineum rather than the vagina; it also requires considerably more effort on the part of the mother, as she attempts to push her baby "uphill." In 1965, Adele Blankfield wrote:

> If, in addition, the woman's back is lifted off the bed, further handicaps may be imposed upon her. Sometimes she is half somersaulted backwards and has to push against gravity as if she is about to launch a spaceman! . . . Frequently her head is unsupported and drops, so that she pushes into her throat. It is unreasonable to expect the patient to achieve this posture (flat back, thigh on abdomen) herself, as it requires exceptional mus-

cular ability even under normal circumstances. Often, the patient is exhausted, and too tired even to grip her thighs—quite apart from raising her heavy torso and her floppy head.[10]

Moreover, the abdominal muscles, which are trying to aid expulsion by raising the intra-abdominal pressure, have first to contract hard to attempt to bring the mother into a "curved-back" position.[11] If the mother does not give up the attempt in despair in the face of the overwhelming mechanical disadvantages, she is likely to find herself running out of time in hospitals where there is a time limit on the second stage. In both instances, the use of forceps or vacuum extraction is increased.

Increased Traction When Forceps Are Used

The obstetrician using forceps is faced with the same mechanical disadvantage as the mother if he or she tries to deliver a baby with the mother lying flat: the pull is horizontal and the baby's weight is vertical. Howard showed that if the mother is upright, only 80 percent of the force needed in the horizontal position is needed to deliver the baby—the average pull exerted is 28 pounds, compared with 33.5 pounds for the horizontal position.[12]

Inhibition of Placental Delivery

In Newton's study, it was found that the delivery of the placenta was faster if the mother was sitting, slower if she was lying down. If the spontaneous expulsion of the placenta is delayed, it is likely to be delivered by pulling on it, forcing it out by pushing the uterus, or by manual removal (putting a hand inside the uterus and scraping the placenta off the walls of the uterus with the fingers). All these procedures increase the risk of fetal blood cells escaping into the mother's circulation, although this is only significant if the mother is Rh negative. Finally, in the case of manual removal of the placenta, the mother is likely to bleed more, sometimes even to the extent of requiring a blood transfusion.[13]

Low-Back Strain

To place a woman's feet in stirrups takes two assistants in order to lift both legs simultaneously; if the legs are lifted separately or unevenly, low-back discomfort or pain can arise from the strain on the sacrum and lumbar vertebrae. It has often been overlooked, however, that this strain can occur simply from overenthusiastic raising of the laboring mother's legs by her attendants.[14]

X-rays and measurements presented in 1937 indicated that squatting alters pelvic shape in a way that helps delivery. A 1969 study showed that the cross-section surface area of the birth canal may increase dramatically, by as much as 30 percent, when a woman changes from the dorsal to the squatting position.[15] Less "civilized" peoples have instinctively made use of this fact to overcome quite marked cephalo-pelvic disproportion. Numerous instances can be cited of women delivering themselves of stillborn fetuses in situations where the degree of disproportion was such that their own lives were at risk from obstructed labor.[16] (In Western societies, the problem of marked cephalo-pelvic disproportion is resolved by cesarean section.) If an attempt is made to rotate the squatting position through 90 degrees or more (the thigh-on-abdomen position, a variation of the lithotomy position), the result is less satisfactory, as the pelvis sways in space instead of being anchored. This in turn prevents the abdominal muscles from contracting to their maximum advantage.

If the mother is lying flat, her legs are "in the way" of the birth attendants, who are principally interested in seeing the perineum. If the mother cannot hold her legs up herself, the alternative to putting them in stirrups is for the attendants to hold them. The danger here is of imposing a sideways strain on the perineal tissues if the thighs are too far apart: this is discussed later in this chapter, as it involves the likelihood of tearing or episiotomy. An additional disadvantage to the mother arises if the attendants brace her feet against their hands (or, very often, their hips). It may be convenient for the midwife if the mother's foot is on her hip, as she will then have both hands free, but the mother's instinctive reaction is to push against the brace with her flexed thighs. This is not only a waste of muscular effort, but may also result in her pushing her body back up toward the head of the bed. It is, in fact, not necessary for either the hands or the legs of the mother to be occupied when she is bearing down in this position: much less extra energy is expended if she is allowed to let her legs flop in a semiflexed position, with her hands limply at her side.

A sitting or propped position requires some mechanical assistance if the mother is to be spared the considerable effort needed to flex herself. No less than thirty-two of the cultures studied from material in the Human Relations Area Files provide the mother with some means of support.[17] Sometimes a stake is driven into the ground for her to hold onto; sometimes a rope is suspended from the ceiling or rafters for her to hang from, or a post or wall situated for her to lean against. Almost always, the mother is assisted by several female helpers—relatives, friends, or midwives. Very commonly, some of this assistance is directly physically supportive—an attendant holding the mother from behind or on a lap.

In Western hospitals, if the husband is not to be actively encouraged to join his wife on the delivery table to support her in his arms, other means of suport must be found. These may be provided in the form of cushions, pillows, beanbags, or foam wedges placed against a wall or a backrest, or may take the form of a birth chair or a bed that adjusts to a chairlike position. The majority of mothers were found by Newton to prefer an angle of inclination between 30 and 45 degrees, although some may wish to be even more upright than this. Properly supported, the woman has her spine curved in such a way as to allow her abdominal muscles to be used solely for their prime action of increasing the intra-abdominal pressure to aid expulsion of the baby. Sitting, compared with seven other postures, was found in another study to produce the greatest intra-abdominal pressure, due not only to the weight of the abdominal contents but also to increased muscular efficiency. Only 65 percent of the force necessary to effect delivery in the horizontal position is required if the mother sits up. Sitting up also allows the mother to bend her head forward slightly, thereby avoiding the uncomfortable feeling of pushing into her throat when she bears down.[18]

In addition to the mechanical and physiological advantages of an upright over a flat position, several psychological advantages are conferred. Mothers who are propped up for the second stage tend to take a more active and positive role in the delivery— the difference between "doing" and "being done to." They are better able to cooperate with their attendants and to see what is happening. Such mothers show pleasure at the first sight of their babies more frequently than those who are flat for delivery, and they are better able to hold them immediately after birth.[19]

A further argument, if one is needed, is the economic one. Simply altering the mother's position—or, more accurately, allowing her to choose it for herself—brings about a decreased need for analgesics, perineal stitching, forceps, or vacuum extraction, all of which add to the cost of a hospital delivery and all of which will require the skills of a doctor, who could be giving more of his or her time and attention to that minority of women who have problems that are not iatrogenic.

The Exhortation to Push

The conduct of the second stage in many Western hospitals is in some respects reminiscent of a football game. The all-too-familiar picture is one of a sweating, panting, pushing mother being instructed to take a deep breath and hold it for as long as possible while bearing down; meanwhile, she is surrounded by an eager and enthusiastic audience, exhorting her to further efforts. It is expected that she should be working very hard, getting hot and red in the face, with her neck veins bulging. Many of the onlookers find themselves holding their breath in sympathy with the woman's exertions. Much cheering and encouragement accompany each expulsive effort, and the atmosphere is tense and urgent, with the emphasis on "aiding, abetting and even coercing the mother into forcing the fetus as fast as she can through the birth canal."[20]

Suzanne Arms, author of *Immaculate Deception*, adds:

> . . . that mothers do not consciously remember the experience as silly and downright humiliating is due to their sincere efforts to please everyone around them, and to the consuming effort of giving birth. . . . The team approach to childbirth . . . even if the delivery occurs without any form of analgesia or anesthesia, is not to be confused with a natural birth, which can only take place in an atmosphere of calm and quiet faith.[21]

The rationale for this insistence that the mother should hold her breath and strain is far from clear. It would appear that, rather like the other nonphysiological traditions in obstetrics, it has been established by habit. There are several good reasons why this habit should be broken.

Taking a deep breath and holding it before attempting to push anything is uncomfortable and inefficient. No man would make an attempt to push a wardrobe by taking a deep breath; he might, however, hold his breath for brief periods, punctuated by a series of short grunts and groans. As long ago as 1965, Adele Blankfield wrote:

> A misconception persists about inspiration in that the patient is told to take a deep breath and then push (Eastman, 1961; Brews, 1963. Negus (1929), together with Clayton, observed and measured the chest expansion of many subjects performing hard physical tasks and straining effort. . . . They noted that the chest was only slightly filled with air for these actions. They observed

that it was most unusual for an initial deep breath to be taken. They concluded that maximal effort could be achieved with a small inspiration. It is extremely difficult to hold a deep breath for the following reasons: the lungs are elastic, and the more they are stretched, the greater the battle against their rebound recoil; . . . and the more the lungs are expanded, the more impulses arrive from higher centers demanding expiration.[22]

It is not necessary, either, to "fix the ribs and diaphragm" to achieve pressure when bearing down.[23] The diaphragm is a sheetlike muscle that tires easily and is largely ineffective in sustaining a contraction when the breath is held.[24] The technical name for the action described (of holding the breath and straining) is the Valsalva maneuver, so called after the seventeenth-century Italian doctor who first described it, not as appropriate to second-stage labor, but as a means of forcing pus out of the middle ear.

When the mother holds her breath, she seals off her windpipe by closing her glottis. If she then bears down, she raises the pressure in the chest cavity. Maintaining this pressure, she dramatically reduces the blood flow back to the heart: the blood is dammed in the venous system (hence the congestion in the mother's face), and the amount of oxygenated blood that the heart can pump out is correspondingly reduced. In the meantime, the levels of carbon dioxide in her blood stream rise (since she is not breathing out) until she feels herself at the bursting point and is forced to gasp for a further breath. This sudden release of pressure in the chest is followed by a backlash or rebound rise in the previously low blood pressure. This sudden and high rise in blood pressure has been shown to cause alterations in heart-rate patterns (EKG), alterations in brain-wave patterns (EEG), and even strokes. While the woman is straining, the pressure in all the vessels and the cerebrospinal fluid is constant. It is during the release that damage may be done; burst capillaries are not uncommon in the faces and eyes of women straining in the second stage.

In addition to these far-reaching changes in the circulatory system, damage may also be done to the vagina, the uterine ligaments, and the skin and muscle of the perineum. Slow, gentle distention of the vagina and perineum is much less likley to cause tearing than the rapid or sudden stretching that occurs if the baby's head is forced to speed down the birth canal by the maneuvers described above (see also page 128).[25] Moreover, if pushing begins simply because the mother is "diagnosed" as being in the second stage rather than because she *wants* to push, the fetus is not simply being pushed down from above like a piston (as it would be if the head had reached the pelvic floor), but is actually causing the ring of contact with the vagina or even cervix to be dragged down, thereby pulling on the transverse cervical ligaments and connective tissue supports of the vagina. Constance Beynon suggests that this may be a causative factor in uterovaginal prolapse.[26]

Finally, if the woman is instructed to push from the very beginning of each contraction, the vagina does not have time to become taut, which it needs to be to prevent the anterior vaginal wall and the bladder with its supports from being pushed down in front of the baby's head. When this happens, a shearing strain is produced between the vaginal tissue and its deeper attachments. This may well be one of the factors in the development of stress incontinence later. Constance Beynon likens the process to a coat sleeve with a loose lining:

> Firstly, the slower the arm is thrust down the sleeve, the less is the tendency for the lining to roll out at the wrist. Secondly, if the lining is held firmly at the top during the maneuver, the amount of resistance to the descending arm is considerably reduced, and its passage down the sleeve becomes much easier.[27]

As might be expected, the cirulatory changes in the mother due to prolonged bearing down (longer than 5 to 7 seconds) will have a pronounced effect on the fetus. If less blood returns to the mother's heart, then less blood leaves it; there is reduced blood flow to the placenta and therefore a drop in the amount of oxygen getting to the unborn baby (fetal hypoxia). This is made worse by the fact that there is already a reduction in the amount of oxygen in the mother's blood.

> Ironically, it is this fetal hypoxia. . . . seen in the second stage of labor that is given as the reason why the second stage should be very short. It is recognized as being dangerous to the fetus, but it has not been understood until now that our instruction to the mother in the second stage to bear down long and hard is *causing* this fetal hypoxia. . . . Her *spontaneous* efforts are normally within physiological limits—about 5 or 6 seconds long.[28]

One physician measured the strength and length of second-stage contractions and bearing-down efforts and related them to simultaneous fetal heart-rate tracings. All bearing-down efforts produced at least a transient drop in the unborn baby's heart rate as a result of head compression. Pushes lasting 5 to 6 seconds produced a quick recovery as the contraction finished and no fall in heart rate after the contractions. When the push lasted 9 seconds, the heart rate fell to lower levels and remained low longer. This, he concluded, was damaging, and pushes sustained for 15 to 18 seconds had a marked hypoxic effect on the fetus.[29]

There have been various articles on the subject of conservative second-stage management in this century. As long ago as 1913, an American practitioner wrote:

> The patient is not allowed to bear down overmuch during the first part of the second stage. The author does not hurry this period of labor without indication. . . . The levator ani and the fascia above and below it making up the pelvic diaphragm can only be spared serious injury by slow dilatation . . . with each pain the head is allowed to come down to distend the perineum a little more.[30]

Another physician, in 1950, made the point that it was better to begin expulsive efforts too late rather than too soon; in 1957, a third added that it was better to strain too little than too much.[31]

When they are permitted to "open up" to the messages coming from the uterus and respond appropriately to them, most mothers do not need to be told when and how to push. But the character of the second-stage responses is likely to be different from the stereotyped labor-ward instructions. The urge to push comes at the height of the contractions, not at the beginning, and there is a clear interval between the onset of the contraction and the mother's urge to exert herself. Also, the amount of effort exerted involuntarily with each contraction will vary considerably. Some contractions may be short and mild, while others will be long and strong. There is no necessity for the mother to fix her diaphragm in order to use it, pistonlike, on the uterus, as it is the abdominal muscles, not the diaphragm, that make the greatest contribution to the expulsive work of the uterus. Furthermore, these can only contract effectively as the mother breathes out (which is also true of other forms of exercise and exertion). Hence grunting, which is often regarded with dismay as a "waste of breath" by labor-ward staff, not only safeguards the mother and baby against the dangers of prolonged breath-holding, but also makes the voluntary pushing efforts more effective.[32]

Some midwives take pride in conducting the second stage by encouraging and supporting the mother without ever mentioning the word "push," thus allowing the laboring woman to follow her physiological inclinations. Those who have witnessed births handled in this way have been impressed by the ease of expulsion of the baby's head and the tranquil atmosphere that can be achieved.

Objections to the conduct of a delivery in this manner are likely to be based on a belief that the second stage will be prolonged, that the forceps rate will rise, and that there may be danger to the unborn baby from a long second stage. A clinical trial in England has shown that these objections are unfounded. Out of 100 mothers with no instructions given to them to push, only two second stages lasted more than 2 hours, and the forceps rate was half that of the control group. The need for stitches and/or episiotomy was, moreover, also half that of the control group. It is appropriate to mention here, too, the conclusion of Butler from his long-term study of 17,000 children (described in the section below on episiotomy) that a second stage lasting as long as 2½ hours did not increase the incidence of neurological impairment in the full-term infant. A subsequent study in 1977 also concluded that the practice of terminating labor after any arbitrary time period in the second stage of labor could not be supported.[33]

Not all women have completely normal labors, and some will need additional guidance on how best to coordinate their efforts. Some will need the assistance of forceps or a vacuum extractor. Each labor is individual and must be considered on its merits and conducted appropriately, but it is surely reasonable to aim at giving every woman the chance to experience an unforced second stage by allowing her to choose her position, and to synchronize her efforts with her own internal instructions, rather than those of an obstetrician or midwife with one eye on the clock. She will then be operating entirely within natural physiological limits, and will also be freer to achieve her own style of birth.

The Use of Fundal Pressure to Assist Delivery

Fundal pressure—that is, pushing down on the top of the uterus in the direction of the vagina—is most commonly used as a method of delivering the placenta, and its use in this context is discussed in the section below dealing with placental delivery. It is, however, still used by some as a method to speed delivery of the baby when there is "delay" in the second stage.

Apart from being an inefficient aid to delivery and causing intense pain to the mother, it has numerous other side effects:

1. It may bruise the abdominal and uterine walls.
2. It may damage the bladder.
3. It puts great strain on the ligaments that support the uterus.

4. It impedes the placental circulation and reduces the amount of oxygen available to the fetus. One study has shown that there is a relationship between this reduction of oxygen due to the use of fundal pressure and clinically observed anoxia in the baby at birth.[34]

The effects of fundal pressure are likely to be compounded by the situation in which it is used. Delay in the second stage is much more common when there are obstetrical complications, when the mother is lying flat, and when drugs with a sedative effect have been used. Unfortunately, these factors by themselves may seriously diminish the oxygen levels in the unborn baby, and pushing hard on the top of the uterus only serves to make matters worse.[35] Consideration of the use of fundal pressure in the second stage is largely omitted from reputable obstetrics textbooks and ought similarly to be omitted from obstetrical practice.

Episiotomy

For most women, discussions on the subject of episiotomy are heavily emotionally charged—and with good reason, as the performance of this surgical incision, and more particularly its subsequent repair, may crucially affect their future sexual well-being and self-image.

An episiotomy, which may be performed for a variety of reasons, is a cut made in the perineum to enlarge the vaginal opening. The perineum or perineal body is made up principally of three of the various muscles that form the pelvic floor. This floor or "sling" of pelvic muscles is responsible for the support of the pelvic organs (and indirectly the abdominal ones), controlling the passage of intestinal gas, feces, or urine, and for sexual responsiveness and satisfaction during intercourse. During the first stage of labor, the normal muscle tone in the sling ensures that direction and guidance is given to the unborn baby's head as it descends—though this is removed if the mother has an epidural[36]—and during the normal and unhurried second stage, the muscles of the perineum thin out slowly and gently to allow the baby's head to emerge. If the skin and muscle of the perineum and vagina do not have time to stretch sufficiently to allow the passage of the head, tearing or laceration will result. These lacerations are usually classified as first-degree, second-degree, and third-degree tears (1°, 2°, 3°). A first-degree tear is a superficial or skin tear; a second-degree one, a skin and muscle tear; and a third-degree one, a skin, muscle, and anal sphincter tear. When an episiotomy is performed, skin and muscle are cut: it would seem logical, therefore, to use episiotomy as a means of preventing a third-degree tear or controlling a possibly extensive second-degree tear.

There are two main types of episiotomy: median and mediolateral. They are usually performed with scissors. A median incision enlarges the vagina outlet in the way that is most likely to happen naturally—by splitting the perineum vertically in the midline toward the anus. This has several advantages over the alternative: it bleeds less, is easier to repair, less painful, and less likely to cause pain during intercourse later. The main danger, and the reason that it is not usually used by midwives, is that if any extension of the incision takes place during delivery, the anal sphincter is likely to be torn—the very situation that the episiotomy was designed to prevent. Median episiotomies are

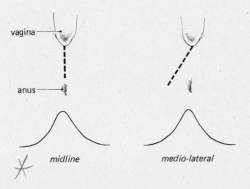

vagina

anus

midline   medio-lateral

much more commonly performed in the United States than in Britain, where medio-lateral is favored.

A medio-lateral incision starts in the midline and is then directed diagonally to the right of the anal sphincter at about 7 o'clock (if the sphincter is considered to be at 6 o'clock); it is 3 to 4 centimeters long. This type of incision has the advantage of protecting the anal sphincter, but it bleeds much more than a median incision and may cause vaginal tearing if it extends during delivery. It is also more difficult to repair, heals more slowly, and is more likely to become infected.

Cutting the perineum in order to hasten delivery has been advocated sporadically since the eighteenth century. Episiotomy procedure was introduced in 1742 by Sir Fielding Ould, the Irish midwife, who cut the vulval outlet when it offered "too great resistance"; Michaelis in 1810 incised the perineum to avoid a dangerous tear.[37] A popular textbook of 1831, however, emphasized the importance of preserving the perineum and discussed in detail labor-slowing techniques whereby this could be accomplished.[38] In 1816, Merriman stated that

> natural labor requires but little assistance on the part of the accoucheur. He must recollect that the dilatation of the soft parts will be effected by the natural pains, assisted by the bag of waters gradually insinuating itself through the uterus and vagina, much more easily and safely than by any artificial means that he can employ.[39]

The term "episiotomy" was attributed in 1857 to Braun, who condemned it as inadvisable and unnecessary.[40]

Before 1967, midwives in England were trained to prevent tears by conservative means, that is, cooperation with the mother to ensure slow delivery of the baby's head and careful delivery of the shoulders. In June 1967, the Central Midwives Board permitted midwives to perform episiotomy as an emergency measure, and today the indications for episiotomy and its technique are a standard part of a British midwife's training. The list of indications for an episiotomy has grown so long in some hospitals that it is now a routine procedure in both Britain and America, and in at least one British hospital it is mandatory.[41] The following are generally considered to be "good" reasons for episiotomy:

1. Any situation that is likely to cause severe and/or third-degree tearing; for example: (a) baby in a face-upward position (persistent occipito-posterior position); (b) prior to a forceps delivery (and therefore, in most hospitals, prior to a breech delivery); (c) a previous third-degree tear (because scar tissue does not stretch well); (d) a perineum that does not stretch in response to the pressure of the unborn baby's head and becomes white and shiny; (e) trickling of blood from the vagina when the baby's head is visible, which suggests that the vaginal tissue is beginning to tear; (f) a narrow pubic arch or android type of pelvis, which pushes the unborn baby's head backward onto the perineum.

2. When there is doubt about the baby's condition in the second stage, an episiotomy will speed up the delivery and also facilitate the use of forceps if necessary.

3. When the baby is premature, an episiotomy may prevent the baby from suffering intracranial damage due to too rapid compression and decompression of the soft skull bones.

4. When the mother's condition necessitates a short second stage with the minimum of pushing (for instance, in severe pre-eclampsia or cardiac disease), or if the mother has ceased to make progress when the head is distending the perineum, an episiotomy may be an alternative to a forceps delivery.

5. When there is a breech delivery—for the reasons given in (1) above, and also to prevent too rapid compression and decompression of the fetal head, which may not be "soft" (as is the case with a premature baby) but which has, in the case of a breech birth, to travel through the pelvis and vagina much more rapidly than is the case when a baby is born head first.

There are unfortunately a great many episiotomies performed for much less defensible reasons:

✳ 1. For a great many practitioners, an episiotomy has become "respectable," whereas a tear or perineal laceration has not. So to avoid the possibility of a first-degree or even a small second-degree tear, an episiotomy—equivalent in most cases to a large second-degree tear—is performed. In hospitals where even a small nick that requires no suturing is considered bad practice, medical students become so anxious lest the perineum tear that an episiotomy becomes the easiest solution. It is very rare to be criticized for an unnecessary episiotomy. This becomes a vicious circle; the next generation of doctors may not know *how* to deliver a mother without an episiotomy, or even how to judge the state of the perineum.

Furthermore, there is evidence to suggest that the increased use of episiotomy does not decrease the incidence of tears. In a comparison between home and hospital deliveries, investigators found that despite a ninefold increase in the episiotomy rate for hospital over home deliveries, the hospital-delivered women still sustained a statistically and significantly greater number of tears of all three degrees. This observation is confirmed by a study carried out in Wales, which showed that while the episiotomy rate doubled between 1965 and 1973 (24.4 percent to 46.7 percent), the incidence of tears remained the same.[42]

2. Although more trained staff were available to look after fewer women in 1970 than in 1946, according to a British study, the proportion of women actually delivered by trained personnel has in fact decreased.[43] Avoiding perineal lacerations and knowing whether an episiotomy is a better alternative to the tear that the attendant believes may be imminent are essentially matters of skill and judgment that come with experience. If, as has already been stated, tears are regarded as a mark of failure, then the inexperienced will perform an episiotomy whenever there is the slightest doubt about the perineum; or, what is even more likely, they will be prevented from performing it only if the mother delivers her baby before there is time for the operation to be carried out.

3. In a great many hospitals in Britain and America, there is

an arbitrary time limit imposed on the second stage of 1 to 1½ hours.[44] After this time, the mother is subjected to an episiotomy and possibly also a forceps delivery, irrespective of the degree of progress she has made and her own and the unborn baby's condition. In some hospitals, notably in London, this time limit may be as little as ½ hour—ludicrously short for the majority of first-time mothers.

This inability to sit quietly and let delivery take place gently and in its own time (assuming that the mother and unborn baby are well and that progress is being made) is justified by the statement that after this length of time the fetus is at risk from possible oxygen shortage or because of the head's being compressed against the perineum. In fact, one obstetrician suggests that for every minute the unborn baby's head is on the perineum, two points can be deducted from its eventual IQ!

There is no evidence to support any of these theories. The director of the Centre for Birth and Human Development has added:

> There does not seem to be any logical rationale for the image of the baby's head as a battering ram against the perineum, especially since in a normal birth the baby's head descends two steps forward and then ascends one step backwards, each time stretching the perineum more and more in a gradual process, rather than against the perineum.[45]

Indeed, Butler's study of 17,000 British children, born during a single week and followed for seven years, found no correlation between the length of the second stage of labor (up to 2½ hours) and the incidence of neurological impairment of any full-term infant who had showed no signs of fetal distress during labor.[46]

4. The last major reason given for episiotomy, which is used to justify 100 percent episiotomy as a routine measure, is that every woman has a built-in pelvic "flaw"; if the midwife or obstetrician does not do her the kindness of cutting the perineum, there will be overstretching and damage to the pelvic supports, leading to prolapse in later life. Proponents of this

argument go on to suggest that if an episiotomy is not performed, after the birth, the husband will no longer be able to enjoy intercourse with his wife, because her vagina will be permanently enlarged and misshapen. Not only is there no evidence to support this theory, but research recently done in America repudiates it. Two groups of women were compared, one of which had delivered without episiotomy, while the other group had had episiotomies. The two populations were matched for age, race, parity (number of children), length of time since delivery, pattern of previous episiotomies, socioeconomic status, nursing status (whether they were breastfeeding), and pregnancy status (whether they were currently pregnant). No statistical difference was found between the two groups with regard to the incidence of rectocele (weakening of the posterior wall of the vagina with protrusion of the rectum into the vagina) or with regard to muscle tone in the vagina and the ability to use the muscles to exert a squeezing action. The study concluded that "episiotomy is definitely *not* prophylactic against pelvic relaxation." Another researcher confirmed that a search of the literature failed to find any evidence to support the claim that episiotomy could be justified on the grounds that it protected the mother.[47]

Even when an episiotomy can be medically justified, it still carries with it a number of side effects by comparison with perineal tears. When tearing occurs, it takes place in most cases at the last possible moment before the head crowns, when the perineal tissue is stretched thin. The timing of an episiotomy, however, is for the most part in the hands of the attendant. If it is done too early, when the perineum is still thick, it will bleed profusely. An episiotomy that has been properly timed is likely to add about 153 milliliters (6 fluid ounces) to the total blood loss; badly timed, an episiotomy may bleed so much that a blood transfusion becomes necessary.[48]

Commonly the tissues are crushed as they are cut. (The crush injury is even worse if the scissors are blunt.) Crushed tissues produce more bruising and swelling than torn tissues and heal slowly; this is likely to account for a fair proportion of those episiotomies that fail to heal spontaneously. The same problem arises when the perineal tissues are liberally injected with local anesthetic: they become thick and spongy and also bleed more. The result of all this is more pain after delivery, compared with that suffered by women who have not received a local anesthetic prior to episiotomy; this is presumably because there is more crushing of the tissues.[49] Normally, when tearing occurs, it does so at the height of a contraction, when the baby's head is distending the perineum; in this situation, the tissues are under pressure and are numb. The tear, if perceived at all, is registered only as a feeling of giving way. If an episiotomy is performed without an anesthetic, as it occasionally is, it will be painless only if it mimics the tear and is done at the height of the contraction, when the tissue is under pressure from the baby's head. If it is not, or if it is done with a local anesthetic that has not been given time to work, it is likely to be extremely painful.

Any woman who has had an episiotomy performed obviously has to have it repaired. This necessitates her lying down (or remaining) flat with her feet in stirrups (the lithotomy position), which is at best a dreadful anticlimax after the excitement of having given birth and at worst a humiliating and traumatic experience. The area to be stitched should always be anesthe-tized, and it should never be assumed that the perineum and vagina are numb simply because delivery took place within half an hour of the stitching, even though this may be true in some cases. It is also indefensible to begin suturing until the anesthetic is fully effective. To a woman who has just given birth, particu-larly if it was arduous, any pain after the delivery is more than she should be asked to tolerate. It is equally appalling that so little attention may be paid to the psychological well-being of the woman while her perineum is being sutured that she feels as if she were demeaned or sullied by the doctor's actions. The

mother needs to be sympathetically included in both the procedure and any conversation about it, not treated as though she
were not present except from the waist downward.

In addition to the problems of being badly cut, a great many
women suffer because they have been badly stitched. "The
stitches were worse than having the baby" is an extremely common complaint among women, and a major factor in the comfort of the perineum is the skill with which it is put back
together. The muscles of the pelvic floor have to be accurately
rejoined with absorbable stitches, sufficient in number to keep
the muscle together and prevent blood from being collected in
pockets under the skin (hematoma), but not so many that there
is no room for expansion caused by the inflammatory process
that is part of healing and that puts the sutures under tension.
It is also vital that the superficial tissues of the vagina and
perineum (skin and mucosa) are correctly aligned and not
stitched too tightly, otherwise great discomfort will be produced
both as the perineum heals and when intercourse is resumed.[50]
It would appear that closing the skin layer with a continuous
running stitch under the skin entails less discomfort and produces faster healing than the use of single stitches, as large areas
of tissue are not trapped under tension—which would increase
as the skin began to heal. Also, nonabsorbable stitches that are
put in too tightly are extremely painful to remove.

The advantage in the early postnatal period of using an absorbable Dexon stitch, which has been shown to cause less
inflammatory reaction and therefore less swelling and wound
tension, is unfortunately counterbalanced by the fact that it
takes 60 to 90 days to be absorbed and is likely to increase the
incidence of pain on intercourse during this period, as the tissues are still being held by the material, thus preventing painless
stretching. It was the conclusion of a 1980 study that Dexon
ought to be used in preference to silk, but that it should be
removed on the fifth day following the delivery.[51]

Apart from the pain a badly stitched perineum may cause, it

is also more likely to become infected, as a result of reducing the blood supply. This will then require frequent bathing with saline or cleansing and debriding solution, dressings, heat lamps, ultraviolet therapy, and eventually restitching. If the restitching is not undertaken, the perineum will slowly heal itself by granulation (filling in from the bottom up, rather than from the sides), and this will cause painful and abundant scar tissue.

The effects of pain due to the stitching of the vagina and perineum may be profound.

> [These] painful associations can have emotional repercussions and deeply affect a woman's capacity for sexual responsiveness. It is with the first attempts at intercourse after childbirth—whether or not it is successful from the man's point of view—that a pattern of anxiety, displeasure and even acute pain can be laid down which may persist long after the time when there is any obvious physical reason for apprehension or discomfort.[52]

This state of affairs is likely to put considerable strain on the marriage. A randomized trial recently conducted in Reading, England, compared the effects of a policy that did *not* restrict episiotomies (in this group, 51 percent were given episiotomies, while 24 percent had intact perineums and 25 percent had tears) with a policy that *did* restrict episiotomies (10 percent episiotomies, 34 percent intact perineums, and 56 percent tears). It found that mothers in the restricted group resumed intercourse, on the average, a month earlier than mothers in the liberal group.[53]

It is of paramount importance that women who are still experiencing pain from their stitches 10 to 14 days after delivery do not wait for their postnatal examination or later in the hope that "it will get better by itself," but seek the aid of their doctor. The longer bad stitching is left, the more scar tissue forms and the harder resuturing becomes: the woman may then be told that the repair should be delayed until she has another baby. In extreme cases, plastic surgery may be necessary. Episiotomies also appear to produce more scarring of the perineum than do tears, and more vaginal numbness.[54] Deaths have even been reported as a result of episiotomies that became infected. Between 1969 and 1977, in one hospital in the state of Washington, three women died from infected episiotomy sites within 10 days of giving birth.[55]

It follows that the person undertaking the perineal repair carries considerable responsibility for the future physical and emotional well-being of the woman in question. Moreover, it is clearly in the mother's interest to avoid episiotomy if possible,

---

Coping with Perineal Stitches: Some Practical Advice

1. As soon as possible after delivery, the mother should start to move the pelvic floor muscles: she should be persuaded to squeeze the muscles and let go, frequently. She will probably be reluctant to do so, because it hurts at first, but such movements, however slight, help to disperse waste products and reduce swelling.[57]

2. While passing urine, an attempt should be made to stop and restart the urine stream. This will again probably be difficult at first, even for a woman who was conscientious about doing pelvic floor exercises prenatally, but with practice the ability will return.

3. While passing urine, she will find that a pitcherful or squeeze bottle of warm water poured over the vulva and perineum will help to dilute the urine and prevent stinging of any lacerations of the labia or vagina.

4. It is vital to keep the stitched area clean and dry. It may be cleaned with running water directed onto the perineum, using a bidet, bath taps, or shower. A plastic squeeze bottle filled with lukewarm water can be used while the woman sits on the toilet or crouches in the bathtub.

5. Tissues or soft toilet paper are best to dry the perineal area; these are gentle and very absorbent.

---

and routine episiotomy in any case. It is difficult to obtain statistical evidence on the episiotomy rate in hospitals, but in England and Wales it was estimated to be 22.3 percent in 1968 and 36.98 percent in 1973. If the increase has continued at the same rate (3 percent per year), it will now (in 1984) be in the region of 72 percent. If trends in London are representative, however, this is a very conservative estimate: in 1977 the West Middlesex Hospital had a rate of 55 percent, and by 1979 two other hospitals had a 90 percent episiotomy rate.[56]

The situation in America seems to be at least as bad. In 1975

---

6. In the early days, a clean sanitary napkin should be put on each time the mother visits the toilet. She needs to experiment to find the texture and type of pad that suits her best. Pads should be detached front first and removed from behind. Mothers who do not find a sanitary belt too uncomfortable may find that it holds a pad firmly against the perineum, where it is less likely to rub on their stitches than the beltless type of pad that sticks onto panties.

7. Wiping after evacuation of the bowel should always be done from front to back to avoid contaminating the stitches.

8. Exposing the stitched perineum to the light and heat of an ordinary light bulb or the warm airstream from a portable hair dryer may be soothing. It also dries the area and speeds healing.

9. The stitched area may be slightly tender even after the skin is healed, so experimentation with positions in lovemaking may be appropriate, to find one that does not put pressure on the scar.

10. It has recently been found that ultrasound is a very effective treatment for thickened scars that cause pain. A 5-minute application three times a week for 6 weeks is a typical treatment scheme. This has been effective even when the woman has not sought help until 15 or even 48 weeks after episiotomy.[58]

Suzanne Arms, in her book *Immaculate Deception*, cited an incidence of 77 percent for all mothers at a large urban teaching hospital and at least 90 percent for all mothers in a major hospital in St. Louis. N.W. Cohen and L. J. Estner, authors of *Silent Knife*, maintain that "the episiotomy rate in the U.S. is well over 90 percent" (in 1983). A third study on episiotomy, published in 1979, reported that the "episiotomy rate in American obstetrics in recent years has been almost 100 percent." A detailed survey of the hospitals in the five-county area of Philadelphia in 1982 revealed that twenty-eight out of the forty-six hospitals studied had episiotomy rates between 80 and 100 percent and in nineteen of these the rate was 90 to 100 percent. The remaining eighteen hospitals had rates ranging from 50 to 80 percent; only three of these had rates of 50 percent, and no hospital had a rate lower than 50 percent.[59]

By contrast, the episiotomy rate in Holland, which has not changed in recent years, is around 8 percent, while the incidence of pelvic relaxation or prolapse there has dramatically declined —yet another argument against the prophylactic use of episiotomy to prevent overstretching. The Reading trial found that the high episiotomy rate (51 percent) in their "liberal" group was not justified: it did not improve the mothers' condition, make them more comfortable, improve their resumption of intercourse, or reduce problems of pain in intercourse. In short, the results of the trial do not suggest that episiotomy is of any benefit in the short or medium term.[60]

A woman who is about to give birth is in no position to argue about whether an episiotomy is necessary in her case. At that point she is obliged to trust the judgment of whoever is aiding her delivery. There are, however, several things that can be done by her, and ideally also by her partner, to reduce the likelihood of an episiotomy being performed:

1. She can make sure that it is recorded on her chart or verbally conveyed to the person delivering her that she wishes

to avoid being cut if at all possible: this will then place the onus on the doctor to justify his or her action subsequently, should an episiotomy be performed. It is to be hoped that this will also reduce the likelihood of a routine incision.

2. She should find a (physiologically) good position for the second stage. The position in which women most commonly find themselves for delivery is the lithotomy or supine position, described by one authority as "the worst conceivable position for . . . delivery, short of being hanged by the feet!"[61] The same is also true of episiotomy and its avoidance. If the woman is horizontal and pushing in the same plane (while gravity as always is acting downward), the combined resultant force is being applied to the perineal tissues rather than, as it should be, simply assisting the baby in the journey down the vagina. If the

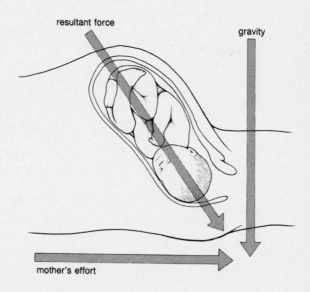

woman in labor sits up (or stands, squats, or kneels on all fours), gravity and her expulsive efforts are working together, and the maximum pressure is being exerted in the plane in which the baby is traveling.

3. The mother's knees should be about a foot apart to ensure that there is no sideways strain on the perineum. Again, with the very common lithotomy position, the feet are either placed in stirrups or held by an attendant: in both cases this nearly always results in the knees being held wide apart, so that the perineum is already stressed before the baby's head begins to distend it; what is more, it is stressed at right angles to the original tension. In this situation, tears and/or the apparent need for an episiotomy are likely. In 1965, Blankfield (referring to the 1955 work of Leak) wrote: "The skin and fascia overlying the perineum are attached to the flexion creases of the thighs. Hyperflexion causes these tissues to become taut and drawn up so that the introitus is narrowed; this can predispose to tears."[62] The mother should either keep her feet rolled with the soles inward and resting on the bed, with her legs flexed slightly, or she may raise her legs and feet by placing her hands around or under her knees. If the woman is permitted to position her legs herself, she is unlikely to choose a position that strains her perineum.

4. In the prenatal period, the performance of pelvic-floor exercises is of great benefit in preparing the mother for her second stage.[63] If she understands and has control of her pelvic-floor muscles, she can respond appropriately to the sensations of the second stage and the midwife's instructions, and she is far more likely to emerge unscathed from the delivery. Most prenatal teachers and books on preparation for childbirth have their own favorite approaches when it comes to teaching pelvic-floor control (such as stopping and starting the urine stream or slowly tightening and relaxing the anal sphincter to learn differentiation and control), but the one that is generally considered to be the most useful is the "elevator shaft" or "invisible elevator" exercise, in which the woman is asked to imagine her pelvic floor as an elevator car that is slowly pulled up four, five, or six floors. (Imagine an elevator on the outside of a building, moving slowly and smoothly up and down.) It is then allowed to descend gradually and is finally "bulged out" to allow the elevator to

enter the basement. This "bulging" is what has to happen in the second stage in order to allow the head to be born. Familiarity with the sensations of pelvic-floor contraction will mean that the woman will recognize whether she starts to tighten up in the second stage—if so, instruction to relax her muscles or allow herself to open up will have much more meaning. Her rapport and her ability to cooperate with the midwife or doctor and to achieve a gentle and unhurried second stage, allowing the uterine contractions and involuntary expulsive efforts alone to push the head down onto the perineum—all this will give the perineal muscles time to thin out and stretch. When the baby's head is about to be born, good pelvic-floor control will enable the mother to "breathe the head out" slowly, rather than forcing it out rapidly—the latter being much more likely to result in perineal tears.

5. If the mother has had an epidural during the first stage of labor and it remains effective during the second stage, the incidence of forceps delivery and therefore episiotomy is greatly increased. If matters can be so managed, however, that the epidural wears off during the second stage, then pushing is likely to be more effective and the need for instrumental delivery reduced.[64]

Naturally, any mother would like to give birth with her perineum intact. However, if an episiotomy is truly necessary and the mother and her partner can appreciate the reason for it, then—provided that it is properly performed and carefully repaired, so that she feels afterward that she is as she was before —the procedure should be one that most mothers can come to terms with. "What is wrong with the practice of episiotomy at present is not episiotomy itself, but that it has become a mere obstetric fashion, and therefore a questionable routine."[65]

CHAPTER SEVEN

The Third Stage:

AFTER THE DELIVERY

Oxytocic Agents

The use of oxytocic agents in the management of the third stage of labor (from the birth of the baby to delivery of the placenta) was the response of obstetricians to the problems of postpartum hemorrhage (blood loss after the birth of the baby amounting to 500 millileters or 20 fluid ounces in volume). "As so often with developments in obstetrics, [in most hospitals] all mothers came to be treated in the same manner, irrespective of the degree of risk [of their bleeding]."[1]

It has been suggested that the prevalence of postpartum hemorrhage (PPH) in Western society is to an extent a man-made problem. One researcher has pointed out that despite detailed biblical references to childbirth, menstruation, and menorrhagia (abnormal menstrual flow), there are no references to retained placenta or PPH. He adds: "Since the sixteenth century much has been written about the third stage of labor; its management seems to present a bigger problem to us than to primitive peoples." He then goes on to describe a Bantu birth in which the woman delivers her baby in a squatting position and remains in the same position while the placenta delivers itself by gravity. The mother then lifts herself onto her haunches, and the membranes fall out. Only when the placenta is completely delivered does she pay any attention to the cord. He continues: "Working among the Bantu for ten years, attending 26,000 Bantu and seeing only abnormal cases, I found many other complications, but a retained placenta was seldom seen. . . .

Blood transfusion for postpartum haemorrhage was never necessary."[2]

In contrast, postpartum hemorrhage (and retained placenta) was responsible for 36 percent of maternal deaths in Texas from 1969 to 1973 and 31 percent of such deaths in Oklahoma between 1965 and 1975 (111 out of 309 and 31 out of 99, respectively). PPH and retained placenta accounted for 14 percent of maternal deaths in England and Wales until 1976, when the proportion fell to 9.2 percent. (In 1932, 450 mothers died; in 1971, 19 mothers.)[3] The commonest cause of PPH is a failure of the uterus to contract and control bleeding from the placental site. This may be due to a number of factors, including twin pregnancy, prolonged or precipitate labor, a lax uterus as a result of repeated pregnancies, and the administration of large doses of sedative drugs or deep anesthesia. There are also circumstances in which the uterus is unable to contract properly, either because there is something inside, (for example, partially separated placenta, retained portions of placenta or membrane, large fibroids) or because there is blood in the muscle wall of the uterus as a result of severe bleeding just before the onset of labor, which makes the wall stiff and inelastic. Occasionally mismanagement of the third stage by the birth attendant is responsible for inefficient contraction of the uterus, for instance, allowing the woman to enter the third stage with a full bladder, or meddling with the uterus ("fundal fiddling"), which may cause irregular contractions and partial separation of the placenta. Other major causes of postpartum hemorrhage are tissue damage—that is, episiotomies; vaginal, cervical, or perineal tears—and coagulation disorders (a failure of the blood to clot). With regard to tissue damage, one study showed that the PPH rate among the women in the sample who required perineal stitches was 7 percent; if the perineum remained intact, the rate was 1 percent.[4]

The use of oxytocic agents is likely to affect only hemorrhage that is caused by the failure of the uterus to contract. In America the most widely used oxytocic agents are oxytocin (also known

as Pitocin), ergonovine (known in Britain as ergometrine), and
Methergine. In Britain, oxytocin and ergometrine can either be
administered individually (intravenously or intramuscularly) as
in America, or, more commonly, in a single intramuscular injection of an oxytocin-ergonovine mixture called Syntometrine,
one ampule of which contains 5 units of oxytocin and 0.5 milligrams of ergometrine.

Ergot

Ergot is a fungal infection of rye, and its effect on the uterus has
been known for centuries.[5] It was first written about by Adam
Loncier in 1582, and European midwives used it throughout the
seventeenth and eighteenth centuries. In its crude form, however, it could be extremely dangerous, and this tended to limit
its usage. Its ability to induce "St. Anthony's fire" (a reddened
face and a burning feeling in the hands and feet, caused by
spasm of the blood vessels, which often led ultimately to gan-
grene) was well known.[6]

In 1807 John Stearns, first president of the New York Academy of Medicine, reintroduced the substance, but failed to
generate much enthusiasm. In 1808 he sent a letter to a colleague (which was subsequently published in a medical journal)
describing how he had been "importuned" by a local midwife
to search in granaries for the diseased heads of rye and to
administer them in a decoction to women whose labors were
abnormally slow; the letter went on to describe the remarkable
effect of ergot.[7]

This letter and others by Dr. Stearns were rediscovered in
1932 by Dr. J. Chassar Moir, who initiated the modern revival
of ergot in obstetrics. Ergotoxine (1906) and ergotamine (1918)
had already been isolated from ergot, but in 1935 simultaneous
announcements of the isolation of a new water-soluble ergot
principle came from Baltimore, Chicago, Basel, and London.
The four substances were found to be identical, but they had
each been given different names—ergonovine and ergotrate

(United States), ergobasine (Switzerland), and ergometrine (United Kingdom). This newly discovered substance could be given by intramuscular or intravenous injection and was thought to be free of dangerous side effects. It was, however, noted to cause the placenta to be trapped within the uterus (retained placenta) if given before the delivery of the placenta.[8]

In 1943, a semisynthetic derivative of ergonovine (ergometrine) called methyl-ergonovine (or methyl-ergometrine) was produced by Stoll and Hoffmann; it was later marketed in America under the brand name of Methergine. Although it gained great popularity in the United States, it did not succeed in replacing ergometrine as the standard preparation in the management of the third stage in Britain, despite over a hundred papers published discussing its use and its lack of side effects compared with ergometrine.[9] The practice of giving ergot preparations intravenously with the birth of the anterior shoulder was regarded favorably by some doctors in America in the 1940s, but in Britain, an authority writing in 1947 considered this practice to be contraindicated before the end of the third stage. Two years later, the routine use of such preparations was condemned by Munro Kerr and Chassar Moir as bringing about "a great and unnatural curtailment of the third stage."[10]

Oxytocin

Natural oxytocin is produced by the pituitary gland which is situated at the base of the brain and has two parts: front (anterior) and back (posterior). In the female, the front portion produces (among other secretions) the milk-stimulating hormone (prolactin); the back portion produces (among other secretions) natural oxytocin, which stimulates the uterus to contract during labor. At the turn of the century, researchers investigating the effect of pituitary gland extract on the blood pressure of a cat discovered that it had the unexpected property of causing instantaneous and intense contraction of the uterus. (Chassar Moir, in recounting the history of pituitary extract, remarks that it was fortunate for medical science that the experimental animal was not a tom!)[11] Unfortunately, the early use of the extract was beset with difficulties, as the strengths of the commercial preparation were very uncertain and varied dramatically. Despite dose standardization in the early 1930s, the response in individual women remained unpredictable. By 1948, a new method of administration was introduced: the slow intravenous infusion of a very dilute solution of the drug (the now well-known oxytocin drip).

A pure form of pituitary extract was developed by Du Vigneaud in 1954, synthesized by Boissonnas shortly afterward, and marketed under the names of Syntocinon and Pitocin. Given *intravenously*, Pitocin is effective in making the uterus contract in 40 seconds; *intramuscularly*, it takes 2½ minutes.

Given *intravenously*, ergonovine is effective in making the uterus contract in 40 seconds; *intramuscularly*, it takes 6 to 7 minutes. With ergonovine, in particular, the dosage is important: for intramuscular use, 0.5 milligrams is recommended, and for intravenous use, 0.25 milligrams (half the intramuscular dose). The two agents act on different parts of the uterus in causing the muscle to contract. "Oxytocin [Pitocin] . . . induces strong rhythmic uterine contractions . . . by affecting primarily the upper uterine segment. . . . Ergometrine [ergonovine] induces unphysiologic uterine spasm . . . and affects the lower uterine segment" and cervix.[12]

The newly discovered ergonovine had to be given intravenously if it was to be effective in stopping or preventing hemorrhage, as 6 to 7 minutes was far too long to wait in the face of a heavy postpartum bleeding. However, advocates of intravenous ergonovine before placental delivery at the University College Hospital in London in 1953 were obliged to recognize that this procedure considerably increased the incidence of retained placenta (in their study the incidence was tripled); they wondered if pulling on the cord might reduce it. In 1962, another researcher working at the same hospital published the results of a preliminary trial in which the administration of intravenous ergonovine with the birth of the anterior shoulder was followed by delivery of the placenta by pulling on the cord ("controlled cord traction"). Despite this scientist's own admission that as far as reducing the need for manual removal of a retained placenta was concerned, her results were "a little disappointing," controlled cord traction became established practice; and this study seems to have formed the basis of what has been taught to British midwives for the past twenty years.[13]

Thus the practice of administering intravenous ergonovine with the anterior shoulder of the baby (the first shoulder born) became widespread. The alternative, also developed in the early 1960s, was a mixture of 5 units of oxytocin and 0.5 milligrams of ergonovine that was administered intramuscularly with the birth of the anterior shoulder, prior to delivery of the placenta by pulling on the cord. In Britain, this alternative was principally for use by midwives, who were not usually trained to give intravenous drugs. (Before this, midwives had been using ergonovine mixed with hyaluronidase in an attempt to speed the action of intramuscular ergonovine. This was unsatisfactory, as the two substances had to be kept in separate ampules and mixed just prior to administration.)

The practice of actively managing the third stage quickly spread, and discussions revolved around which drug was best; when to give it (with crowning of the head, with the anterior shoulder, after the birth of the baby, or after delivery of the placenta); how to give it (intravenously or intramuscularly); and how to deliver the placenta after having given an oxytocic drug, (that is, by pulling on the cord [controlled cord traction, or CCT], maternal effort, or fundal pressure [pushing downward on the uterus]). Many papers were published comparing the effectiveness of the two drugs, the alternative routes of administration, and the methods of placental delivery. With the introduction of ergonovine and Syntometrine, the PPH rate fell; undoubtedly many lives were saved by their use. Postpartum hemorrhage is a terrifying event for mother, midwife, and obstetrician alike, and the discovery and application of these oxytocic drugs stands as one of the "enduring achievements of modern science."[14]The use of these drugs, however, rapidly became routine "prophylaxis" for all women, irrespective of the degree of risk, and few researchers actually studied the use of oxytocic drugs using a nontreated control group of mothers for comparison.

In America, the management of the third stage has tended to be more conservative than in Britain. The authors of one standard obstetrics textbook state that "oxytocin, ergonovine, and Methergine are all employed widely in the conduct of the normal third stage of labor, but the timing of their administration differs in various institutions." They go on to say that in their hospital it is usual to add 20 units of oxytocin to the intravenous infusion after placental delivery and to let it run at a rate of 10 milliliters per minute until the uterus is firm, continuing it at the rate or 1 to 2 milliliters per minute for the next hour. They do not comment on the procedure if there is no IV in progress, possibly because most mothers have one set up at some time during labor at this hospital; if this is the case, it would be in agreement with the findings of a survey of forty-six hospitals in Philadelphia, in which twenty-nine reported an IV rate of 90 to 100 percent, and a further six a rate of 70 to 90 percent. Taking Pennsylvania as a whole, about 40 percent of mothers had Pitocin administered during labor. Similarly, Suzanne Arms cites a rate of 45 percent of all mothers receiving Pitocin during labor in a large teaching hospital.[15] If these findings are typical, they may explain why an oxytocic agent is less likely to be given before the delivery of the placenta in America than in Britain —if a Pitocin drip is already in progress, it would be superfluous. If an oxytocic agent is given with the birth of the anterior shoulder, it is more likely to be Pitocin than ergonovine; either Pitocin or, in some areas, intravenous Methergine may be given after the delivery of the placenta.[16]

Ergonovine, particularly when given intravenously, has unpleasant and occasionally dangerous side effects, probably due to its indiscriminate action on smooth muscle, including the heart and blood vessels. Headache, dizziness, ringing in the ears, chest pain, palpitations, and cramplike pain in the back and legs have been reported.[17] Nausea and vomiting (which may occur to a mild extent following delivery when no oxytocic drugs are used) is made worse by ergonovine: 4.5 percent of mothers in a control group were nauseated and 19.5 percent in an ergonovine group, as reported in a study that also found intractable nausea and vomiting in 2 percent of the mothers who received ergonovine, but none in the control group.[18]

Work done by the Department of Anaesthetics in Manchester suggests that intravenous ergonovine given to women who have been delivered under anesthesia may occasionally predispose to the development after delivery of acute pulmonary or cerebral edema (engorgement or congestion of the lungs or brain with fluid from the circulatory system, causing severe breathlessness in the case of the lungs; in the case of the brain, headaches, vomiting, blurring of the vision, and, in severe cases, increased drowsiness and eventual coma).[19]

The most common serious effect concerns the impact of ergonovine on the blood pressure. Much research has shown that ergonovine can produce a sharp rise in blood pressure in susceptible women, which would appear to correspond to 12 percent of subjects.[20] This figure may be a conservative estimate, as it has been shown that if raised blood pressure is monitored continuously, rises of 20 mmHg may occur without symptoms. "Minor and even moderate degrees of blood pressure may be much more common than we realize."[21]

Even a moderate rise in blood pressure may be dangerous in women who already have high blood pressure or toxemia (preeclampsia). Several instances of the development of very high blood pressure with accompanying severe frontal headaches have been documented. Having a seizure as a result of the sudden elevation in blood pressure (eclampsia) has occurred in some cases as a result of ergonovine administration. There have also been reported instances of cardiac arrest and at least one death due to the effects of high blood pressure; other deaths

occurred because of uterine rupture following the routine administration of the oxytocin-ergonovine mixture in cases where
it was later discovered that there was difficulty in delivering the
baby's shoulders.[22]

There are other drawbacks associated with the use of ergonovine and the oxytocin-ergonovine mixture:

1. The obstetrician has to decide between clamping the cord
immediately when the baby is born, thereby denying the newborn the extra physiological quota of 90 milliliters (3 fluid
ounces) of blood; or, alternatively, leaving the cord and risking
the possibility of the baby's becoming overtransfused as blood
is forced into the newborn by the energetic contractions of the
uterus.[23]

In 1960, one scientist wrote:

> Unfavorable also is the practice of administering intravenous
> ergotrate [ergonovine] immediately upon the birth of the ante-
> rior shoulder of the newborn. This unphysiological procedure
> necessitates a choice between immediate clamping of the cord
> upon the birth of the newborn, or submitting the fetal circula-
> tion to a large quantity of blood forced over from the placenta
> by the vigorous contraction of the uterus and the influence of
> IV ergotrate. All this is over and above the unfavorable effect IV
> ergotrate may have on the circulation of the mother.[24]

It has also been suggested that this process of overtransfusion
may begin in utero when the placenta is squeezed like a sponge
following the administration of oxytocic agents; this may be the
main reason for the rise in the number of newborn infants with
"physiological jaundice" severe enough to cause anxiety to
pediatricians. An investigation was begun in 1980 in England in
an attempt to clarify this issue.[25]

There is evidence that clamping the cord immediately predis-
poses to transplacental hemorrhage and increased incidence of
maternal bleeding, because of interference with the mechanisms
of placental separation (see page 148).[26] Ergonovine itself inter-

feres with the physiology of placental separation by inducing an "unphysiologic uterine spasm . . . which may result in partial retention of the placenta. This carries a higher risk of heavy bleeding and . . . general anesthetic for manual removal."[27]

2. The obstetrician is rushed into getting the placenta out before the ergonovine (given intramuscularly mixed with oxytocin) starts to work (7 minutes); this inevitably means interfering with the mother's response to her newborn baby. The physician must interrupt these first moments to ask the mother to push out the placenta; more commonly, the doctor will pull it out by the cord, with his or her other hand on the mother's abdomen, "guarding" the uterus (see page 161). If the delivery of the placenta is delayed and the ergonovine is given time to come into action, the placenta may be trapped as the circular muscle fibers at the lower part of the uterus and cervix contract. In this situation, the spasm must be relieved either by giving the mother amyl nitrate to inhale (which relaxes smooth muscle and will make the mother feel very flushed for a few moments as the blood vessels also "relax"—precisely the state of affairs that the ergonovine was given to prevent); or by the administration of a general anesthetic, followed by manual removal of the placenta.

The combination of these two factors (partial separation or trapping of the placenta) means that the incidence of general anesthetic for manual removal of the placenta is increased when ergonovine is used. This, as Professor Dewhurst remarks, may not be too high a price to pay for preventing excessive blood loss when women are at "high risk," having previously had problems in the third stage of labor—as was the case in his study; but it is open to question whether the routine prophylactic use of ergonovine (on its own or as mixed with oxytocin) is justified in cases where there is no anticipated problem, since it increases the likelihood of a general anesthetic, itself a potential cause of maternal death.[28]

A further problem encountered with the routine use of ergonovine in some form before the delivery of the baby is that of trapping the undiagnosed second twin or third triplet. Undiagnosed "extra" babies are not common, and a large maternity hospital might expect one or two per year—for example, the Royal Women's Hospital in Melbourne had eight cases between 1970 and 1977. But there is a high mortality rate (35 percent) and a high incidence of brain damage in survivors for those babies who suffer the devastating effects of having ergonovine administered to their mothers while they are still *in utero*. [29] This might be considered an argument against routine administration of oxytocic agents in low-risk women, at least before the baby is completely born and the presence of an unexpected sibling has been excluded.

Apparently the fear of hemorrhage has meant that, since the isolation and widespread use of ergonovine and Pitocin, most investigations of the use of drugs in the management of the third stage of labor have been restricted to a comparison of specific oxytocic drugs, without the benefit of a nontreated control group as a base line. The few studies that have included a control (placebo) group have, however, yielded some interesting information. In 1964, researchers divided 1,500 pregnant women into three groups, one of which was given oxytocin, one an ergot derivative, and one saline solution. In each case, neither the mother nor her attendant knew which "drug" was being given, and in each case the drug was administered after the delivery of the placenta. They found that there was no significant difference in blood loss between the three groups in those mothers who lost less than 500 milliliters of blood (approximately 1 pint); but there was among mothers who lost more than 500 milliliters— 3.2 percent of the oxytocin group, 1.8 percent of the ergot group, and 5.3 percent of the placebo group. The conclusion was that since 5 percent of the mothers in the oxytocin and in the ergot group still needed further treatment (because the uterus failed to contract properly), while 12 percent of the mothers in the placebo group required further treatment (this figure falls to 10 percent if the mothers who needed uterine massage only are excluded), the routine use of oxytocic drugs benefited only *seven* women in every hundred. The influence on blood pressure revealed by this study has already been referred to: significant increases in blood pressure in women whose blood pressure had been normal prior to delivery were recorded in 47 percent of the ergot group, 38 percent of the oxytocin group, and 31 percent of the placebo group. In women who already had high blood pressure, the increases were 30.7 percent of the ergot group, 11.5 percent of the oxytocin group, and 7.9 percent of the placebo group.[30]

A 1961 study had compared two groups of fifty women: one group received oxytocin routinely after the delivery of the placenta and the other did not. No significant difference was found between the two groups in the amount of blood lost during delivery and the first hour after delivery, although more of the control group required additional treatment. (There were no notable changes in blood pressure in either group.)[31] Both these trials appear to suggest that a woman who receives an oxytocic agent on an individual basis (that is, when she needs it) is no worse off in terms of postpartum hemorrhage than the woman who receives it prophylactically; in fact, she may be significantly better off in terms of escaping the side effects of oxytocic agents.

Two British scientists compared three small groups of mothers who received intravenous ergonovine, intramuscular ergonovine-oxytocin mixture, and nothing, respectively, 20 minutes after delivery of the baby and placenta. No other drugs were given to any of the women during the recording period. They found a postpartum blood loss of less than 200 milliliters (approximately 8 fluid ounces) in each mother. However, despite the fact that all the mothers in the study had normal blood pressure to start with, *all* the mothers in the ergonovine group and 60 percent in the oxytocin-ergonovine mixture group experienced moderate to severe increases in blood pressure, while there were no moderate to severe increases in the control group.[32]

In another study, five groups were compared, of whom the

first received nothing and the second, oxytocin intramuscularly; the other three each received one of three different kinds of ergot derivative, all administered after delivery of the placenta. The conclusion was "that the proper management of the fourth stage of labor (the first hour after delivery) did not require routine use of an oxytocic agent [as] illustrated in the control group of patients, 78 percent of whom did quite well without medication." (This figure is similar to the 1961 study above.) Of the 22 percent who did require treatment, a proportion (unspecified) responded to uterine massage without the use of oxytocic drugs. A statistically significant increase in the incidence of nausea and vomiting and of high blood pressure following the use of ergot derivatives was also observed.[33] In addition, it has been shown that oxytocin is as effective as ergot preparations in preventing postpartum hemorrhage and does not have the same severe side effects.[34]

Two more researchers compared the use of ergonovine and oxytocin, singly and in combination, with a control group. All the mothers in the trial except those having their first babies were at high risk by virtue of a bad obstetrical history, emergency admission, toxemia, anemia, or grand multiparity (seven pregnancies or more). The only mothers excluded from the randomized trial were those who had previously had third-stage difficulties, postpartum hemorrhage, or retained placenta, as it was thought dangerous to use mothers in this category as inert controls. Even in this study, it was found that 60 percent of women in the control group "had efficient uterine action and were in no danger of haemorrhage."[35]

Finally, a study compared three groups, receiving intravenous ergonovine, intravenous oxytocin, and nothing, respectively. It found that the ergonovine group had significantly more instances of retained placenta (and therefore manual removal and blood loss) than the other two; consequently, the rate of postpartum hemorrhage was slightly lower in the oxytocin group, than in the other two. It found that 80 percent of the control group had a blood loss of less than 500 milliliters (1 pint), compared with 88 percent in the ergonovine group and 90 percent in the oxytocin group. It concluded that when an oxytocic drug was required, oxytocin given intravenously in adequate doses (in this study, 10 units) reduced the PPH rate almost as well as ergonovine but without interfering with the physiological mechanism of placental separation. This result confirmed work by Finnish researchers in 1964, who compared the oxytocin-ergonovine mixture with oxytocin and found that the PPH rate was the same in both groups (although the third stage took longer to complete in the oxytocin group), but that the incidence of retained placenta was greater with the mixture.[36.]

There is no doubt that at the time when ergot was reintroduced, postpartum hemorrhage was responsible for the deaths of hundreds of women every year, nor that subsequently ergonovine has prevented a great many deaths, as well as forestalling significant hemorrhaging in women who started to bleed. Ergonovine, however, is not the only factor that can possibly be related to the drop in the number of deaths from PPH. Since 1932, more women at risk from third-stage complications have been confined in hospitals; moreover, the "fourth stage of labor" has been recognized as potentially hazardous, and closer watch has been kept on women for the first hour after delivery.[37] Blood banks and blood transfusion services are available, as are emergency medical service (EMS) facilities. Deaths due to secondary PPH (that is, hemorrhage occurring after 24 hours) have been reduced by the wider availability of good anesthetics and surgical techniques (to remove retained placental fragments), and antibiotics have reduced deaths from secondary PPH due to infection of these retained fragment. In addition, a pure synthetic form of oxytocin has been developed that has a more physiological action on the uterus than ergonovine.

There may now be sufficient evidence to suggest that the routine use of ergonovine should be abandoned altogether and that it should be used only in selected high-risk situations. One physician, discussing the death of a 17-year-old girl who had had a normal pregnancy, labor, and delivery, stated, "It is likely that blind adherence to the postpartum ritual was contributory or causative in this death [from intracranial hemorrhage]. It is possible that the prophylactic use of ergot is . . . fraught with danger and not to be condoned unless definite indications are present."[38]

In view of the dangers associated with the prophylatic use of any oxytocic drug (Pitocin or ergonovine), why are they still being used for women who are not considered to be at risk? "Those women who have a normal first and second stage could be allowed to complete the process normally."[39] Unhurried by the obstetrician (since there would be no urgency to deliver the placenta within 7 minutes), the mother could then experience the full tide of emotion that would itself stimulate the release of her own natural oxytocin, with its contracting effect on the uterus.[40] The baby who was interested in sucking right away could be put to the breast, causing the release of yet more natural oxytocin. Since there would be no risk of overtransfusion for the normal infant, the cord could be allowed to finish pulsating before being divided, and this would allow rapid physiological separation of the placenta and reduce the blood loss still further (see also page 148.)[41] Again, while the third stage is progressing normally, there is no reason to hurry delivery of the placenta by pushing on the uterus or pulling on the cord; the mother should be allowed to expel it herself, making use of the effects of gravity.

A potential objection to the abandonment of routine oxytocics in the management of the third stage, even with low-risk women, is the difficulty of predicting which women make up the 10 to 20 percent who would bleed if untreated. Several factors have been suggested by various researchers as predisposing to postpartum hemorrhage (apart from previous third-stage problems, twins, placenta previa, prenatal hemorrhage due to partial separation of the placenta [abruption], or anemia—all of which would probably be known before the onset of labor). Among these suggested factors are a prolonged first or second stage, poor second-stage contractions, or a precipitate labor; the pres-

ence of such factors might alert the mother's attendants to the
possibility of bleeding, and the original decision—to withhold
prophylactic oxytocics—could be reversed. In other words, a
potentially low-risk situation could be treated individually, on its
merits.

It should also be noted that with the unplanned use of oxytocics in the case of 12 percent of an unselected control group who
started to bleed, only 5 percent lost more than 500 milliliters of
blood (that is, had a postpartum hemorrhage); moreover, in the
case of the other two oxytocic groups in this study, 5 percent
of the mothers experienced failure of the uterus to contract
properly, thereby necessitating further treatment, in spite of
receiving prophylactic drugs.[42] Further, as was pointed out at
the beginning of this section, postpartum hemorrhages are not
100 percent preventable even if oxytocic drugs are used prophylactically for all mothers, as some of these hemorrhages may
be due to causes other than uterine atony (failure of the uterus
to contract).

As long ago as 1966, J. H. Patterson expressed the view that
ergonovine should be avoided before the birth of the baby and
only used before completion of the third stage in cases with
significant bleeding; that Pitocin rather than ergonovine should
be given in cases with a history of PPH or other special circumstances; and that cord traction (pulling on the cord) should be
tried for removal of the undescended placenta only when bleeding indicates immediate action, or if after 30 minutes the natural
process has not occurred. This should be backed up by manual
removal if cord traction fails. Others had earlier maintained that
in high-risk cases Pitocin should be given alone with the birth
of the anterior shoulder (intramusclarly), and that ergonovine
should be given intramuscularly only after placental delivery. If
bleeding occurs and intravenous ergonovine is necessary, further research has shown that the administration of 0.25 milligrams was associated with fewer side effects (without affecting
the incidence of PPH or manual removal later) than the 0.5
dosage that is currently employed in most hospitals (this despite

the fact that Chassar Moir himself recommended that the intravenous dose should not exceed 0.25 milligrams).[43]

Very little research to reassess the management of the third stage has been undertaken in the last fifteen years. Practices vary from country to country and from hospital to hospital within a given country, and up-to-date randomized, controlled studies are urgently needed to clarify the situation. At present, the evidence that does exist calls into question the current practice of routinely using oxytocics, particularly ergonovine, in the management of the third stage.

The Umbilical Cord

In the sections considering the positions that may be adopted by the laboring woman for the first and second stages of labor, it was indicated that over 80 percent of "primitive" peoples adopt some variation of an upright position. As a consequence, the baby when born is initially placed between the mother's legs, while the mother delivers herself of the placenta (in the manner described in the previous section). If she has adopted a sitting position, the baby may be brought up onto her abdomen for her to hold, or she may lean forward and put it to the breast. In both instances, the baby is approximately at or below the level of the placental site for the time it takes the cord to stop pulsating. It is also the practice of the vast majority of these peoples to delay the cutting of the cord for an average of 15 to 20 minutes *after the delivery of the placenta.* [44] (If the cord is cut before delivery of the placenta, one must depend on the invention of methods to staunch the extra bleeding that results.) In many cultures there are delays of several hours before the cord is cut. Commenting on her investigations, Margaret Mead notes:

> The Manus of the Admiralty Islands place the crying neonate, cord uncut, facing the mother, in the belief that sight and sound together will facilitate delivery of the placenta. This raises the

question of whether the sight of the neonate as well as the sound of its crying is involved in a biological releasing mechanism which should be taken into account in planning delivery style.[45]

It would certainly seem that the normal physiological process involves delivery of both baby and placenta before anything happens to the cord. A woman giving birth unaided is not likely to have anything about her with which to sever the cord, and she could not easily transport herself and her baby while the placenta was still in the uterus, even assuming that she shared the urgency of many obstetricians to separate the baby from the placenta as quickly as possible. (One physician has commented: "This practice [of leaving the cord to finish pulsating] appears to have gone into abeyance in a number of places—due no doubt to the haste in producing the babies and getting on with the next case!"[46]

Intuitively, it seems likely that the physiological process has evolved for good reason, and that in the majority of cases it cannot be improved upon. Any interference with the natural order of things is apt (with few exceptions) to be detrimental to mother, child, or both. As might be expected, however, the third stage of labor has not escaped Western influence. In the mid-seventeenth century, as more and more men entered the field of midwifery, cord clamping became the rule, for no better reason than that the bed linen was spared if the maternal end of the cord was clamped. It was also then easier to tell when the cord lengthened—indicating that the placenta had separated and descended into the lower portion of the uterus.[47] Despite warnings that this practice might be harmful—Erasmus Darwin in 1803 counseled that "another thing very injurious to the child is the tying and cutting of the navel string too soon," and Meadows in 1881 referred in his manual on midwifery to Dewees's observation that the uterus contracted better and facilitated the expulsion of the placenta if the maternal side was not clamped[48]—cord clamping has continued to the present day, and it is likely that, by interfering with the physiology of placental separation, it has contributed to the deaths of many women as a result of postpartum hemorrhage.

As the baby is born, the contracting uterus rapidly reduces its own size and that of the placental site by a process of contraction and retraction of the uterine muscle fibers (retraction is the progressive shortening and "fattening" of the muscle fibers as the uterus contracts and relaxes). This process has been taking place throughout labor and assists the dilation of the cervix and expulsion of the baby. The placenta does not separate during the normal first and second stages, as the placental site has to be reduced by approximately half its original size before separation begins. Once the baby is being born, the uterus can reduce itself sufficiently for the process of separation to begin. As the placental site is reduced, the placenta itself is squeezed, and the blood in the spaces between the fronds or villi of the placenta (from which the unborn baby obtained by selective absorption all the substances necessary for its development) is forced back into the veins and spongy lining layer of the uterus, making them tense and congested. These are kept under pressure by the muscle layer of the uterus, which, having retracted, does not allow the blood from these tense veins to drain back into the maternal bloodstream. During this process the cord is still pulsating, and some of the fetal blood residual in the placenta is "pumped" back into the baby, thus allowing further thickening of the placental wall.[49]

When the uterus contracts again (and there is evidence that contractions are stronger at the placental site than elsewhere in the third stage),[50] the congested veins burst; the small amount of extravasated blood (blood that escapes the vessels) causes tearing of the very fine septa of the spongy layer, thereby detaching the placenta from its uterine site. With the same contractions, the criss-crossed muscle fibers surrounding the maternal blood vessels seal off the torn end as the placenta is detached (these fibers are referred to by many as "living ligatures"). Because of the simultaneous sealing of the blood vessels and the peeling off of the placenta, maternal blood loss is only on the order of 60 to 100 milliliters (2–3 fluid ounces). The placenta normally separates from the center and then descends into the cavity of the uterus, pushed in the direction of least resistance, which is the lower portion of the uterus and the cervix, peeling off the membranes as it does so. This process is usually so rapid that contraction and retraction of the cervix do not take place before the placenta is expelled without resistance into the vagina. If the mother is sitting on her haunches, it will fall out of the vagina by the force of gravity,[51] and the small quantity of blood lost (see above) will in this case be kept inside the inverted sac of placenta and membranes. If separation is not quite symmetrical, the placenta will slide down sideways; then the blood escapes from the vagina. Following the expulsion of the placenta, the uterus shrinks still more in size, the contraction and retraction of the muscles ensuring that the "living ligatures" are tightened further.

This process relies on the ability of the uterus to contract and retract rapidly throughout, and initially to contract against a compressed, compact placenta. Any interference may jeopardize the mother's safety by increasing the time before which the living ligatures can act effectively. If the cord is clamped, a counterresistance is set up in the placenta, the extra fetal blood being trapped within it, so that it cannot become compressed and compact. Retraction of the uterus may then be prevented and separation slowed, with consequent delay in the sealing off of the torn blood vessels.

If the placenta cannot separate by rapidly peeling off (like a postage stamp from a rapidly deflated balloon), it will try to separate by the formation behind it of a large blood clot, resulting from the oozing of the torn but incompletely sealed blood vessels. This is not normal; it is abnormal. By the time the placenta has separated by this method, not only has more blood been lost from the mother's circulation in order to form the clot, but the cervical muscle has also retracted; this, combined with a bulkier placenta, will make placental expulsion more difficult, if not impossible. The longer the placenta remains undelivered, the greater is the likelihood of more bleeding, as the uterus cannot contract firmly while the bulky placenta is still inside it. This state of affairs is compounded if the uterus is handled at this time, as "fundal fiddling" may detach the membranes at one point, allowing the blood behind the placenta to escape without clotting— thereby further increasing maternal blood loss and further delaying the complete separation of the placenta. The increased incidence of retained placenta, necessitating a general anesthetic and manual removal, is itself associated with an increase in blood loss.[52]

In 1968, two similar studies each compared a group of mothers who received no routine oxytocics prior to placental delivery and who had cord clamping delayed with a control group who also did not receive routine oxytocics but had the cord clamped immediately. The first researcher found that the duration of the third stage was the same in both groups (about 10 minutes), but that blood loss after delivery of the placenta was doubled in the early-clamped group (133 milliliters, as opposed to 67); the total blood loss in the early-clamped group was also significantly higher than in the late-clamped group (364 milliliters, as opposed to 268). Moreover, retained placenta requiring manual removal occurred in 9 percent of the cases in the early-clamped group, but in none of the late-clamped group. In all cases, such retention was due to faulty separation and not to faulty implantation.[53]

The second researcher's finding was that the mean duration of the third stage was much shorter when the cord was not clamped (4 minutes, as opposed to 12); the total blood loss was also far less in the unclamped group (an approximate range of 16 to 182 milliliters, compared with 100 to 371 milliliters). Among the mothers in the late-clamped group were two who had had postpartum hemorrhages in previous deliveries: they lost only 450 milliliters (15 fluid ounces) and 120 milliliters (4 fluid ounces) of blood, respectively, in this trial. By contrast, the early-clamped group had one mother who lost 780 milliliters (26 fluid ounces) and required intervention to prevent further bleeding.[54]

It is interesting to note that the total maternal blood loss in the former study was greater than that in the latter study, for the groups in which the cords were unclamped; it is possible that this reflects the method of placental delivery. In the former study, the placenta was delivered by fundal pressure on a contracted uterus, while in the latter study, the placenta "was not handled until the mother felt the urge to bear down herself, and was only received when it appeared outside the vagina."[55] It has been argued that "compressing or pushing the uterus downwards towards the pelvic cavity . . . contuses and bruises the uterine wall and causes a passive congestion of the uterus which may produce bleeding during subsequent relaxation."[56]

A further maternal hazard associated with cord clamping is that of isoimmunization (that is, stimulating the production of antibodies in the mother by allowing fetal blood cells to escape into her bloodstream). As the placenta separates (physiologically), some fetal blood from the placenta escapes into the torn blood vessels of the mother's circulation. This appears to happen to a varying degree in all pregnancies, but it is the Rh-negative mother carrying an Rh-positive baby who may be affected by the "transfusion," if it is great enough to stimulate antibody production.[57] (Small transfusions do not appear to provoke antibody production.) It has been postulated that as much as 215 milliliters of fetal blood may be trapped in the placenta by early clamping of the cord, with a subsequent rise in pressure within this closed system, and that when the uterus contracts (particularly following the use of an oxytocic agent in the third stage), the further increase in pressure—as much as 150 mmHg—may be sufficient to burst the tensely distended umbilical vessels. It is suggested that such circumstances might facilitate the passage of fetal cells into the mother's circulation. This suggestion is supported by work done in the last twenty years, including a study that found the incidence of feto-maternal transfusion to be doubled when the cord was clamped, compared with no clamping—66 percent versus 33 percent. Further research confirmed the suggestion that oxytocic drugs given before placental delivery also increased the incidence of feto-maternal transfusion.[58]

Since the introduction of RhoGAM (to be administered to Rh-negative mothers within 72 hours of delivery of an Rh-positive baby), the incidence of an Rh-negative mother developing antibodies after the birth of her first child has been dramatically reduced, but failures still occur if the feto-maternal transfusion is large.[59] Any procedure that will reduce the magnitude and incidence of third-stage transfusions (that is, late clamping of the cord and not giving oxytocics prior to placental delivery) will reduce the number of mothers thus affected.

Considered purely from the mother's point of view, it would appear from the evidence that the treatment of choice in cases that are still low-risk at the end of the second stage would be to allow a physiological third stage (no oxytocic drugs prior to delivery of the placenta and the cord left unclamped or cut and allowed to bleed freely); in cases of high risk, Pitocin would be given prior to delivery of the placenta and the cord treated in the same manner as for low-risk cases, with ergonovine backing up the Pitocin in selected cases.[60]

Leaving the cord unclamped, or cutting it and allowing free bleeding, obviates the problems of transplacental hemorrhage and interference with the separation of the placenta, and therefore of increased blood loss; but the situation is "complicated" by the fact that the newborn is at the other end of the cord. The only physiological sequence of events for the baby is that described at the beginning of this section: if the cord is cut or clamped before the placenta is delivered, the newborn may receive less than his or her physiological "quota" of blood; but if oxytocic agents are given prior to placental delivery, the infant may receive more than his or her quota, if the cord is *not* clamped or cut.

One researcher considered the treatment of the umbilical

cord in some detail, with reference particularly to the baby's welfare. During any mammalian birth, the expulsion of the placenta follows a short time after that of the offspring. In the intervening period, the young newborn is either at its mother's feet (if she is standing) or near her vulva (if she is lying down), and unless the cord is torn during expulsion or chewed off by the mother, it remains intact until the placenta is delivered. When ultimately severed, the cord is not tied or clamped in any way. "This mechanism, which evidently evolved for a purpose, provides the newborn with its full allotment of blood from the placenta and assures that no stagnant blood is then retained within the stump of the umbilical cord." This observer also points out that the only difference between general mammalian and early human reproduction was that the cord was severed in the case of the humans by rubbing it between two stones rather than by chewing it in half. (Whatever method is used, the umbilical stump of the infant shrivels and drops off in three to ten days, leaving the neat navel or "belly button," the shape of which is determined by nature, not man.) Tying of the cord was never employed until the ligature became common practice in surgery:

> As the physician became more skillful with the use of hemostats [clamps], scissors and ligatures, the umbilical cord presented an inviting site for surgical procedure, and the present custom of immediate severance and immediate ligation of the cord followed. Ligation of the cord makes it possible to get babies and mothers out of the delivery room more rapidly, just as low forceps contribute to more rapid care. Whether they have added to the ultimate welfare of the newborn is a question.[61]

Various workers have shown that vital physiological changes take place in the baby's heart and lungs in the moments following birth. It has been suggested that the uninterrupted flow of blood through the cord vessels from the "reservoir" of placental blood acts as a safety valve and "volume-maintenance system" as adjustments take place in the baby's heart and circulatory system. The flow of blood from the placenta to the baby occurs under the influence of gravity, uterine contractions, and the onset of respiration in the newborn, and the scientist just quoted maintains that immediate clamping of the cord inter-feres with the physiological chain of events, in particular the return to the fetal circulation of 75 to 125 milliliters (2½ to 4 fluid ounces) of blood. It also traps in the cord "stagnant blood which provides an inviting culture medium for bacterial growth." He advocates delaying the clamping and division of the cord until 15 to 20 minutes after the delivery of the placenta. Apart from condemning the administration of oxytocic drugs in the third stage, he also criticizes the practice of cord stripping (or "milking" the blood from the cord by pinching it between finger and thumb and stroking it toward the baby), claiming that this procedure:

> brings at each stroke some 10–15 cc [cubic centimeters] of blood quite abruptly into the fetal circulation. It is the equivalent almost of introducing within 1–2 seconds 200 ml [milliliters] of blood into the adult circulation [which could cause heart failure]. It is a difficult to understand how the delicate circulatory channel of the newborn can accommodate this blood so abruptly.[62]

A survey of relevant research has suggested that the only time cord stripping may be of value as a procedure is following a cesarean section, when it may compensate for the absent uterine contractions and possibly reduce chilling of the baby, which may occur while waiting for the cord to cease pulsating. But this study, too, admits that the problem is to know precisely how much and how long the cord should be stripped. On the basis of information currently available, the authors of this review article felt it reasonable to assume that delayed clamping of the umbilical cord is associated with an increase in blood volume in the newborn. Another study estimated that the total blood volume of a newborn baby varied between 65 milliliters per kilogram (if the cord was clamped at birth) and 120 milliliters per kilogram (if the cord was clamped at 3 minutes). Assuming an average birth weight of 7½ pounds (3.38 kilograms), this means a range of 219 to 405 milliliters of blood. This confirms earlier findings that "when the cord clamping was delayed by five minutes the blood volume increased by 61 percent to 126 ml/kg." Again assuming a birth weight of 7½ pounds, the range is 263 to 425 milliliters. This is consistent with the statement made in a letter to the *British Medical Journal* in 1973 estimating "that (particularly if ergometrine [ergonovine] is given to the mother and the cord is not clamped) a baby can receive a volume of blood from the placenta equivalent to as much as half its entire blood volume after delivery." It is possible that this may be more than was intended physiologically. An investigation of the extra blood transfused by gravity and delaying cord clamping concluded that the baby received an extra 89 milliliters of blood. Williams—writing in 1909, well before the routine use of third-stage oxytocic drugs—refers to Budin, who showed that if the cord is not tied early, the newborn may receive an extra 92 milliliters of blood.[63]

If it is the case that the extra blood that "should" be transfused physiologically is approximately equal to 100 milliliters, rather than the 200 apparently received if oxytocics are given to the mother, it would explain the observation of J. M. Gate and his colleagues that the baby is overtransfused as a result of the "almost universal use of oxytocics to expedite placental separation." Gate further states that in these circumstances the placenta is squeezed like a sponge, and the newborn may receive a blood transfusion that is not needed. "One would expect the surplus blood to be haemolysed and that could well be the source of the bilirubin [the pigment that gives rise to yellowing of the skin—"jaundice"—when in excess] which is causing anxiety to our paediatric colleagues."[64] It would also explain the finding that the large placental transfusion that infants receive if cord clamping is delayed may acutely distend the circulatory system of normal newborns, who, despite possessing "a great capability to adapt to this circulatory overloading, show evidence of increased effort and duration in the extrauterine adaptive processes." The study goes on to assert, however, that no harmful effects have been shown to follow in normal, full-term infants. (It does not say whether or not the mothers of the babies thus observed received oxytocic drugs prior to placental delivery.)[65]

On the other side of the coin, it has been suggested that respiratory distress syndrome may be a consequence of clamping the cord too early. In this case the baby is deprived of the full complement of placental blood, and the increased volume of blood required by the pulmonary circulation must be drawn from the baby's own bloodstream. Dr. Courtney, writing in the *British Medical Journal*, remarks: "Hypovolaemia [low blood volume] seems a logical cause for failure of pulmonary expansion which this simple precaution [delaying cord clamping] helps to prevent. . . . If the cord is pulsating well it is important not to cut [the baby] off from this significant, warm, oxygenated blood transfusion." He believes that this extra blood is even more significant in preventing respiratory distress syndrome if the baby is premature or undersize, an opinion borne out by a study that found an increased incidence of the syndrome in premature babies whose cords were clamped before the onset of respiration. Most research on the subject has been carried out on normal, full-term infants; the exact relationship, if any, of cord clamping to respiratory distress syndrome remains the subject of considerable controversy. The review article on cord clamping concludes:

> In full-term, vigorous infants, "early" versus "late" clamping is not a vital issue [in physiological terms]. These babies seem to endure the physiologic consequences of either . . . with no apparent untoward effects. In depressed full-term infants (those slow to breathe or respond) the factor of time may be more significant, since further insult may not be so well tolerated. In premature infants, even if not depressed, the issue assumes still greater importance.[66]

Circumstances alter cases, and nowhere does this occur as rapidly as in the practice of obstetrics and perinatology. It may not be possible to attend satisfactorily to the mother or the baby with the cord still intact if either needs swift medical attention; nor is it possible to deliver a baby with the cord wrapped tightly around the baby's neck without clamping, cutting, and unwinding it. But where the labor and delivery are normal in all respects, and particularly if no oxytocic drugs are given prior to delivery, it appears to be detrimental to the mother and the newborn to clamp the cord before the placenta is delivered.

The issue of early versus late cord clamping remains controversial for the medical profession, and further investigations are needed if the issue is to be decided scientifically. Until then, we might still listen to R. D. Laing, who, at the meeting of the International Society for Psychosomatic Obstetrics and Gynaecology in 1972, said, "And I should like to know why in our society the cord might not be left to be cut as late as possible, rather than as quickly as possible."[67]

Placental Delivery

While it is the case that a good proportion of mothers are concerned about the way in which the umbilical cord is managed in the interest of their babies, and some may have strong feelings about the routine use of oxytocic drugs, relatively few will have considered the way in which the placenta will be delivered or the implications of the method chosen by the birth attendant. In Western societies, placental delivery methods are described as either "maternal effort" (the so-called natural method) or "mechanical," involving some form of pushing, pulling, or uterine manipulation.

As was seen in the previous section, physiological placental separation occurs when the uterus contracts strongly and the placenta, made thick and compact by the "escape" of fetal blood via the intact cord to the baby, peels off the uterus at the "perforation layer." The placenta then folds in on itself and is pushed toward the lower portion of the uterus by the strongly contracting upper portion, or fundus. This process happens so quickly that no retraction has yet taken place in the cervix, and the placenta is "expelled without resistance into the vagina," after which it will "fall out by gravity," in the words of one physician. This presupposes that a physiological position is adopted for the third stage, so that gravity can act in the same plane as the vagina. The physician just quoted, who attended 26,000 Bantu mothers over a ten-year period, reports that he rarely had to deal with a retained placenta (when he did, it normally entailed only lifting out the terminal part of the membranes from the vagina); never did he have to resort to blood transfusion for a postpartum hemorrhage.[68]

An undrugged, cooperative mother in a Western hospital may, if permitted, push out her own placenta unaided. But she will have to do so when the birth attendant urges rather than when her own inclinations prompt her (unless the two happily coincide), as she will probably have been given an oxytocic drug with the birth of the baby's first shoulder. As was noted in the section on oxytocic drugs, ergonovine components become effective within 7 minutes of intramuscular administration; the placenta must be delivered before this happens, lest it be trapped behind the closed, contracted cervix.

The other problem faced by the mother is likely to be the position in which she finds herself. She is probably lying flat, and the sensations of the uterus as it contracts once the baby is born are quite unlike the powerful, positive, "bearing-down" sensations of the second stage. No stage of labor can accurately or aptly be likened to the act of defecation, which denotes "getting rid of waste material" and also serves to confuse a mother whose baby in the second stage is in fact traveling up and forward following the sacral curve; but one may wonder how many of those who urge a mother to expel her placenta when lying flat have ever tried to evacuate their bowels in a similar position? Certainly it will require more effort from her than from her "primitive," upright counterpart.

Pulling on the cord to effect delivery of the placenta probably became fashionable in the West following the translation into English of Mauriceau's treatise of 1673. He recommended this procedure because he feared that the uterus might close before the placenta was delivered spontaneously. For the next hundred years, this was the "recognized procedure of experienced accoucheurs."[69] Any interference with the normal physiological process of parturition, however, as has been illustrated throughout this book, is accompanied by disadvantages as well as its intended advantages. In the case of cord traction, these potential disadvantages are: (a) pulling off or snapping (avulsing) a cord, either because it is very delicate or inserted into the membranes rather than the substance of the placenta; (b) pulling out a placenta that had not completely separated from the lining of the uterus, and consequently leaving a portion behind; and (c) inverting the uterus by pulling on the cord when the placenta is still completely attached.

Pulling off the cord is not in itself detrimental to the mother. If she can deliver the placenta herself by her own efforts, all is well. If it is delivered by other, mechanical means (pushing on the uterus), there are all the disadvantages associated with that technique; if a manual removal is required because ergonovine has taken full effect and the cervix is closed, so that the placenta cannot be delivered by other means, the situation is graver. Patterson, in addition to the above, recalls the need for an emergency ambulance crew to attend a "shocked patient without much blood loss but with the placenta in utero and the cord avulsed." Leaving a portion of the placenta behind is a serious matter, as severe bleeding may result if the uterus is unable to contract properly and manual removal is necessary. If the retained fragments are not noticed at the time of delivery, they may become infected and/or give rise to secondary bleeding, which will then require antibiotics, manual removal, and possibly a blood transfusion. It may even result in a generalized bloodstream infection (septicemia) and other complications. Inversion of the uterus (which may be complete—in which case the fundus of the uterus is visible between the mother's thighs—or partial—

in which case the fundus is not externalized) will result in a state of profound maternal shock and possibly hemorrhage.[70]

Although Crede in 1853 agreed that in the hands of accomplished obstetricians, cord pulling was a satisfactory method, he showed that complications were frequently encountered by the unskilled. Consequently, he devised a method of manual compression of the uterus at the height of a contraction, thus expressing, or pushing out, the placenta. This method is now considered by most obstetricians to be dangerous, although a few still use it. One authority has stated:

> Maternal shock may follow an attempt to deliver the placenta by Crede's method. The dangers of forcible manipulation of the uterus cannot be overemphasized and indeed Crede's method has now been entirely abandoned by many obstetricians who feel that they prefer manual removal of the placenta as the safer method.[71]

The other alternative was fundal pressure: pushing downward on the contracted uterus and using it as a sort of piston or battering ram. This procedure, besides having "no useful effect if the placenta is still in the uterine cavity, whether separated or not," may cause bruising and contusing of the uterine wall and a passive congestion of the uterus that may cause bleeding when the uterus relaxes. It may also result in a prolapse of the cervix into the vagina as a result of the strain placed upon the uterine ligaments.[72] Moreover, it is painful.

Ahlfeld, who worked with Crede, found that the same complications condemned by his teacher in the cord-traction method occurred not infrequently when expression was performed by "incompetent midwives." He therefore postulated his famous doctrine of "Hands off the uterus." Writing more recently, Patterson stated that "the oldtimers learnt in a hard school, and through the experience which has been built up by midwives for centuries. They knew that the commonest cause of third-stage trouble was fiddling about. It still is, and it behooves us to remember it."[73]

Cord traction, however, became popular once again with the wider use of oxytocic drugs in the active management of the third stage. The remedy of some obstetricians for the problem of fundal fiddling was "decisive action":

> From the point of view of training undergraduates and pupil midwives, decisive action is more easily presented and more readily accepted than tentative inaction, with its associated temptations. The popularity of cord traction with the midwifery staff indicates the attractions which the method holds.[74]

In some cases, the attendants await the classic signs of (separation and) descent—namely, an escape of blood, lengthening of the cord, and rising up of the uterus—before attempting to pull on the cord, but others regard these signs as unreliable ones, often missed in the general activity of the delivery; they therefore advocate cord traction as soon as the uterus has contracted, with the free hand "guarding" the uterus to prevent uterine inversion (a modification of the technique described by Brandt, who advocated pushing the uterus *upward* with the free hand).[75] Some go even further and recommend cutting the cord the moment the baby is delivered and immediately pulling on the cord, with the other hand pressing the uterus upward and backward. Continuous traction is applied, so that the instant of placental separation is recognized by a slackening of tension in the cord, which is then delivered by further traction (the "cord sign of separation"). This whole procedure presupposes giving oxytocin mixed with ergonovine upon the delivery of the baby's first shoulder.[76]

If mechanical methods of delivering the placenta, as described above, fail, manual removal is indicated. This entails giving the mother a general anesthetic so that a hand may be passed into the uterus to separate the placenta by moving the fingers from side to side. This procedure, while lifesaving in some situations, is not without its hazards both in terms of damage to the uterus and anesthetic complications. The complications of cord traction may be rare, but they do occur; in 1966, the year in which

Fliegner and Hibbard published their paper advocating the "Active Management of the Third Stage of Labour," there were three cases in one English hospital alone of acute inversion of the uterus for which active management was responsible. Furthermore, "there seems little doubt that this hazard is increased if an active policy of management of the third stage is practised."[77]

The development of the techniques and drugs necessary for pursuing such a policy has meant that they have been, and undoubtedly will continue to be, lifesaving in some circumstances and will dramatically reduce the postpartum hemorrhage rate in others. But that is not necessarily an argument for applying them routinely. The situation in which they were shown to reduce the PPH rate most dramatically and significantly was when the third stage lasted for over 30 minutes; but in the majority of cases, the normal third stage lasts only about one-third of this time. Two studies by physicians who managed the third stage physiologically (no oxytocic drugs and no cord clamping) found an average duration of 10 minutes, with no manual removals required. Third-stage delay was the situation in which Patterson, a staunch opponent of routine active management, himself recommended cord traction "with early resort to manual removal should cord traction prove ineffective."[78]

When the mother is not deemed to be at risk and has had a normal first and second stage, she "could be allowed to complete the process normally."[79] One obstetrician, formerly a supporter of the active approach to the third stage, confesses to having reversed his opinion and reverted to old-fashioned management, being now "utterly convinced of its superiority." He concludes his letter to the British Medical Journal, "It is gratifying and instructive to see how well the uterus will do its job if left alone."[80]

The Newborn Baby

Gentle Birth

Dr. Frederick Leboyer published his book *Birth without Violence* in 1975, at a time when many people were expressing concern about the widespread use of drugs in labor, routine separation of the baby from the mother, and the increase in the use of obstetrical techniques such as induction, monitoring, and forceps deliveries. The focus of his book (and also his film) was that birth should be a gentle transition from the womb to the outside world, rather than a tidal wave of "sensation." To this end, he suggested specific actions that he believed would minimize the "shock" of being born: a dark, quiet room; placing the newborn on the mother's abdomen; delaying the cord clamping; massaging the baby and placing him or her in a warm bath.[81]

Although Leboyer was at pains to impress upon those who questioned him that he wished to impart an *attitude* and not a technique, his procedures became the subject of considerable controversy. Delivering in the dark, delaying cord cutting, and bathing the newborn received particular criticism.[82] It is not difficult for even a sympathetic audience to find objections to some of Leboyer's actions and assumptions. There is now some evidence that toward the end of pregnancy the baby is not in total darkness in the uterus, but that enough light penetrates the mother's stretched abdominal and uterine walls to allow a diffuse pink glow throughout the amniotic fluid—rather like holding one's hand over the end of a flashlight. The intensity of this glow will depend on the brightness of the external light and the thickness of the clothing covering the abdomen, but it may be reasonable to suggest that the newborn has some knowledge and even some "expectation" of light, so that darkness may be just as strange as overhead fluorescent lights.[83] From the practical point of view, birth attendants obviously must have enough light to see what they are doing and an immediate source of *bright* light should the situation suddenly warrant it.

There are similar objections to trying to deliver a baby into silence. There is good evidence that the womb is quite a noisy place: there is a loud, continuous, rhythmical, "whooshing" sound, which is punctuated by occasional rumbles of air. Researchers have found that the unborn baby also responds to external sound (independent of what the mother hears), but this must be very loud to exceed the internal noise the fetus is constantly hearing. Silence as the baby is born is likely not only to be strange for the infant, but also to impose considerable restraints on the mother, father, and birth attendant, "robbing" the newborn of the cries of joy and spontaneous greetings that are characteristic of normal undrugged deliveries. Lind, who had 130 normal, full-term births photographed, felt that the expressions on the faces of the babies confirmed his impression that a normal delivery is not as a rule a painful experience for the infant. In his photographs, none of the newborns showed signs of anxiety or pain, but rather curiosity and great expectation, despite not being delivered into a silent environment.[84]

Bathing the baby immediately after delivery may indeed cause a drop in the newborn's temperature, which is the objection usually put forward by critics of Leboyer's technique; but presumably this could be avoided if the room temperature were high enough. It is, however, quite likely that "high enough" is considerably higher than anyone else in the room would find comfortable (or economical). The McMaster study, which compared babies delivered at 80 degrees Fahrenheit and given a warm-water bath with babies delivered at 75 degrees Fahrenheit and not bathed, found that the underarm temperatures of the bathed group were significantly lower than those of the controls for up to an hour following delivery—although none was dangerously low, that is, below 95 degrees. This suggests, among other things, that room temperature must be well above 80 degrees Fahrenheit to avoid cooling the baby. (The alternative would be to use an infrared heater, positioned about 28 inches above the baby.) The McMaster study also found that "the Leboyer bath did not appear to have a calming effect: of the 19 babies observed, 9 reacted with irritable crying and 10 maintained or achieved an alert state."[85]

The debate over the details of the Leboyer birth should not, however, detract from the central issue—Leboyer's belief in the baby as an important, sensitive individual who should be treated as gently and respectfully as the situation will allow. It may or may not be possible to prove that his approach confers measurable long-term benefits (one uncontrolled follow-up study suggested that development was generally superior in infants delivered by Leboyer's "method"); but proof is not usually required to substantiate the assertion that it is better to treat human beings gently rather than roughly or thoughtlessly.[86]

The only scientific randomized trial applied to the Leboyer technique to date is the McMaster study, referred to above. Although it produced some interesting results, it failed to find any clear-cut differences in either the mother's perception of her birth experience or in the behavior of the baby, whether during the neonatal period or at 8 months of age. The researchers did point out, however, that there were only minimal differences between the two methods of delivery used. "The control deliveries though more conventional were intended to be equally gentle, and differed from the Leboyer group only in location, lighting, room temperature, draping, time of cord clamping, type of contact with the mother, and bath." (In both groups the mother held her baby right after birth, but in the Leboyer group, the baby was placed in immediate, direct skin-to-skin contact with the mother's abdomen and was massaged by the mother. In the control group, the attendant took the newborn, cut the cord, wrapped the baby up and then gave him or her to the mother.) The McMaster researchers felt that they could not ethically compare "the Leboyer protocol with the anachronistic practices which he and many others had condemned," and they set up their study "to avoid confounding the controversial specifics of

Leboyer's method with the *principles of gentleness*"[87] (emphasis added).

It could therefore be argued that their attitude to birth and the newborn was already similar to that of Leboyer. In their hospital they pay sufficient attention to the wishes of expectant parents to provide Leboyer deliveries for those who request them (this prompted the study). But in their institution, this may be simply "gilding the lily," considering the responsive and Leboyer-like spirit that evidently already prevails.

It is difficult to see, as they point out, how anyone ethically convinced by the "Leboyer" techniques could willingly compare them with "anachronistic practices" in the same study; for this reason, it may be that Leboyer's principles will not be satisfactorily subjected to the scientific application of a randomized, controlled trial. If they are accepted, it will be because mothers want them and feel them to be right. In the meantime, it is possible to argue against specific "anachronistic" practices that are a feature of many conventional deliveries.

Extracting Mucus from the Baby's Nose and Mouth

In the hospital, nearly all newborns are subjected to the routine suctioning of the nose and mouth "to clear the airway," without any regard to whether or not such a procedure is necessary. The suction is usually performed with a bulb syringe or a nasogastric mucus extractor with a glass trap. Most babies born normally and unaffected by drugs have the nose and mouth cleared spontaneously as they are born by the pressure exerted on the chest wall by the vagina, and breathing begins within seconds of the chest being delivered. To subject an infant who is breathing peacefully to oral and nasal suction "just in case" is a totally unnecessary assault.

Babies who have difficulty in breathing (and it is five times more common in the hospital than at home)[88] are far more likely to owe their problems to the use of narcotics and anesthetics during labor (and/or to the reasons for their use) than to a blocked airway; if this is the case, mucus extraction will not improve the situation. A British pediatrician with special knowledge of cardiac and respiratory rhythms in newborn babies has said: "Sticking a catheter down a baby's throat is bad: pushing it into a baby's nose and mouth does nothing at all to help it breathe. Mucus catheters should be banned as dangerous instruments."[89] Pushing a mucus extractor "blindly" into the nasopharynx, larynx, or trachea of the newborn, via the nose or mouth, may stimulate the endings of the vagus nerve that are situated there. If the vagus nerve is stimulated, the impulses will pass over the vagal network to the medulla (the part of the brain that contains the respiratory and cardiac centers). The net result may be a disturbance of heart rhythm, slowing or even stopping of the heart, and inhibition or cessation of breathing (apnea). In a study conducted at the New Haven Medical Center, researchers found that following "blind" nasopharyngeal suction, of forty-six infants, seven developed serious slowing of the heartbeat; one of the seven had a cardiac arrest (the heart stopped beating altogether), and five of the seven stopped breathing. The authors conclude that blind suction of the nasopharynx is a hazardous procedure, particularly in the first critical minutes of life, when the baby is physiologically unstable, and they suggest that their results are sufficiently serious "to warrant re-examination and careful clinical evaluation of the use of the nasopharyngeal catheter immediately after birth."[90] In instances where thick mucus, blood, or meconium is thought to be obstructing the baby's lungs, it should be removed under direct vision by a pediatrician. The use of a bulb syringe may be unpleasant and in many cases unnecessary, but the bulb cannot usually reach the larynx or trachea and is therefore less likely to cause damage.

Holding the Baby Upside Down

It is still the practice in a great many hospitals to hold the baby upside down, suspended by the ankles, for the purpose of allowing "any fluid in the trachea to drain out" and to facilitate breathing.[91] While in this position, the baby may also be smacked on the bottom to startle him or her into crying.

These practices show a total disregard for the baby as an independent human being. Newborns have been shown repeatedly to be acutely sensitive in their perceptions, and it must be a terrifying sensation to be suddenly hung upside down in space, having just come from the confines of the womb. Dr. Leboyer's photograph of a screaming newborn with clenched fists next to his face speaks volumes on the subject of the needless suffering imposed upon the newborn. Moreover, this suffering is not solely psychological. One Canadian authority has condemned the practice of suspending babies by the feet because of the enormous strain it places on the hip joints. Such straining may, he says, cause untold damage that may lead to serious complications later on. He adds that this potential damage may be compounded if the baby's bottom is slapped while the baby is held in this position, as this can further damage the hip joints. There are less traumatic and more effective ways of clearing the air passages, should the need arise.[92]

Wrapping the Baby

One of the chief concerns of midwives and doctors, once the baby is born safely and breathing properly, is that the infant not become chilled. Wet newborns cool down very rapidly for several reasons: the room is usually much cooler than the uterus from which they have just come; their surface area is large in relation to their body weight; and their metabolic response is not yet sufficient to compensate for rapid heat loss. If the newborn is allowed to get cold and stay cold, the consequences may be serious. The baby will use up all his or her available energy stores in trying to keep warm, which may lead to hypoglycemia (low blood sugar). "Cold stress" may also delay the baby's adjustment from fetal to newborn circulation and adversely affect thyroid, adrenal, water, and fat metabolism.[93]

For these good reasons, the usual response of the birth attendants is to dry the infant thoroughly and wrap him or her in a warm blanket, leaving only a small portion of the face exposed. This is an effective way to cut down heat loss, but it unfortunately has the effect of greatly altering the mother's interaction with her baby in the first minutes after birth. (This is compounded if the newborn is removed from the mother's arms and placed in a heated crib. This practice was common in the past, in the belief that the baby would be warmer in a crib, but a study conducted in 1974 suggests that this belief is mistaken. The study, carried out on normal infants (over 5 pounds, no breathing problems, high Apgar scores, normal delivery) compared the body temperature of newborns placed in cribs with those placed in their mothers' arms at 5 and 16 minutes after birth. It found that "the temperatures of both groups remained within the acceptable range of heat loss . . . and . . . the differences in the mean temperatures of the two groups was not significant."[94]

Klaus and Kennell filmed twelve mothers with their full-term infants, allowing each mother total freedom in handling her baby by placing them both under a radiant heater to prevent them from getting cold. They noted that each mother went through an "orderly and predictable" pattern of behavior when she first examined her infant. She began hesitantly to touch the baby's hands and feet with her fingertips, and within 4 or 5 minutes began to caress the baby's body with the palms of her hands. This intense examination continued for several minutes, and then diminished as the mother dozed off with the naked infant at her side.[95]

Another scientist found that his own observations of mothers' initial contact with their newborn babies in a conventional delivery room "differed in many ways from Klaus and Kennell's . . . because in this situation the baby was well wrapped up and the only exposed parts were his head and face, and sometimes small, pink hands and feet!"[96] Other researchers comparing the effects of early contact with delayed contact have specifically given the early contact groups their *naked* babies.[97] Not only does placing mother and infant under a radiant heater facilitate this spontaneous "examination" of the newborn by the mother, but it also appears to be more effective in preventing heat loss than the usual procedure of wrapping. One study compared five groups of infants: three groups were in room air 72.5 to 79.7 degrees Fahrenheit (22.5 to 26.5 degrees Centigrade) with one group wet, one group dry, and one group both dry and wrapped; the two remaining groups were under a radiant heater, one wet and one dried. They found that the heat loss in wet infants exposed to room air was five times as great as in those that were both dried and warmed. The temperatures of babies dry and wrapped were similar to those of babies wet and warmed, and none were quite as good as those dried and warmed. The researchers conclude:

> In vigorous infants, the simple maneuver of drying and wrapping in a warm blanket is almost as effective in diminishing heat loss as placing them under a radiant heater. However, in depressed or immature infants who may be more asphyxiated [short of oxygen] or have reduced energy stores, radiant heat maintains body temperature while allowing access to [the baby].

They also suggest that the heat loss in the dry and warmed group could be reduced still further if the output of the heater was increased (in their study the power was set at 400 watts and was 28 inches above the baby) and if air currents in the delivery room were reduced.[98] Some hospitals now have a radiant heater above the delivery table to facilitate early mother-infant contact without risk of the baby's cooling down, and there seems to be no reason on physiological grounds why their careful use should not be extended.[99]

Using Silver Nitrate

Ophthalmia neonatorum is any puslike discharge from a baby's eyes within 3 weeks of birth. In many countries, the law requires that this event be reported to public health authorities. Ophthalmia neonatorum can be caused by a variety of organisms, but the one for which silver nitrate is specifically given is responsible for the sexually transmitted disease gonorrhea.[100] If the gonococcus organism gets into the baby's eyes (either by passing through an infected vagina or by coming into contact with contaminated hands), the infant may suffer permanent impairment of vision or even blindness.[101]

It was not until the mid-eighteenth century that the connection was made between vaginal infection in the mother and eye infection in the child, and not until the mid-nineteenth century was the bacterium responsible finally identified. Shortly after this, in 1831, the German physician Crede introduced a preventive treatment (Crede's prophylaxis) that consisted of putting one drop of 2 percent silver nitrate solution into each eye of every baby immediately after delivery. This method spread rapidly throughout Europe and to America, with little change except for the general acceptance of a 1 percent solution instead of a 2 percent solution. (Crede himself considered a solution of less than 2 percent to be less than effective; this was endorsed by further research in 1934.)[102]

When silver nitrate is put into the eye, the silver binds with the surface protein of any organisms present and prevents their growth. Unfortunately, it also binds with the surface proteins of the transparent membrane covering the eye (the conjunctiva), and this causes the intense irritation commonly associated with silver nitrate administration. As a result, the baby usually cries; if tears are produced, the salt in them combines with the silver nitrate to produce particles that further irritate the eye. This irritation, producing redness and swelling, and the associated pain, which even in adults may last for several days, is the reason that silver nitrate is not longer used in cases of adult eye infection now that alternative treatments are available.[103]

It should be said that at the time silver nitrate prophylaxis was introduced, gonococcal ophthalmia was responsible for a considerable number of childhood admissions to schools for the blind, and there was no simple, effective treatment for gonorrhea once contracted. Silver nitrate was also cheap and simple to use. In that historical situation, pain and conjunctivitis were certainly the lesser evils.

In the hundred years since its introduction, however, there have been numerous relevant changes, particularly in the developed countries of the West. Women in general are better nourished, better housed, and receive very much better prenatal care. Even more important in relation to gonorrhea has been the introduction of antibiotics for its safe and effective treatment, both in adults and babies. As the incidence of gonorrhea in pregant women at the time of delivery drops, the incidence of gonococcal opthalmia neonatorum also drops. (Investigations in both Philadelphia and Copenhagen suggest that only about 20 percent of infected mothers subsequently infect their babies.)[104]

Against this background, it is appropriate to question the continued routine use of silver nitrate for all newborns. Over the years, various investigations have been carried out in an attempt to determine the effectiveness of the use of silver nitrate in preventing gonococcal eye infection, but most of these have either failed to use an untreated comparison group or failed to produce groups that were truly comparable with each other before treatment began; in any case, their results have generally been doubtful or conflicting. Greenberg and Vandow in 1961 concluded from their reading of the literature that "no proper evaluation has ever been made of silver nitrate solution as a prophylactic drug against ophthalmia neonatorum."[105] Since 1960, many individual countries and states have either abandoned the use of silver nitrate or, conversely, established either its use or that of some other prophylactic agent as compulsory. In the first case, there is no further incentive for an evaluative study; in the second, it is not possible to include a control group without special dispensation.

The results published in 1961 by Greenberg and Vandow of their survey of 96 hospitals in New York City, however, go a long way toward explaining the widely differing conclusions of other researchers on the efficacy of silver nitrate prophylaxis. In 1955, the New York City Board of Health amended the sanitary code to permit substances other than silver nitrate to be administered prophylactically to prevent gonococcal ophthalmia; moreover, it gave special dispensation to some institutions to omit all prophylaxis so that comparisons could be made. Over the three years covered by the survey, nearly half a million babies were born in the hospitals under consideration. The resulting data were analyzed according to the type of treatment given, the type of hospital, and the type of service.

Overall, the researchers found 17 cases of gonococcal ophthalmia among the 258,621 babies who received silver nitrate (a rate of 6.6 per 100,000 live births); 22 cases among the 86,407 who received no prophylaxis (25.5 per 100,000); 1 case among 13,438 who received saline (common salt) solution (7.4 per 100,-000); 9 cases among the 80,311 who received antibiotic ointment or drops (11.2 per 100,000); and no cases among the 33,199 newborns who received 50,000 units of penicillin by intramuscular injection. It would appear, when the data are analyzed according to the type of prophylaxis used (in the above manner), that saline solution is almost as effective as silver nitrate in preventing gonococcal eye infections and considerably better than antibiotic drops or nothing.

When the data are analyzed according to the type of hospital, however, and more specifically, according to the type of service —that is, public or private—a different pattern emerges. There were no cases among the 78,000 babies born to mothers in private hospitals, 28 cases among the 102,000 born to mothers in public hospitals, and 21 among the 292,000 born to mothers in voluntary hospitals, regardless of the type of prophylaxis used. If the voluntary hospitals' cases are split into private and public patients, then those 21 cases show the same distribution: 1 case out of 213,000 "private" patients, as opposed to 20 cases among 79,000 "public" patients. Adding the two categories together, it will be seen that only 1 baby developed a gonococcal eye infection among the 291,000 babies born to mothers who were private patients, while 48 infants were affected among the 181,000 born to mothers on public wards, regardless of whether any prophylaxis was used or, if it was, what type was employed.

Thus the importance of the socioeconomic level of the population in determining the incidence of gonococcal infection is clear. The worst-housed and poorest-paid sector of the community tends to have the worst health conditions and the worst prenatal care. Between 1955 and 1958, the black population of New York City had the worst socioeconomic environment, and this was reflected in the proportion of black babies who developed gonococcal eye infections within the total who did so: 40 out of a total of 49. Of the white population, Hispanics had the worst socioeconomic environment; again, this was reflected in the incidence of gonococcal eye infections among their babies: 5 out of the remaining 9, despite the fact that Hispanics represented only 15 percent of the total white population.

If the different treatments are now compared *within the same socioeconomic groups,* the results are as follows. The only case of gonococcal ophthalmia in the "private" group occurred in a baby given prophylactic silver nitrate. Of the other 48 in the "public" group, there were 22 in the "no prophylaxis" group (121.4 per 100,000); 1 in the saline group (130.4 per 100,000); 16 in the silver nitrate group (15.5 per 100,000); 9 in the antibiotic ointment-or-solution group (20.8 per 100,000); and none in the group (numbering 15,761) who received antibiotic by intramuscular injection.

It must be remembered that in most of these hospitals, the trials conducted were neither randomized nor controlled, and thus the results have to be interpreted with caution; but they do seem to indicate that both the need for and the type of prophylaxis is strongly related to the socioeconomic level of the mother and therefore to the likelihood of a particular mother suffering from gonorrhea. It would appear from the evidence so far presented that silver nitrate is not 100 percent effective in the prevention of gonococcal ophthalmia and that its usefulness is probably limited prophylactically to populations of low socioeconomic status. The authors of this survey recommended that compulsory routine prophylaxis should be abandoned in areas where the risk of infection is low.[106]

One of the few papers to give the results of a randomized, controlled trial was published in Sweden in 1982 by Kallings and Wahlberg. They randomly assigned 544 babies to three groups at birth, each receiving either 1 percent silver nitrate, 10 percent hexargium (a less irritating silver compound), or saline solution (as a control). A further 83 babies in the study had nothing at all put in their eyes, having been delivered by cesarean section (which minimizes the risk of gonococcal infection). None of the 627 babies developed gonococcal ophthalmia, a result that came as no surprise to the authors, who calculated that the probable incidence of gonococcal ophthalmia was 1 in 6,000 in Sweden.[107]

The most important aspect of silver nitrate prophylaxis as far as most mothers are concerned, however, is not its efficacy but the pain, redness, and swelling that are produced as soon as the drops are put in the baby's eyes. This chemically induced conjunctivitis has long been associated with silver nitrate and varies in severity from very little reaction to copious purulent discharge. The Swedish study found that irritation persisted for as long as 8 to 10 weeks in some infants.[108] A number of studies have been undertaken to find either alternatives to silver nitrate, such as antibiotics, or methods of reducing the severity of the reaction by rinsing the eyes after silver nitrate is administered.[109] In the latter case, the results seem to suggest that rinsing with sterile water might be preferable to anything else, but by and large rinsing the eyes is probably ineffective.

Most of the studies that compare antibiotics with silver nitrate for prophylactic use have been too small to show differences in the incidence of gonococcal opthalmia—but they do show that antibiotics are much less irritating. Antibiotics used prophylactically, however, have their own disadvantages: they are more expensive; maintaining consistent fresh solutions is impractical; there is a risk of penicillin sensitization; and their use may encourage the emergence of antibiotic-resistant strains of certain organisms. In spite of this, in 1980 the American Academy of Pediatrics for the first time approved the use of tetracycline or erythromycin as alternatives to silver nitrate.[110]

Other disadvantages of the routine use of silver nitrate include using either the wrong drug or the wrong concentration of silver nitrate, thereby causing permanent damage to the eyes.[111] A more common disadvantage is the response of professionals to the fact that silver nitrate itself quite often produces "ophthalmia neonatorum, i.e. a purulent discharge from the eyes within 21 days of birth"—as many as 39 percent of babies were thus affected in the Swedish study.[112] If this high rate of chemically induced purulence is common and is known to be chemically induced more often than not, professionals will either disregard a purulent discharge occurring within 24 hours of birth—hence increasing the risk that therapy for genuine infection will be delayed—or take swabs for culture from every eye discharge so that none are missed, thus wasting much time and money on a high number of negative results.

The final disadvantage is that babies who have had silver nitrate put into their eyes are in pain and do not open their eyes widely. This has been observed to affect the response of parents (particularly of fathers) to the newborn to a certain extent.[113] Among the infants themselves, one researcher found less alertness and scanning behavior on the second day of life in the silver nitrate group, although this effect had ceased by the fourth day. The mothers of these newborns, however, made significantly fewer attempts to make eye contact with their babies, even after the conjunctivitis had passed, and this negative effect was potentiated when it coincided with other stress factors, such as a difficult delivery.[114]

Since the introduction of antibiotics in the 1940s, it has been possible to treat both gonorrhea and gonococcal ophthalmia simply and effectively. In none of the studies mentioned was antibiotic therapy ineffective when gonococcal ophthalmia occurred. If silver nitrate does not prevent it (in all cases), and if antibiotic therapy will cure an affected mother and/or child, what would be the consequences of abandoning Crede's prophylaxis?

In Britain, where ophthalmia neonatorum is still a disease

that must be reported to public health authorities, all forms of prophylaxis were abandoned long ago. Various centers collect statistics on the incidence of ophthalmia neonatorum, gonococcal ophthalmia, and gonorrhea, as well as the number of children who are registered as blind or partially sighted as a result of opthalmia neonatorum. Thus it is possible to show that from 1969 to 1976, the number of females treated for gonorrhea at hospital clinics in England rose from 14,518 to 21,537. Over the same period, the number of legally reported instances of opthalmia neonatorum in England and Wales fell from 434 to 222. (These data suggest that *more* mothers were being effectively treated for gonorrhea over this period, despite the rise in incidence.) Again over the same period, there were no registered cases of blindness attributable to ophthalmia neonatorum and only one registered case of partial sight attributable to ophthalmia neonatorum (occurring in 1975–76). It is not possible to determine from the published records whether this case was due to the gonococcus bacterium or not. In the year in which this one registration was made, there were 584,270 live births in England and Wales and 222 reported cases of ophthalmia neonatorum. There were also 20 laboratory-identified cases of gonococcal ophthalmia. This indicates a low incidence of ophthalmia neonatorum and an even lower incidence of gonococcal ophthalmia, and furthermore suggests that the few cases that do occur are being effectively treated.[115]

The main difference between Britain and America in postnatal care of mothers and babies is that in Britain there is a statutory obligation for every mother and newborn to be seen everyday by a midwife until the baby is 10 days old. Accordingly, there is an effective community midwifery service to fulfill the legal requirement. In the United States, unless the mother is cared for by a midwife (either lay or certified), she is not likely to see a professional soon after she leaves the hospital—which occurs, on the average, about 3 days after the birth.

Gonococcal conjunctivitis usually has a short onset (1 to 5 days after delivery),[116] and a heavy amount of discharge associated with redness of the eyes and swelling of the eyelids will be readily observed by anyone responsible for a baby's care. Any mother whose child does not receive routine professional care soon after the third day postdelivery should be strongly advised before leaving the hospital to report any eye discharge immediately to a doctor, so that immediate microscopic examination can be performed and the appropriate treatment or advice given. This should be the case regardless of whether the baby has received any form of prophylaxis, since none has been shown to be 100 percent effective. Every effort, moreover, should be made to identify pregnant women with gonorrhea, either by taking vaginal swabs for culture in late pregnancy or for microscopy following admission in labor, if a mother is considered to be at high risk from the disease.

In high-risk areas in America, it may be appropriate to retain some form of prophylaxis, especially when it is felt that a mother may not seek treatment promptly should her baby develop an eye infection. But the work of Wahlberg and of Greenberg and Vandow has suggested that in areas or countries that enjoy a low frequency of gonorrhea, good prenatal care, and similar positive factors, routine prophylaxis should be discontinued.[117] The British experience seems to support this suggestion.

Where silver nitrate prophylaxis is required by law, that law is binding on the persons present at delivery or the doctor responsible for the mother's care, depending on the state; it is not binding on the mother, and she is not obliged to accept the procedure. George Annas, director of the Center for Law and Health Sciences at the Boston University School of Law, maintains that a woman has the legal right to "refuse any procedure, including silver nitrate."[118] Some hospitals have printed release forms that absolve both the institution and its employees of any liability as a result of the parent(s) refusing to permit the administration of prophylactic medication.[119] At the same time, the efforts of many organizations are directed toward bringing about a change in those state laws that still require mandatory prophylaxis, particularly with respect to silver nitrate.

Removing the Baby to a Nursery

It is the custom in all but a very few hospitals to remove the newborn from the mother after she has seen her baby and possibly held him or her for a short period. There are various reasons given for this practice if the mother should happen to question it (which very few do—such is the effects of institutions): "The baby needs to rest after the exertions of being born," "needs weighing," "cleaning up," or "warming up." Sometimes the mother may even be told that the infant requires a "period of observation."

Unless the baby is in need of the care of a pediatrician and intensive-care nurses, there is no need to remove the newborn from the mother. Keeping the baby warm has already been discussed; the baby can quite happily "wait" to be weighed or cleaned until the mother is ready for this to be done, and then it can be done at her bedside. Researchers have shown repeatedly that the normal baby is especially alert and receptive after birth, ready to interact with the mother; any rest the newborn needs will be taken later. Moreover, unless the infant is in need of specialist observation, or unless the mother has been given narcotic drugs, there is no one who will "observe" her baby better or more keenly than she. All the necessary procedures can be and are carried out perfectly satisfactorily at home when that is the place of delivery. In fact, aside from the wish to escape any unnecessary interference during labor, the desire not to be separated from the newborn was the main reason women gave for wanting their later confinements at home, according to Sheila Kitzinger's study. She points out that every mother in the study who had already had one baby in the hospital wrote to emphasize this reason, often at great length. In these letters, many women expressed a passionate sense of urgency about being able to care for their babies themselves from the first seconds of life, and it is a great indictment of our hospitals that they felt that this was possible only in the home environment.[120]

Only in our "civilized" society is the continuum of the mother-baby relationship so regularly interrupted, and it appears that in some circumstances we may pay a high price for arbitrarily separating the mother and the newborn. A controlled study carried out in Nashville, Tennessee, on 301 mothers and babies found that there was a significantly higher incidence of child abuse and "parenting disorders" among mothers who were deprived of contact with their babies for 12 hours following delivery and thereafter permitted contact only for 30 minutes every 4 hours for the next 2 days; this was in comparison with those who had their newborns rooming-in after an initial 7-hour period of separation. (It should be stressed that these were all normal, vigorous, full-term babies, born spontaneously, and both mothers and infants remained healthy throughout their stay in the hospital.)[121] This study is one of eleven reviewed by Marshall Klaus at the Rainbow Babies' and Children's Hospital Symposium on Parent-Infant Attachment in Cleveland, Ohio, in November 1977. The other ten studies concentrated on early mother-infant contact: two compared extra contact in the first 3 hours plus extra time over the next 3 days with controls; eight compared extra time in just the first hour with controls. Dr. Klaus found that no matter when increased amounts of contact are added in the first 3 days after birth, there appears to be improved mothering behavior.[122]

Much of the behavior that is involved in parenting is learned rather than instinctive.[123] Nevertheless, Dr. Klaus believes that increased contact with her infant may somehow set in motion a sequence of innate behavior so that the mother may recapitulate what was once normal human maternal behavior (that is, nearly continuous feeding and carrying of the baby). A Swedish study has found that 20 minutes' extra skin-to-skin contact between mother and newborn made women with their first babies behave more as if they were handling their second (or subsequent) infants.[124]

The evidence of the past thirty years tends to argue against a "critical" period for bonding and attachment in humans (bonding is defined by infant researcher T. Berry Brazelton as the initial attraction of a mother to her baby and her desire to form an emotional relationship; attachment is defined as the long, hard process of developing the bond). Mothers and infants in Western hospitals have, by and large, been allowed minimal contact, yet most have managed to form close attachments and most mothers have provided adequate mothering (even if their early separation has meant that they have had to work harder at it, and that a greater proportion of women has failed to form a satisfactory relationship than might otherwise have done so).[125]

Since the human infant depends for survival (to a far greater extent than the young of any other species) on the mother's bonding with and attending to him or her, it would seem unlikely that this life-sustaining relationship would be dependent on a single process. Dr. Klaus suggests that an analogy may be drawn between the bonding-attachment process and that which triggers the first breath in the newborn. A lengthy search by respiratory physiologists for the "key" factor that initiated respiration in the newborn revealed that there were many factors, each of which played some part; if one or more factors were absent, the combined effect of those that remained was in most cases sufficient to cause the infant to take his or her first breath.[126]

Keeping mother and baby together from birth onward, however, is likely to facilitate and enhance the many behavioral, hormonal, physiological, and immunological mechanisms that serve to bind them together, and they ought not to be separated without good reasons. Once researcher summarizes the situation thus: "For a non-specific time after birth, there does seem to be a period in the developing relationship between mothers, fathers, and babies when separation may be detrimental."[127]

How detrimental such separation is appears to depend on the mother's socioeconomic class. The better the socioeconomic environment, the greater is the chance of repairing any damage done at birth. But the poorer the socioeconomic environment, the more likely it is that any harm done at birth will be compounded. The impact that socioeconomic class may have in the

longer term on the mother-infant relationship in cases where the
two have been separated at birth is illustrated by two separate
studies. A pair of scientists studied the effects of separation on
three groups of white, middle-class mothers, using two groups
whose premature babies had been in a special-care unit for 3
weeks or more. One group could see but not touch their infants,
while the second group could touch and handle their babies in
the incubators and cribs; the third (control) group had normal,
full-term babies and were not separated.

The researchers found that the separation had little effect on
interaction between the mothers and babies, although the "no-
contact" group smiled at and cuddled their infants significantly
less than the others in the initial period. At 1 year, these differences had almost disappeared. The only striking variation found
at the 21-month follow-up was that five mothers (out of twenty-
two) in the "no-contact" group were now divorced; one mother
in the "premature-plus-contact" group was divorced, while
there were no divorces in the control group.[128]

A second study, on the other hand, shows striking differences
in the attachment behavior of the mothers and babies in two
groups (numbering fourteen each) of black, inner-city, mostly
unmarried mothers of low socioeconomic class, none of whom
were breastfeeding but all of whom had had normal, full-term
deliveries. The control-group mothers were given the traditional
American contact with their newborns—a glimpse of the baby
at birth, a brief visit 6 to 12 hours later for identification and
feeding, and thereafter visits of 20 to 30 minutes every 4 hours
for feeding. The mothers in the other group were given their
naked babies for 1 hour within the first 3 hours after birth, and
an extra 5 hours' contact each afternoon for the next 3 days—
a total of 16 hours' extra contact. Follow-up observations
showed that the "extra-contact" mothers were more likely to
pick up and comfort their babies when they cried (even when
the mothers knew they were not wet or hungry), stood closer to
and were more likely to soothe their babies during physical
examinations, and were more likely to fondle and establish eye

contact with their babies during feeding periods. These differences were still obvious at 1 year, and at 2 years the children of
the "extra-contact" group of mothers had much better linguistic
ability—their mothers used twice as many questions, fewer
words per proposition, more adjectives, and fewer commands
than the control group. This study seems to suggest that early
separation combined with low socioeconomic class may make a
substantial difference to maternal behavior, and these effects
may continue to manifest themselves for up to 2 years after
delivery.[129] But it must be said that like the evidence is as yet
insufficient to justify generalizations about all mothers in low
socioeconomic groups.

Chemical Separation

If the mother has received drugs during labor (particularly
Demerol), the chances of her being able to interact satisfactorily
with her baby at birth are reduced. If the drugs are mistakenly
given right at the end of labor (which is likely if the mother is
not examined vaginally before administering the drug), she may
be interested only in going to sleep after the birth, as the sedative aspect of the drug takes effect. If the drug is given earlier
in labor, it is the newborn who is more likely to be drowsy and
unresponsive to the mother's attentions. Unfortunately, this
state may persist in the baby for several days and may interfere
with the mother's ability to bond to her infant. It is difficult to
like someone who does not respond to any of your advances and
turns a feeding session into a chore because of the number of
times he or she has to be jostled and coaxed to feed.

It would seem that there is plenty of evidence to support the
contention that mothers and babies should not be separated in
any way or at any point from birth onward without good reason;
when such separation is essential (for instance, if the newborn
is premature or requires urgent medical attention), strenuous
attempts should be made to give the mother as much physical
and emotional access to her infant as is possible.

Hospitalization and the Mother-Infant Relationship

Although many hospitals now have an (optional) policy of rooming-in—that is, allowing babies to remain beside their mothers' beds during the day, rather than in the central nursery —it is still common for the baby to be removed from the mother at night so that he or she can be observed by the hospital staff. This is particularly true of the first night, when the mother is assumed to need sleep and is thus given sleeping medication, while the infant is removed.

A mother's need for sleep on the first night following delivery will depend on what time her baby was born. Healthy infants, born normally and undrugged, commonly feed two or three times in the first hour or so, when they are "quietly alert," and will then sleep for 7 or 8 hours if undisturbed. During this time, the mother can also sleep if she needs to. However, she is apt to want to use some of that rest time to begin to come to terms with the birth of the child, particularly if it is her first, and to relive the events of the labor and delivery in her mind, coupled with frequent glances at the baby by her side to remind herself of the baby's reality. When a child is born at home, this natural sequence of events can take place uninterrupted, and the mother can slowly absorb the vastness and complexity of motherhood and begin to know and care for her baby.

It is very difficult for this to happen in a hospital. A mother cannot mentally order the events of the birth if her mind is clouded with drugs. It is hard enough for her to absorb the fact that she and her husband are now a family if her husband must go home and leave her; if the baby is also removed, it must be almost impossible. If she does not sleep, she may lie awake, emotionally isolated, imagining that every cry she hears is her baby.

Furthermore, a newborn whose mother intends to breastfeed needs to be given the breast when he or she cries—not water, dextrose, or worse still, infant formula. It will take longer for the mother to build up her milk supply and cause her more discomfort if she misses feedings because her baby is given water or other fluids at night. Moreover, a totally breastfed baby does not need extra water; the baby's fluid and food intake are perfectly balanced in breast milk. This is true even if the newborn is jaundiced: a trial done in England showed that water supplements made no difference to the onset of jaundice, to the mean age of the peak serum bilirubin (bilirubin is the pigment in the blood that causes the yellow "jaundice" color), or to the number of babies requiring phototherapy (treatment under lights).[130] Water is inadequate if the newborn is hungry, and it cannot be presumed that the baby is *not* hungry when crying simply because it is less than 2 hours since the last feeding. Many young infants who are allowed to feed as often as they want take highly variable numbers of feedings during a 24-hour period, at intervals that also vary widely. "In the early days some babies may want feeding every hour or so, and the greatest number of feeds often occurs on the fifth day. In the Sheffield survey . . . 29 per cent of babies wanted eight feeds on the fifth day and 10 per cent wanted more than nine."[131] Allowing mothers to believe that feeding every 3 to 4 hours is the norm for breastfed babies will only serve to undermine their confidence in their ability to feed their infants properly on their own milk alone, when they find that the baby wants to be fed more frequently.

Among the other common fallacies perpetuated by many hospitals and professionals is the notion that it is necessary to time feedings and limit sucking time on succesive days to 2, 5, 7, and finally 10 minutes, in order to prevent sore nipples.[132] Nipple soreness is actually due to a baby's being incorrectly positioned at the breast. (Infants properly latched onto the breast have the nipple so far back in their mouths that they compress the milk ducts—which are located well behind the nipple, under the areola—between the tongue and the roof of the mouth when feeding. At no time are they sucking the nipple itself.) Reciprocally, however, it does not matter how short the mother makes the feeding, if the baby is not properly latched on—she will experience some nipple soreness. Initial breastfeeding is not necessarily painful in itself, but it may well become so through incorrect positioning.[133] Mothers may also be told that they should feed the baby from both sides at each feeding, but if the infant is content and/or asleep after an unrestricted feeding at the first breast, there is nothing else the mother needs to do except remember to offer the other side first the next time her baby wants feeding.

There are other respects (apart from this regular separation of mother and baby, with its potential impairment of the feeding relationship) in which many hospitals are not good places to learn about mothering in the psychological sense. The mother may have no privacy in which to develop a relationship with her newborn. Single (private) rooms are expensive and not always available; drawn curtains are rarely respected by professionals, aides, or cleaning staff. The mother may be told that she must not cuddle her baby (unless the baby is being fed), for fear of "spoiling" him or her; she must not place or change her baby on her own bed, for fear of "contaminating" him or her—let alone actually have the baby in her bed. Some hospitals have such a poor opinion of new mothers that they forbid them to carry their newborns, lest they drop them (despite the fact that in many cases they will be carried for a substantial part of every day once they are at home). The mother is even encouraged— frequently, though implicitly—to be dependent on the hospital "experts" in the care of her baby, rather than to think for herself. Some new mothers even feel it necessary to ask if they may change their own babies, if they wish to do this outside of the scheduled time. Consequently, many go home with tiny total strangers, whom they may find it hard even to like, and with no confidence in their own abilities. The time spent in the hospital may be regarded retrospectively as a sort of limbo period, and it may be weeks or even months before such mothers can recover their lost self-esteem.

CHAPTER EIGHT

Alternatives and Improvements

The Birth Environment

One major nonmedical influence on a woman's experience of childbirth is the environment in which she receives her care and has her baby. Although there are a variety of different options in the United States, in practice they are not equally available to all women.

For many, the only alternative is giving birth in a teaching hospital—a large institution that, in addition to offering care for low-risk mothers, provides specialists for high-risk situations. As the name implies, teaching hospitals are also the training grounds for doctors, nurses, and sometimes student midwives. For most American women, however, the nearest institution is a community hospital. (Unlike many European countries—Britain, for instance—America has very few maternity hospitals.) Community hospitals are smaller than teaching hospitals and are generally found outside large urban areas. They are staffed by obstetricians, family practitioners, pediatricians, and possibly nurse-midwives, but are not usually technologically equipped to deal with mothers with preexisting medical difficulties or babies who need special care facilities; should problems develop, the mother and infant are transferred to the nearest primary health care center, probably a teaching hospital.

Free-standing birth centers, another alternative, are increasing in number in America as their popularity rises. They provide low-risk, family-centered care for women who do not want to (or are not able to) have their babies at home. Most of these centers, which are not usually on hospital grounds, are run by nurse-midwives, using a physician for back-up. Others are run by obstetricians or nurse-midwife/obstetrician teams. If any problems arise during pregnancy or labor, the woman is transferred to the nearest hospital.

Some hospitals (teaching, community, or maternity) now provide "birth" or "birthing" rooms. These are an attempt to provide the best of both worlds—a homelike atmosphere, but within an institution in which additional staff and facilities are available at a moment's notice. The type of staff available will depend on the institution, as will the prevailing attitude toward birth. Once again, this is an option that is usually reserved for those not considered to be at increased risk.

It is perfectly legal to have a baby at home, but individual state laws determine who may assist the mother in a professional capacity. All but two states—North Dakota and Nebraska—provide for the practice of certified nurse-midwives. Although she is responsible for the independent management of the mother and newborn, in no state may the nurse-midwife *practice* independently; she must always work in conjunction with a physician (unlike her European counterpart, who is legally an independent practitioner in her own right). There are, however, only about 2,000 qualified nurse-midwives in America, who work largely in hospitals and birth centers, so their services are not yet available to all the women who may want them. Moreover, many states specifically prohibit these certified nurse-midwives from attending births at home. In 1980, these nurse-midwives delivered just under 2 percent of the nation's babies; by contrast, the approximately 22,000 midwives in Britain delivered 75 percent of all the babies born in that country in the same year.[1]

In order to be recognized as professionals by law in the United States, nurse-midwives must be certified by the American College of Nurse-Midwives. The certificate is earned in eighteen to twenty-four months of university-based training, on top of qualification as a registered nurse; alternatively, college graduates who are not nurses can take a three-year master's degree at some universities (such as Yale), which includes licensing as an R.N.

The legality of the practice of midwives who have no formal qualification—that is, lay midwives—varies from state to state. In a few states—for instance, New Mexico, Texas, and Washington—lay midwives are recognized by law and licensed. In others, their practice is legal only if they were licensed before a certain date, as in Kentucky and Virginia. In states such as Arizona, Arkansas, Florida, and Mississippi, lay midwifery is legal but no licenses are issued. Other states either tolerate lay midwifery (Alaska, Nevada, Oregon, and Wyoming, for example) or prohibit it through judicial interpretation (California, Colorado, and North and South Dakota). In New York, Pennsylvania, Ohio, North Carolina, and certain other states, lay midwifery is clearly prohibited.[2]

Lay midwives are usually women who have gained their experience empirically by apprenticing with other midwives, attending births, and reading. They work mostly in homes, but sometimes in birth centers. Almost all consult with doctors, who are available if difficulties arise. If there is no physician back-up, the lay midwife has to rely on an emergency medical service or take the mother to the emergency room of the nearest hospital herself, should severe problems arise.

Although in theory the American mother has the same sort of options as her British counterpart—birth at home, in a teaching hospital, or in one of the other establishments discussed above—in practice the choice may not be so wide, depending on where she lives. If there are no birth centers nearby, she must choose between birth in a hospital, where most American women have their babies, and a home birth—an option sought by only a determined minority. Some physicians will attend births at home.

Any discussion of home births, even in those countries where the law allows qualified midwives to conduct them, tends to arouse strong reactions on both sides. But as Eva Alberman, a lecturer on childbirth at the London School of Hygiene and Tropical Medicine, has remarked:

> A true comparison between home and institutional delivery will never be achieved until it is possible to study outcomes such as the long-term quality of births in terms of physical, psychological and mental health, the benefits to the mother of relief of pain or anxiety, the long-term benefits in terms of incidence of complications such as prolapse, urinary incontinence and other similar measures.[3]

In the meantime the arguments surrounding home births center on safety and emotional well-being, sometimes as if these two factors were mutually exclusive. What follows is a summary of the advantages and disadvantages of both hospital and home deliveries. While free-standing birth centers vary considerably, in general what is said here about home deliveries applies to deliveries in birth centers as well.

Hospital Delivery: The Advantages

1. The most obvious and undisputed advantage is the immediate availability of the necessary equipment and expertise to cope with difficulties and emergencies that may arise during labor or with the newborn. Any woman who has good reason to anticipate such problems would be wise to elect to give birth in a suitably equipped and staffed hospital.

2. There may be social advantages when a mother's domestic situation or home surroundings are problematic. The most important social factor at home is whether the mother has sufficient *willing* help right after the baby is born. The fact that the home may be crowded or lack hot running water is not necessarily reason for advising against home confinement, but the mother may prefer or feel that she would be better off using the facilities provided in a hospital.

3. For some women, hospital birth may carry psychological advantages. Women have been told repeatedly that hospital

birth is safer for them. The fact that this statement is not supported by evidence (see Chapter One) does not stop a substantial number of women from believing it, and it would be just as bad to compel a woman who has no anticipated medical need for hospital facilities to give birth at home as it would be to insist that she go to a hospital. In all labor, peace of mind is an important factor; a woman should be able to give birth in the place where she feels safe and secure—which for a proportion of women will mean a hospital.

Some advantage may also be gained from the contacts made by the newly delivered mother with others in the same position. Friendships made in this situation may be valuable and supportive both in the hospital and when the mothers go home.

Hospital Delivery: The Disadvantages

1. The mother is usually subjected to all the routine hospital procedures, regardless of her individual needs. (Her chances of a cesarean are at least 1 in 6 and maybe as high as 1 in 3 in some teaching hospitals.[4])

2. Friends and relations are greatly restricted in the support they can give the mother, both during labor and once the baby is born.

3. The mother may have to contend with the whims of individual members of the hospital staff, who have a territorial advantage.

4. She is more likely to receive unnecessary intervention simply because the facilities are there (see Chapter One).

5. She is more likely to be given drugs as a first, rather than last, resort (see Chapter Five).

6. She is much less free to respond to her own feelings about what is right for her—what she wears, eats, drinks, the position she adopts during the first and second stages, where and how she actually gives birth, what happens to the baby and cord after birth, when she feeds the baby, and so forth (as elaborated earlier in this book).

7. The chances of serious infection to the newborn may be significantly higher in the hospital than at home.[5]

Home Delivery: The Disadvantages

The reason most often given by professionals for opposing delivery at home (or in a birth center) is that it is not safe, or not as safe as a hospital. They do not mean that more babies (or mothers) die at home, since the perinatal mortality rate for babies born at home is very much lower than for those born in hospitals, particularly when one considers those babies whose mothers were actually selected for a home confinement.[6] They mean, rather, that if something should go wrong, the facilities are not available at home to remedy it. First, this assumes that if something goes wrong in a hospital, it is always possible to correct it. Unfortunately, certain unpredictable disasters befall mothers and babies that simply cannot be put right, no matter where they take place (for example, amniotic fluid embolism in the mother, or congenital malformations in the baby that preclude life). The concept of absolute safety in childbirth is an illusion and should be accepted as such by mothers and professionals alike.

The claim of increased hospital safety also assumes that birth attendants are ill equipped to deal with unpredictable emergencies arising at home. In fact, the overwhelming majority of complications are not emergencies requiring split-second action. Nonetheless, British midwives attending home deliveries are not only trained in how to handle, for example, a postpartum hemorrhage or a baby who does not breathe immediately, but also have at their disposal most of the same drugs and equipment as their hospital counterparts. The midwife at home also has—or should have—access to an emergency medical service (rescue squad) should the need arise, or may arrange to transport the mother to a hospital by car or ambulance if she feels that the woman or her baby need the help of an obstetrician or pediatrician. Most American midwives have similar training and usually have life-sustaining equipment to use until transfer to a hospital can be completed.

With proper selection at the beginning of the pregnancy (see the risk factors in Chapter One), revised if necessary as a result of the good prenatal care the mother should receive, the incidence of avoidable mishaps in home births is very low. (A study of 5,000 home births in Holland showed that of the few deaths that occurred, none could have been prevented had the birth taken place in a hospital; the British birth survey, moreover, has shown that babies born in hospitals are five times more likely to have breathing difficulties than those born at home. One American study of 1,000 births showed that severe perineal tears were ten times more likely in a hospital than at home.)[7]

Finally, there is the question of the degree of risk. Many aspects of our lives involve calculated risks; every time we cross a street, drive a car, or board an airplane, we are taking a calculated risk. If we did not on occasion put our trust in ourselves or in someone else, life would come to a standstill. Deciding to embark on a pregnancy involves taking a calculated risk; so, too, does deciding where and how to give birth. Every mother, consciously or unconsciously, makes a choice. If she allows herself to be confined in a hospital without discussing the reasons for it, she is taking the risk that her advisers may not be considering her individual needs but merely following policy; once she is in the hospital, the risk of unnecessary intervention may be greater than the potential benefits conferred on her by being there. If she consciously makes this choice, then she must have considered the relative advantages and disadvantages. Should she decide that she wants her baby born at home, then, similarly, she has judged that in her circumstances the benefits outweigh the hazards. All that professionals and others can do is to make sure that the mother has as much accurate information at her disposal as possible in order to make an informed choice, since it is she who bears the child and copes in the long term with the consequence of the decisions taken at the time of birth.

Home Delivery: The Advantages

1. Before giving birth, the mother is likely to have been cared for by *one* physician and midwife and to have met other midwives and had the chance to talk to and develop a trusting relationship with the people who will help her during labor.

2. When prenatal visits take place at home or in a birth center, the mother is relaxed. Other children in the family have a chance to get to know the midwife and become involved in the preparations for their new sister or brother.

3. There is much less disturbance in the lives of the mother's other children if the birth of the new baby does not coincide with the disappearance of the mother. Jealousy is more likely to be avoided if the only problem the other children have to cope with is the arrival of the baby.

4. The expectant parents are not faced with the need to decide when labor has really started and when to go to the hospital; the midwife can be contacted by telephone and will visit the mother at home or recommend that she come to the birth center.

5. At home, in very early labor, the midwife may leave the couple or family for a period, returning when either she or the mother feels that her presence is necessary. In a birth center, the attendants do not leave, but the couple is free to go and return later.

6. Once labor is established, the midwife stays with the mother until the baby is delivered, thus providing continuous emotional and practical support.

7. There are no admission procedures and no forms for the mother to complete. Perineal shaving is rarely performed, and enemas or suppositories are given only if they are needed.

8. The mother can choose what she wears for labor.

9. She can move around during labor, experimenting with different positions to increase her comfort.

10. She may eat or drink, as she feels inclined.

11. There is no audience at the birth except of her own choosing; her other children may be present if she desires.

12. She is able to use the breathing and relaxation techniques that she has learned with the understanding and support of the midwife, who is more likely than unfamiliar attendants to know the sort of childbirth instruction the mother has received.

13. Drugs are not routinely available and may be used only in emergencies.

14. The mother is much less likely to have her labor interfered with or actively "managed."

15. Familiar surroundings and an atmosphere of calm are likely to assist the mother in relaxing and tuning in to her labor so that she can follow her own body rhythms.

16. At home, the midwife and doctor are the mother's guests; in the birth center, she is encouraged to act as if she were at home. Throughout labor, attention is focused on her and her individual wishes are respected.

17. The mother can decide the place and position for the second stage: it is not necessary for her to give birth in or on a bed if she would rather be on the floor, or to give birth sitting or lying if she would rather be squatting, standing, or on all fours.

18. Episiotomy (a subject that the mother can discuss with the midwife beforehand) is much less likely to be performed. Usually, no arbitrary time limit is imposed on labor, so the second stage can be allowed to progress at its own pace, provided mother and baby show no signs of distress.

19. The way in which the newborn is treated is again up to the mother; she can hold and feed her baby when she feels she wants to, without asking permission.

20. The baby's father is able to play a more positive role and will be more confident in his attitude toward his wife. He can wear his own clothes and sit beside or behind his wife, holding her in his arms if that seems appropriate. He may even help deliver the baby if he wants to and if the mother and midwife have no objection.

21. The mother at no point surrenders her responsibility for herself, her labor, her family, or her newborn baby. Feeling close to and learning about caring for a new baby is easier when the mother can avoid prescribed routines.

22. Breastfeeding is easier to establish at home. Unlimited sucking time and feeding on demand help to minimize engorgement and to promote a good milk supply. Night feeding is much less tiring if the mother can simply take the baby into bed with her and lie down to feed the baby when he or she cries, thus avoiding the necessity of being fully awakened several times a night; moreover, there is no one to create difficulties by giving the baby a bottle without the mother's permission. (Thirty percent of babies in British hospitals are still bottle-fed by hospital staff without their mothers' consent, according to a survey published in the April 1981 issue of *Parents* magazine.) In addition, the advice given to the mother on all aspects of the postnatal period, but in particular on breastfeeding, is likely to be consistent: she will not be bombarded with conflicting information from whichever nurse happens to be on duty.

23. The newborn is much less likely to acquire an infection at home or in a birth center, since the baby's skin is rapidly colonized by the harmless germs of his or her parents, brothers, and sisters.[8] Hospital staff, on the other hand, have to be constantly alert, particularly in maternity units, to the dangers of cross-infection by harmful strains of staphylococcus aureous (yellow, pus-forming bacteria). Usually such bacteria are relatively harmless, but through continual exposure to antibiotics in powders and sprays, penicillin-resistant strains have developed in hospitals, and these strains are the organisms most often responsible for epidemics in nurseries and maternity wards.

24. Postpartum blues (*not* postpartum depression) virtually never occur following a delivery at home or in a birth center, as the mother does not have to cope with a sharp change in her environment (going home from the hospital) or suddenly take over the total responsibility for her baby from others; nor does

she have to share the early days with strange women and their infants.

It can be seen from this list that for an expectant mother who is not in a category of increased risk, who is within reach of emergency facilities, and who is in the care of a skilled and confident midwife, there are considerable advantages in staying at home or going to a birth center for the birth of her baby, if that is what she wants to do. There is more to childbirth than simply the production of a live baby and live mother. For many women, how the baby is born is also extremely important. Giving birth is now an event that, for most women, will occur only once or twice in a lifetime, and it is a significant experience that cannot be shrugged off with "better luck next time" if it is not a happy event. The mother's perception of herself and her child may be greatly affected by the circumstances and atmosphere surrounding the birth and by the care, consideration, and respect she receives from her attendants.

The actual obstetrical details may be less important than the way the mother *feels* about the birth. A woman who has had a perfectly straightforward labor and delivery, but who was frightened, neglected, spoken to unkindly, or given drugs against her wishes, may remember the experience as a nightmare, whereas a mother who has had a benignly abnormal, possibly long and tedious labor, but who was supported and encouraged, given explanations, and not left alone, may remember it as "all right." The experience of childbirth, whether good or bad, is not forgotten, although the memory may be buried. It can color the mother's thinking and her relationship with her child and the rest of her family for many years.

An Alternative

There is now a hospital alternative that goes a long way toward achieving many of the emotional advantages, described above, of home birth. This alternative is in France, where almost all confinements take place in either municipal hospitals or in private clinics. Many French women have become increasingly vocal, and they are demanding an improvement in service. Their grievance is not with the lack of home confinement facilities but with the unfeeling attitude shown in many maternity units.

Dr. Michael Odent is the director of a nineteen-bed maternity unit at the local community hospital in Pithiviers, France, a town 35 miles south of Paris with a population of about 45,000. The hospital provides maternity care for the local population without selection: all mothers, including those with obstetrical complications, are admitted. In addition, about 40 percent of the 900 mothers delivered there each year come from outside the area, sometimes from outside the country. Professional care is provided by Dr. Odent (or a colleague) and six midwives. The midwives work in pairs for periods of 48 hours, which they spend entirely in the unit; they then have four days off duty. Prenatal care is shared between the mother's own family doctor and the maternity unit.

In this setting, Dr. Odent has been able to put into practice his own philosophy, evolved in part from ideas first launched by the French obstetrician Frederick Leboyer in his book *Birth without Violence*. (A detailed and illustrated account of Odent's theory and practice is now available in his own book *Birth Reborn*.)[9]

One of the central beliefs that colors much of what is done in his maternity unit is that the normal physiology of the birth process should not be disturbed and that the atmosphere of the hospital, the behavior of the staff, and the environment in which the mother gives birth should all facilitate the change in level of consciousness that Odent sees as an integral part of normal labor. He describes this process as "regression": the woman in labor separates herself from the modern world, forgets what is learned or cultural, and instead responds to what is instinctive inside herself, as if listening to an older, more "primitive" part of her brain. This turning inward frees the emotions and releases the body. The mother can then adopt positions that she finds helpful and relax both sphincter and perineal muscles. Odent suggests that this altering of the state of consciousness protects the mother against the effects of pain and produces a positive sense of well-being. One possible explanation for this is that there is an optimum state of consciousness for the *inhibition* of those hormones such as adrenaline (which produces the "fight or flight" response in humans as well as other animals) and the *release* of oxytocin and even perhaps endorphins—the natural opiates of the brain.

Accordingly, preparations for birth at Pithiviers take the form of weekly group discussions with expectant parents that emphasize the excitement, happiness, and normality of birth. They include evenings of singing as well as discussions with new parents. Most mothers are admitted to the unit in labor, since induction is not practiced. Each mother is given her own bed in a single or double room, which she keeps throughout her stay. There are few rules, and the mother wears her own nightclothes. She is encouraged to stay upright and walk about during the first stage of labor, and as labor advances she makes her way to the delivery suite, which includes two conventional labor rooms rarely used except for medical procedures and instrumental deliveries) and the *salle sauvage*, or birth room. (Cesarean sections are done in the surgical department of the hospital.)

The birth room is predominantly brown, with orange curtains at the windows. There is no clock, and a raffia shade covers the light. In one corner of the room there is a large, firm, low-level platform with many brightly colored cushions, a record player, and a birth chair. Extra heating is always available from a small heater. The lighting in the birth room is subdued to minimize unnecessary sensory stimuli, and the birth attendants recognize the importance of silence and of substituting soothing music for distracting noises. Communication with the mother is also on a basic level, using simple words that spare the intellect, or touch and gesture. The mother is emotionally supported in labor by as a few people as possible, those she knows and trusts—the midwife, her husband, her mother. The male doctor stays in the background. A small, inflatable pool of warm water is also available for the mother to use as an aid to relaxation. Some mothers find this so helpful that they spend all of labor in the pool. Although this is not actively encouraged, about eighty babies a year are born while the mother is in the water; they suffer no harm.

During the second stage, the mother is again encouraged to be attentive to her own body's needs and to adopt positions conducive to her comfort and relaxation. Odent believes that the positions a mother adopts in labor and her state of consciousness are reciprocal—that the mother needs to be free to find postures that, traditionally, have been used to facilitate altered states of consciousness (such as resting on all fours or kneeling as if praying) and that, conversely, "liberating the instinctive brain" increases the capacity to spontaneously find positions that are physiologically effective (for example, the baby's head rotates more easily in the pelvis when the mother is on all fours). Over the years, mothers delivering in the unit have been observed to adopt a variety of positions: kneeling, standing, sitting, curled up on the side, crouching, squatting, and bending forward from a standing or kneeling position, as well as a variety of asymmetrical positions (for example, with one leg straight out, or leaning to one side).

At the end of the second stage, when a standing woman experiences a contraction she is normally observed to bend her knees to squat, especially if one or two assistants are supporting her shoulders. This position seems to be the most efficient, as it produces the maximum pressure in the pelvis, the greatest increase in the surface areas of the pelvic outlet, the minimum muscular effort, and the optimum relaxation of the pelvic muscles. (If the mother is giving birth to a breech baby, Dr. Odent feels that this supported squatting position is essential to avoid delay between the delivery of the body and umbilical cord, and the delivery of the head; during this interval the baby's blood [and therefore oxygen] supply is being reduced as the cord is compressed [at least partially] between the baby's head and the mother's pelvis.) The upright position also greatly reduces the need for episiotomy, the incidence of which is only 7 percent for the whole unit.

The baby is delivered toward the mother, who sits down or sits back on her heels, takes the newborn in her arms, and puts him or her to her breast within minutes of birth. The cord is not clamped or cut until the baby is at least 5 minutes old and the cord has stopped pulsating; nor are oxytocic agents routinely given to the mother. The placenta is delivered by gravity and the mother's own effort, or by gentle cord traction.

The mother is given a bowl of warm water, which is placed between her legs. Into this she lowers her infant for a few minutes, washing, observing, and talking to him or her. After this, the newborn is dried, wrapped, and given to the father while the mother is washed. Then the mother and father, carrying their new baby, walk back to the mother's room.

The whole policy is one of nonintervention and minimum disturbance of the normal physiology. The mother is given no analgesics or other drugs during labor and her membranes are not broken artificially. Forceps are not used in the unit. If obstetrical assistance is required, the mother is either delivered using the vacuum extractor or by cesarean section.

During the years 1977 and 1978, Dr. Odent and his midwives acted chiefly as observers; no directions or instructions were given to the mother that would influence or limit her own inclinations during labor. Over this period, 1,799 babies were delivered, of which 1,592 (88.5 percent) were delivered spontaneously, 58 (3.2 percent) by vacuum extractor, and 149 (8.3 percent) by cesarean section. During the same period, 16 babies died (0.9 percent), 31 (1.7 percent) were transferred after birth to special units because of major neonatal problems, and 17 (1 percent) of the mothers required manual removal for the delivery of the placenta. The significance of these figures, however, can be established only by comparison with figures from a unit or hospital that serves a similar population; unfortunately, because so many women at the hospital in Pithiviers come from outside the community, it is difficult to imagine where a comparable hospital might be found.

The Birth Attendant

The second major influence on a woman's experience of birth is the person (or people) who cares for her prenatally and at delivery. Again, as with the place of birth, the choice of an attendant may not be as wide in practice as it is in theory. Some mothers will be limited by geographic and financial factors, so that, for many, the "choice" will be the nearest hospital, with a doctor as the principal caregiver. Some will live in areas where the services of a nurse-midwife or a lay midwife are realistic alternatives. Information concerning the options in a given area may come by word of mouth (family, friends, other pregnant or recently delivered women), from an already known and trusted professional, or from consumer-oriented information organizations. In addition, women may turn to the American College of Nurse-Midwives, which provides a list of all the nurse-midwifery services available in the United States.[10]

Some mothers have a fairly clear idea of what they expect from their caregivers before they go to them for the first time; for others, the possible options and their reactions to them emerge only gradually. Unless the mother is content to leave all the decision making to her attendants (in itself a form of choice), at some point during her pregnancy she will have to communicate her hopes and concerns to her caregivers. Caregivers are not mindreaders: if the mother does not say what she wants, the best her attendants can do is to give her the care and treatment that they consider to be in her best interest—which may or may not be in keeping with her own expectations. At worst she will be subjected to the prescribed routine of that physician or that institution. Most prospective mothers, especially first-time mothers, will have some anxieties and certain questions that they will want to ask. One way for a mother-to-be to ensure that, when face to face with her caregivers, she does not forget what she was going to say, is for her to write it down. If the mother has strong feelings about any aspect of her care during the birth itself, these are much better discussed beforehand—labor is no time to be arguing with the obstetrician or midwife. If the mother's attendants during labor are not the same as her prenatal caregivers, any relevant instructions can be recorded on the hospital chart or wherever her birth attendants will see them.

A memory aid of this sort is rather different from a birth plan —a device advocated by some childbirth educators and consumer organizations. A birth plan is a much more detailed, formal list of the options that the woman or couple would prefer for the birth. It may even be a printed form which the mother fills in and which covers all aspects of her care, before, during, and after birth. Sometimes it is compiled before the attendant or place of birth is selected, as a sort of checklist for those who have the time, the motivation, and the money to "shop around." Or it may evolve during the course of pregnancy and be brought for discussion with the already-selected caregiver.

If a birth plan is used, its wording should reflect a cooperative and flexible attitude. A list of demands that begins "I do not want and do not consent to the following . . ." may well be resented by physicians and midwives, partly because it assumes that they will be aggressive and hostile in their treatment of the couple and partly because, in some forms, the birth plan may tie the hands of the mother's attendants if her labor deviates from normal or her baby requires special care. Should emergencies arise, whether at home or in a hospital, the mother should give her caretakers the same cooperation that she would expect from them in a straightforward birth.

When and if a birth plan has been worked out that meets the approval of both the parents and the attendants, it "can be initialled by the caregiver and entered into the chart as part of the care plan for the mother and baby."[11] During labor it can serve as a convenient set of reminders for whoever is caring for the mother, thus relieving her and her partner of continually having to repeat their requests. This is particularly useful if there are changes of staff during the woman's labor.

A birth plan is generally seen by couples as a way of assuming some sort of control over events once the mother is in the hospital. In most instances, however, this is an illusion. Prospective parents become relatively powerless once they enter a hospital, and the birth plan, since it is not a contract, really functions only on the level of a convenient set of reminders. Apart from this, its main value is probably in the prenatal period, where it serves to identify the basic philosophies and flexibility of the caregivers and to reveal any important areas of disagreement at a time when it is still possible for the mother to change her birth attendants.

The optimum setting for any laboring woman is a place where she feels comfortable and secure, attended by a person she knows and trusts.

A couple who attempts to use a birth plan as a substitute for trust may find that they end up with more, rather than less, of the intervention that they sought to avoid.[12] If the mother does not trust her attendants during labor, she cannot let go emotionally, allowing her body and mind to open up to the sensations coming from her uterus in order to work with them. Fear, anxiety, and a generalized mistrust will instead cause her body to produce the hormones appropriate to that emotional state— namely, adrenaline and noradrenaline.

The muscle fibers of the uterus react to the presence of these hormones in different ways. The activity of the muscle fibers in the body of the uterus is reduced (so contractions become weaker), while the activity of those in the lower part of the uterus and cervix is increased (and the cervix starts to close). In addition, adrenaline and noradrenaline cause the constriction of blood vessels in any organ not directly concerned with the mother's survival (the "flight or fight" response), and the blood supply to the actively contracting uterus is reduced.[13] If this situation is not relieved, it may reduce the amount of oxygen available to the fetus, cause pain in the muscles of the uterus, and slow labor. Several recent studies have demonstrated a direct correlation between maternal anxiety and problems during labor.[14]

One of the ways to avoid this situation is to establish a relationship of trust prenatally, bearing in mind that relationships take time to develop. A birth plan, which may initially provide a useful basis for discussion, is likely to prove ultimately unnecessary when there is real continuity of care and the mother in labor is looked after by the person she has come to know (and trust) before labor begins. If it is impossible to find a setup that offers this sort of care, it may well be possible at least to choose one with which the mother is in agreement about basic issues.

In either case, the better informed the mother is, the better she will be able to articulate her point of view and to understand the doctor's or midwife's response to it if it differs from her own. However strongly she may feel emotionally about certain issues, she is more likely to gain the cooperation and respect of her caregivers if she demonstrates her ability to discuss matters rationally and factually.

The power to create change in the field of obstetrics and midwifery lies—as it always has—in the hands of the consumer. The extent to which a range of options is available to childbearing women is a reflection of the use that they make of that power. The hierarchy and technology prevalent at many hospitals today may impose considerable restrictions on choice within the hospital setting, so the most useful exercise of a prospective mother's power to choose (especially when the professionals' income derives directly from the consumer) may be her decision *where* to have her baby and *whom* she will rely on for her care.

APPENDIX: THE CASCADE OF INTERVENTION

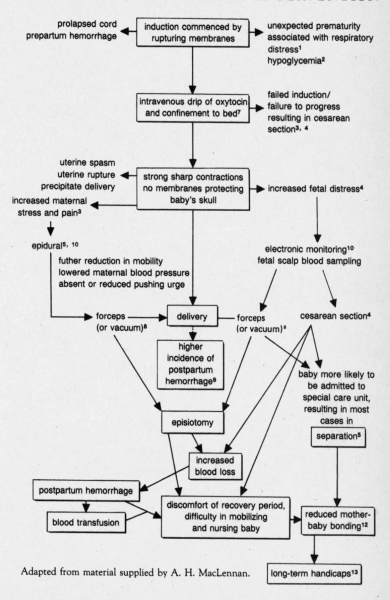

prolapsed cord
prepartum hemorrhage

induction commenced by
rupturing membranes

unexpected prematurity
associated with respiratory
distress[1]
hypoglycemia[2]

intravenous drip of oxytocin
and confinement to bed[7]

failed induction/
failure to progress
resulting in cesarean
section[3, 4]

uterine spasm
uterine rupture
precipitate delivery

strong sharp contractions
no membranes protecting
baby's skull

increased fetal distress[4]

increased maternal
stress and pain[3]

epidural[5, 10]
futher reduction in mobility
lowered maternal blood pressure
absent or reduced pushing urge

electronic monitoring[10]
fetal scalp blood sampling

forceps
(or vacuum)[8]

delivery

forceps
(or vacuum)[8]

cesarean section[4]

higher
incidence of
postpartum
hemorrhage[9]

baby more likely to
be admitted to
special care unit,
resulting in most
cases in

episiotomy

separation[5]

increased
blood loss

postpartum hemorrhage

blood transfusion

discomfort of recovery period,
difficulty in mobilizing
and nursing baby

reduced mother-
baby bonding[12]

long-term handicaps[13]

Adapted from material supplied by A. H. MacLennan.

REFERENCES

Chapter One   Birth As Pathology

1. M. Tew, "Obstetrics vs. Midwifery—the Verdict of the Statistics," *Journal of Maternal and Child Health*, May 1982, pp. 193–201.
2. J. G. Fryer and J. R. Ashford, in *British Journal of Preventative and Social Medicine* 26 (1982), pp. 1–9.
3. M. Tew, "Obstetricians Over-ruled: The Myth of Hospital Safety," *Journal of the Association for Improvements in Maternity Services*, Spring 1984, p. 3. For the 1970 study, see G. Chamberlain et al., *British Births 1970*, vol. 2: *Obstetric Care* (London: Heinemann, 1978).
4. C. N. Barry, "Home versus Hospital Confinement," *Journal of the Royal College of General Practitioners* 30 (1980), pp. 102–7.
5. See Fryer and Ashford (note 1); Tew (note 1); M. Tew, in *Place of Birth*, ed. S. Kitzinger and J. Davis (London: Oxford University Press, 1978), p. 56.
6. G. L. Kloosterman, quoted in S. Arms, *Immaculate Deception* (Boston: Houghton Mifflin, 1975), p. 237.
7. W. O. M. Moore, in Kitzinger and Davis (see note 5), p. 4.
8. K. R. Niswander and M. Gordon, *The Women and Their Pregnancies*, Collaborative Study of the National Institute of Neurological Diseases and Stroke (Philadelphia: W. B. Saunders, 1972), p. 126.
9. B. Brennan, in *The Complete Book of Midwifery* by B. Brennan and J. R. Heilman (New York: E. P. Dutton, 1977), p. 81; J. Epstein, "A Safe Homebirth Program That Works," in *Safe Alternatives in Childbirth*, 3rd ed. (Marble Hill, Mo.: National Association of Parents and Professionals for Safe Alternatives in Childbirth [NAPSAC], 1976), p. 105; L. E. Mehl, "Statistical Outcomes of Homebirths in the U.S.: Current Status," in ibid., p. 88.
10. M. Tew, "The Safest Place of Birth—Further Evidence," *Lancet*, 30 June 1979, pp. 1388–90; 8 September 1979, pp. 523–24.
11. L. E. Mehl, "Home versus Hospital Delivery: Comparison of Matched Populations" (paper presented at annual meeting of American Public Health Association, Miami Beach, 20 October 1976), reported in Kitzinger and Davis (see note 5).
12. M. Klein et al., in *British Journal of Obstetrics and Gynaecology* 90 (February 1983), pp. 118–28.
13. M. P. M. Richards, "An Evaluation of the Risks of Hospital Delivery," in Kitzinger and Davis (see note 5), p. 72.
14. M. P. M. Richards, "Obstetricians and the Induction of Labour in Britain," *Social Science and Medicine* 9 (1975), pp. 595–602; M. P. M. Richards, "The Induction and Acceleration of Labour: Some Benefits and Complications," *Early Human Development* 1, no. 3A (1977).
15. J. H. E. Carmichael and R. J. Berry, "Diagnostic X-rays in Late Pregnancy and in the Neonate," *Lancet* 1 (1976), p. 351.
16. Richards (see note 16), p.78.

17. Carmichael and Berry (see note 15).
18. Richards (see note 16); I. Chalmers, "Evaluation of Different Approaches to Obstetric Care" (paper presented to seminar on Human Relations and Obstetric Practice, University of Warwick, October 1975).
19. H. Mahler, in *Lancet* 2 (1 November 1975), pp. 829–33.
20. K. O'Driscoll et al., "Selective Induction of Labour," *British Medical Journal* 4 (1975), pp. 727–29.
21. See A. L. Cochrane, *Effectiveness and Efficiency* (London: Oxford University Press for the Nuffield Perinatal Hospitals Trust, 1972); D. P. Byar, R. M. Simon, W. T. Friedewald, et al., "Randomized Clinical Trials," *New England Journal of Medicine* 295 (1976), p. 74; L. W. Shaw and T. C. Chalmers, "Ethics in Cooperative Clinical Trials," *Annals of the New York Academy of Science* 169 (1970), p. 487.
22. W. R. Rosengren and S. De Vault, "Impact of Hospital Routines on the Management of the Different Stages of Birth," in *The Hospital in Modern Society*, ed. E. Friedson (New York: Free Press, 1963).
23. Kloosterman (see note 6), pp. 160, 286–87; P. Dunn, "Obstetric Delivery Today," *Lancet*, 10 April 1976, pp. 790–93.
24. A. H. MacLennan, "An Audit of Obstetric Practice in the Management of Labour," *Australian and New Zealand Journal of Obstetrics and Gynecology* 18 (1978), pp. 287–88. The diagram is from A. H. MacLennan, personal communication, 1980 (reproduced by kind permission).
25. D. Riley, "What Do Women Want? The Question of Choice in the Conduct of Labour," in *Benefits and Hazards of the New Obstetrics*, ed. T. Chard and M. Richards (London: Heinemann, 1977).
26. E. Shabanah, A. Toth, and G. B. Maughan, in *American Journal of Obstetrics and Gynecology* 89 (1977), p. 841.
27. M. Newton, N. Newton, and D. Peeler, "Effects of Disturbance on Labor," *American Journal of Obstetrics and Gynecology* 101 (1968), pp. 1096–1102.
28. E. A. Williams, in *Journal of Obstetrics and Gynaecology of the British Empire* 59 (1952), p. 635.
29. J. Kelly, "Effect of Fear on Uterine Motility," *American Journal of Obstetrics and Gynecology* 83 (1962), pp. 576–81.
30. H. Fox, in *Birth and the Family Journal* 6, no. 3 (1979), p. 162.
31. M. Enkin, in *Birth and the Family Journal* 4, no. 3 (1977), p. 101.
32. Richards (see note 13), p. 71.
33. A. W. Franklin, "A Fresh Look at Childbirth," *Journal of Maternal and Child Health*, January 1980.

Chapter Three   The First Stage: Altering the Physiological Pattern

1. For the textbooks, see J. B. De Lee, *Obstetrics for Nurses* (Philadelphia: W. B. Saunders, 1904); M. Myles, *Textbook for Midwives*, 7th ed. (Edinburgh and London: Churchill Livingstone, 1972). For the study, see M. Romney, "Predelivery Shaving: An Unjustified Assault?," *Journal of Obstetrics and Gynecology* 1, no. 1 (1980), pp. 33–35.
2. T. Denman, *An Introduction to the Practice of Midwifery* (New York: E. Bliss & E. White, 1821); F. Churchill, *On the Theory and Practice of Midwifery*, 3rd ed. (Philadelphia: Lea, 1848); G. S. Bedford, *The Principles and Practice of Obstetrics*, 4th ed. (New York: William Wood, 1868); S. P. Warren, "Technique of Labor in Private Practice," *American Journal of Obstetrics and Diseases of Woman and Child*

45 (1902), p. 26; J. W. Williams, *Obstetrics: A Textbook for the Use of Students and Practitioners*, 1st–4th eds. (New York: Appleton, 1903–1919).

3. R. A. Johnston and R. S. Sidall, "Is the Usual Method of Preparing Patients for Delivery Beneficial or Necessary?," *American Journal of Obstetrics and Gynecology* 4 (1922), pp. 645–50; H. Lankford, in ibid., 2 (1921), pp. 176–78.

4. J. W. Williams, *Obstetrics: A Textbook for the Use of Students and Practitioners*, 5th ed. (New York: Appleton, 1924).

5. R. Burchell, "Predelivery Removal of Pubic Hair," *Obstetrics and Gynecology* 24 (1964), pp. 272–73.

6. H. Kantor et al., "Value of Shaving the Pudental-Perineal Area in Delivery Preparation," *Obstetrics and Gynecology* 25 (1965), pp. 509–12.

7. P. Lomas, in *Place of Birth*, ed. S. Kitzinger and J. Davis (London: Oxford University Press, 1978).

8. F. Mauriceau, *Observations sur la grossesse et l'accouchement* (1668), trans. by H. Chamberlen as *The Accomplisht Midwife* (1673); also published as *The Diseases of Women with Child and in Childbed* (1697).

9. S. Merriman, *A Synopsis of the Various Kinds of Difficult Parturition, with Practical Remarks on the Management of Labors* (Philadelphia: Stonehouse, 1816).

10. G. J. Engelmann, *Labor among Primitive Peoples* (St. Louis, 1882).

11. W. T. Lusk, *The Science and Art of Midwifery* (New York: Appleton, 1894).

12. W. Smellie, in *Treatise on the Theory and Practice of Midwifery*, ed. A. H. McClintoch (London, 1876).

13. D. B. Scott and M. G. Kerr, in *Journal of Obstetrics and Gynecology* 7 (1963), p. 1044.

14. C. J. Mendez-Bauer, in *Journal of Perinatal Medicine* 3 (1975), p. 89.

15. R. Schwarcz, A. G. Diaz, R. Fescina, and R. Caldeyro-Barcia, *Latin American Collaborative Study on Maternal Posture in Labor* (1977); reported in *Birth and the Family Journal* 6, no. 1 (1979). For the other study cited above, see R. Schwarcz et al., *Proceedings of the VII World Congress of Gynaecology and Obstetrics* (Amsterdam: Excerpta Medica, 1976), pp. 377–91.

16. P. Dunn, "Obstetric Delivery Today," *Lancet*, 10 April 1976, pp. 790–93.

17. Lusk, (see note 11).

18. M. Mead, in *Childbearing: Its Social and Psychological Aspects*, ed. S. A. Richardson and A. F. Guttmacher (Baltimore: Williams & Wilkins, 1967), p. 201; M. Mead, *Male and Female: A Study of the Sexes in a Changing World* (New York: William Morrow, 1946).

19. Merriman (see note 9).

20. E. E. Phillip, *Obstetrics and Gynaecology Combined for Students* (London: H. K. Lewis, 1962); D. Llewellyn-Jones, *Fundamentals of Obstetrics and Gynaecology* (London: Faber & Faber, 1969).

21. J. Foulkes and J. G. Dumoulin, in *British Journal of Hospital Medicine*, June 1983, pp. 562–64.

22. Ibid.

23. Myles (see note 1).

Chapter Four   The First Stage: The Active Management of Labor

1. T. Chard, "The Physiology of Labour and Its Initiation," in *Benefits and Hazards of the New Obstetrics*, ed. T. Chard and M. Richards (London: Heinemann, 1977), p. 81.

2. Garvey, Govan, Hodge, and Callander, *Obstetrics Illustrated*, 2nd ed. (Edinburgh: Churchill Livingstone, 1974), p. 458.

3. W. Patterson, "Amniotomy, with or without Simultaneous Oxytocin Infusion," *Journal of Obstetrics and Gynaecology of the British Commonwealth* 78 (1971), pp. 310 –16.

4. P. Howie, "Induction of Labour," in Chard (see note 1), p.83.

5. Garvey et al. (see note 2); Setna et al., in *Journal of Obstetrics and Gynaecology of the British Commonwealth* 74 (1967), p. 262; A. C. Turnbull and A. M. B. Anderson, in *ibid.* 75 (1968), p. 32; Patterson (see note 3); W. P. Bradford and G. Gordon, in *Journal of Obstetrics and Gynaecology of the British Commonwealth* 75 (1968), p. 698; M. A. Garud and S. C. Simmons, in ibid. 75 (1968), p. 702; M. E. Pawson and S. C. Simmons, in *British Medical Journal* 3 (1970), p. 191.

6. Patterson (see note 3); P. J. Steer et al., "Uterine Activity in Induced Labour," *British Journal of Obstetrics and Gynaecology* 83 (1975), pp. 454–59.

7. N. G. Caseby, "Epidural Analgesia for the Surgical Induction of Labour," *British Journal of Anaesthesia* 46 (1974), pp. 747–51.

8. Chard (see note 1), p. 80.

9. Caseby (see note 7).

10. For information in this paragraph, see S. M. M. Karim et al., "Response of the Pregnant Human Uterus to Prostaglandin F_2X Induction of Labour," *British Medical Journal* 4 (1968), pp. 621–23; Chard (note 1); I. Z. Mackenzie and M. P. Embrey, in *British Medical Journal* 2 (1977), p. 1381; A. A. Calder and M. P. Embrey, "Induction of Labour," in *The Management of Labour: Proceedings of the Third Study Group of the Royal College of Obstetricians and Gynaecologists,* ed. R. Beard, M. Brudenell, P. Dunn, and D. Fairweather (London, 1975), p. 62; D. R. Bromham and R. S. Anderson, "Uterine Scar Rupture in Labour Induced with Vaginal Prostaglandin E_2," *Lancet,* 30 August 1980, p. 485.

11. On intravenous administration, see Howie (note 4). On oral administration, see A. P. Gordon-Wright and M. G. Elder, in *British Journal of Obstetrics and Gynaecology* 86 (1979), pp. 32–36; J. F. Miller, G. A. Welply, and M. Elstein, in *British Medical Journal* 1 (1975), p. 14.

12. Gordon-Wright and Elder (see note 11); Calder and Embrey (see note 10).

13. Howie (see note 4).

14. P. Yudkin, A. M. Frumar, A. M. B. Anderson, and A. C. Turnbull, "A Retrospective Study of Induction of Labour," *British Journal of Obstetrics and Gynaecology* 86, no. 4 (1979), pp. 257–65.

15. Ibid.

16. Calder and Embrey (see note 10); I. Chalmers, "Evaluation of Different Approaches to Obstetric Care" (paper presented to Seminar on Human Relations and Obstetric Practice, University of Warwick, October 1975).

17. Yudkin et al. (see note 14).

18. Ibid.; J. Bonner, "Induction and Acceleration of Labour in Modern Obstetric Practice" (paper presented to Study Group on Problems in Obstetrics, Medical Information Unit of the Spastics Society, London, 1975); H. Arthure et al., "Report on Confidential Inquiries into Maternal Deaths: Tunbridge Wells, April 1975," in *England and Wales 1970–72,* Department of Health and Social Services Report on Health and Social Subjects, no. 11 (London: HMSO, 1975); K. O'Driscoll, "An Obstetrician's View of Pain," *British Journal of Anaesthesia* 47 (1975), pp. 1053–59; I. J. Hoult, A. H. MacLennan, and L. E. S. Carrie, in *British Medical Journal* 1 (1977), p. 14; W. A. Liston and A. J. Campbell, in ibid. 3 (1974), p. 606.

19. Hoult et al. (see note 18).

20. Yudkin et al. (see note 14).

21. P. R. S. Brinsden and A. D. Clarke, "Postpartum Haemorrhage after Induced and

Spontaneous Labours," *British Medical Journal* 2 (1978), pp. 855–56; M. E. Pawson and S. C. Simmons, in ibid. 3 (1970), p. 191.

22. Yudkin et al. (see note 14); K. Hartman, paper presented to meeting on the MM2 of the GP Obstetric Unit, John Radcliffe Hospital, Oxford, March 1979.

23. Brinsden and Clarke (see note 21).

24. For Welsh study, see I. Chalmers et al., "Obstetric Practice and Outcome of Pregnancy in Cardiff Residents, 1965–73," *British Medical Journal* 1 (1976), pp. 735 –38. Compare M. Richards, "Induction and Acceleration of Labour—Some Benefits and Complications," *Early Human Development* 1 (1977), pp. 3–17; Turnbull and Anderson (note 5); A. Ghosh, "Oxytocic Agents and Neonatal Morbidity," *Lancet* 1 (1975), pp. 3–17.

25. Liston and Campbell (see note 18).

26. R. Caldeyro-Barcia, quoted in S. Arms, *Immaculate Deception* (Boston: Houghton Mifflin, 1975).

27. Yudkin et al. (see note 14).

28. Ibid.

29. Chalmers et al. (see note 24).

30. M. Richards, "An Examination of the Risks of Hospital Delivery," in *Place of Birth*, ed. S. Kitzinger and J. Davis (London: Oxford University Press, 1978). For other findings cited in this paragraph, see Calder and Embrey (note 10); Yudkin et al., (note 14); Chalmers (note 16); W. A. Bowes, Y. Brackbill, E. Conway, and A. Steinschneider, eds., "The Effects of Obstetric Induction on Fetus and Infant," *Monographs of the Society for Research in Child Development* 4 (1970), p. 137; M. K. Aleksandrowicz, "The Effects of Pain-relieving Drugs Administered during Labor and Delivery on the Behavior of the Newborn: A Review," *Merrill-Palmer Quarterly* 20 (1974), pp. 121–41; J. W. Scanlon, "Obstetric Anesthesia as a Neonatal Risk Factor in Normal Labor and Delivery," *Clinics in Perinatology* 1 (1974), pp. 465– 82; J. S. McDonald, L. L. Bjorkman, and E. C. Reed, "Epidural Anesthesia for Obstetrics," *American Journal of Obstetrics and Gynecology* 120 (1974), p. 1055.

31. Yudkin et al. (see note 14).

32. I. Chalmers, H. Campbell, and A. C. Turnbull, "Use of Oxytocin and Incidence of Neonatal Jaundice," *British Medical Journal* 1 (1975), pp. 116–18; Hartman, (see note 22); H. Campbell et al., "Increased Frequency of Neonatal Jaundice in a Maternity Hospital," *British Medical Journal* 3 (1975), pp. 548–52; E. A. Friedman and M. R. Sachtleben, "Neonatal Jaundice in Association with Oxytocin Stimulation of Labour and Operative Delivery," *British Medical Journal* 1 (1976), pp. 198–99.

33. D. Llewellyn-Jones, *Fundamentals of Obstetrics and Gynaecology*, vol. 1: *Obstetrics* (London: Faber & Faber, 1969), pt. 3. The percentages for the incidence of these conditions mentioned in the listing below are from this source.

34. K. O'Driscoll, C. J. Carroll, and M. Coughlan, "Selective Induction of Labour," *British Medical Journal* 4 (1975), pp. 727–29.

35. E. G. Knox, "Control of Haemolytic Disease in the Newborn," *British Journal of Preventative and Social Medicine* 30 (1976), pp. 163–69; percentage from Llewellyn-Jones (see note 33).

36. E. Alberman, "Facts and Figures," in Chard and Richards (see note 1); see also Llewellyn-Jones (note 33).

37. J. Leeson and A. Smith, Letter, *British Medical Journal*, 12 March 1977.

38. O'Driscoll et al., (see note 34).

39. M. B. McNay, G. W. McIlwaine, P. W. Howie, and M. C. MacNaughton, in *British Medical Journal* 1 (5 February 1977), p. 347.

40. I. Chalmers, R. G. Newcombe, and H. Campbell, Letter, *British Medical Journal*, 12 March 1977, p. 707.

41. McNay et al., (see note 39).
42. Leeson and Smith (see note 37).
43. Chalmers et al. (see note 40).
44. D. Meager and K. O'Driscoll, Letter, *British Medical Journal*, 12 March 1977.
45. Chalmers et al. (see note 24); I. Chalmers, "Implications of the Current Debate on Obstetric Practice," in Kitzinger and Davis (see note 1); I. Chalmers, J. G. Lawson, and A. C. Turnbull, "An Evaluation of Different Approaches to Obstetric Care," *British Journal of Obstetrics and Gynaecology* 83 (1976), p. 921.
46. The two studies are, respectively: M. Hall et. al., "Is Routine Antenatal Care Worthwhile?," *Lancet*, 12 July 1980, pp. 78–80; O'Driscoll et al., (see note 34).
47. For the first two studies mentioned, see Chalmers, Lawson, and Turnbull (note 45); R. W. Beard in *Prevention of Handicap through Antenatal Care*, ed. A. C. Turnbull and F. P. Woodford (Amsterdam: Excerpta Medica, 1976), p. 169. For the last, see J. F. Pearson and J. B. Weaver, "Foetal Activity and Foetal Wellbeing: An Evaluation," *British Medical Journal* 1 (1976), pp. 1305–7.
48. The comparison here is between N. R. Butler and D. G. Bonham, *Perinatal Mortality* (Edinburgh: Livingstone, 1963), pp. 113, 89; and O'Driscoll et al. (see note 34); the Glasglow study is McNay et al. (see note 39).
49. Butler and Bonham (see note 48); Richards (see note 30).
50. Yudkin et al. (see note 14).
51. J. Schneider et al., "Screening for Fetal and Neonatal Risk in Postdate Pregnancy," *American Journal of Obstetrics and Gynecology* 131, no. 5 (1978), p. 473.
52. G. E. Knox et al., "Management of Prolonged Pregnancy: Results of a Prospective Randomized Trial," *American Journal of Obstetrics and Gynecology* 134, no. 4 (1979), pp. 376–84.
53. The study reviewed is R. Homburg et al., "Detection of Foetal Risk in Postmaturity," *British Journal of Obstetrics and Gynaecology* 86 (1979), pp. 759–64; it is in agreement with A. MacLennan, "An Audit of Obstetric Practice in the Management of Labour," *Australian and New Zealand Journal of Obstetrics and Gynecology* 18, no. 4 (1978), pp. 287–88.
54. D. M. F. Gibb et al., "Prolonged Pregnancy: Is Induction of Labour Indicated? A Prospective Study," *British Journal of Obstetrics and Gynaecology* 89 (April 1982), pp. 292–95.
55. I. Chalmers and M. Richards, "Intervention and Causal Inference in Obstetric Practice," in Chard and Richards (see note 1).
56. D. Llewellyn-Jones (see note 33), chap. 45.
57. J. Sturrock and R. Brown, in ibid.
58. O'Driscoll (see note 18), p. 1053.
59. R. Schwarcz et al., "Third Progress Report on the Latin American Collaborative Study of the Effects of Late Rupture of the Membranes on Labor and the Neonate" (submitted to the director of the Pan-American Health Organization and the participating groups, Latin American Center of Perinatology and Human Development, Montevideo, 1974), reported in *Modern Perinatal Medicine*, ed. L. Gluck (Chicago: Year Book Medical Publishers, December 1974), p. 435.
60. R. Schwarcz et al., "Foetal Heart-Rate Patterns in Labour with Intact and Ruptured Membranes," *Journal of Perinatal Medicine* 1 (1973), p. 153.
61. R. Caldeyro-Barcia, "Possible Iatrogenic Effects of Rupture of the Membranes during Foetal Monitoring," in *Perinatale Medizin*, vol. 4, Proceedings of German Congress on Perinatal Medicine, ed. J. W. Dudenhausen and E. Saling (Stuttgart: Georg Thieme, 1973), p. 5; R. Caldeyro-Barcia et al., "Fetal Monitoring in Labor," in *Maternal and Child Health Practices: Problems, Resources and Methods of Delivery,*

ed. H. M. Wallace, E. M. Gold, and E. F. Lis (Springfield, Ill.: Charles C Thomas, 1973).

62. Schwarcz et al., in Gluck (see note 59), p. 432; R. Schwarcz, A. G. Diaz, R. Fescina, and R. Caldeyro-Barcia, "Latin American Collaborative Study on Maternal Position in Labor," reported in *Birth and the Family Journal* 6, no. 1 (1979).

63. Schwarcz et al., in Gluck (see note 59), p. 433; R. Caldeyro-Barcia, in *Birth and the Family Journal* 2, no. 2 (1975).

64. R. Caldeyro-Barcia, at Conference of the American Foundation for Maternal and Child Health, March 1974; reported in Arms (see note 26).

65. Schwarcz, Diaz, et al. (see note 62).

66. L. Lindgren, "The Causes of Foetal Head Moulding in Labour," *Acta Obstetrica et Gynaecologica Scandinavica* 38 (1959), p. 211; R. Schwarcz et al., "Pressure Exerted by Uterine Contractions on the Head of the Human Fetus in Labor," in *Perinatal Factors Affecting Human Development,* ed. R. Caldeyro-Barcia (Washington, D.C.: Pan-American Health Organization, 1969).

67. E. Holland, "Cranial Stress in the Foetus during Labour and the Effects of Excessive Stress on the Intercranial Contents, with an Analysis of 81 Cases of Torn Tenterium Cerebrelli and Subdural Cerebral Haemorrhage," *Journal of Obstetrics and Gynaecology of the British Empire* 29 (1922), p. 549.

68. J. Frederick and N. R. Butler, "Certain Causes of Neonatal Death: Cerebral Birth Trauma," *Bioloigy of the Neonate* 18 (1971), p. 321; P. F. Muller et al., "Perinatal Factors and Their Relationship to Mental Retardation and Other Parameters of Development," *American Journal of Obstetrics and Gynecology* 109 (1971), p. 1205.

69. Schwarcz et al., in Gluck (see note 59), pp. 437, 439; P. Schwartz, "Birth Injuries in the Newborn," in *Morphology, Parthogenesis, Clinical Pathology and Prevention* (New York: Hofner Publishing Co., 1961).

70. G. Aramburu, O. Althabe, and R. Caldeyro-Barcia, "Obstetrical Factors Influencing Compression of the Fetal Head and the Incidence of Dips I in Fetal Heart Rate," in *Physiological Trauma as an Etiological Agent in Mental Retardation* (Bethesda, Md.: National Institute of Neurological Diseases and Stroke, U.S. Department of Health, Education and Welfare, 1970); Schwarcz et al., in Gluck (see note 59), p. 439.

71. Schwarcz et al. (see note 63); O. Althabe et al., "Influence of the Rupture of the Membranes on Compression of the Fetal Head in Labor," in Caldeyro-Barcia (see note 66).

72. Caldeyro-Barcia et al. (see note 61); see also Schwarcz et al., in Gluck (note 59), p. 442.

73. K. R. Niswander and M. Gordon, *The Women and Their Pregnancies,* Collaborative Study of the National Institute of Neurological Diseases and Stroke (Philadelphia: W. B. Saunders, 1972).

74. Compare H. A. Gabert and M. A. Stenchever, "Continuous Electronic Monitoring of Fetal Heart Rate during Labor," *American Journal of Obstetrics and Gynecology* 115 (1973), pp. 919–23, and R. W. Beard et al., "The Effects of Routine Ultrapartum Monitoring on Clinical Practice," *Gynecology and Obstetrics* 3 (1977), pp. 14–21; with I. M. Kelso et al., "An Assessment of Continuous Fetal Heart-Rate Monitoring in Labor," *American Journal of Obstetrics and Gynecology* 131 (1978), pp. 526–32.

75. J. Wennberg, paper presented to the arrival meeting of the American Public Health Association, Los Angeles, October 1978.

76. E. J. Quilligan, "The Obstetric Intensive-Care Unit," *Hospital Practice* 7 (1972), pp. 61–69; T. Chard, "The Foetus at Risk," *Lancet* 2 (1974), pp. 880–83.

77. R. Caldeyro-Barcia, in *Birth and the Family Journal*, 2, no. 1 (1975), p. 38.
78. M. Balfour et al., "Complications of Fetal Blood Sampling," *American Journal of Obstetrics and Gynecology* 107 (1970), pp. 288–94; H. M. Feder et al., "Scalp Abscess Secondary to Foetal Scalp Electrode," *Journal of Pediatrics* 89 (1976), pp. 808–9; F. J. Plavidal and A. Weroh, "Fetal Scalp Abscess Secondary to Intrauterine Monitoring," *American Journal of Obstetrics and Gynecology* 125 (1976), pp. 65 –70; D. M. Okada et al., "Neonatal Scalp Abscesses and Fetal Monitoring Factors Associated with Infection," *American Journal of Obstetrics and Gynecology* 129 (1977), pp. 185–89; M. Atlas and D. Serr, "Hazards of Foetal Scalp Electrodes," *Lancet* 1 (20 March 1976), p. 648; G. Thomas and R. J. Blacknell, in *American Journal of Obstetrics and Gynecology* 123 (1973), p. 2118; R. C. Goodlin and J. R. Harrod, in *Lancet* 1 (1973), p. 559; D. F. Tuberville et al., in *American Journal of Obstetrics and Gynecology* 122 (1975), p. 630.
79. C. B. Gassner and W. J. Ledger, "The Relationship of Hospital-Acquired Maternal Infection to Invasion Intrapartum Monitoring Techniques," *American Journal of Obstetrics and Gynecology* 52 (1978), pp. 193–97; D. Hagen, "Maternal Febrile Morbidity Associated with Foetal Monitoring and Cesarean Section," *Obstetrics and Gynecology* 46 (1975), pp. 260–62.
80. R. H. Paul and E. Mon, "Clinical Fetal Monitoring versus Effect on Perinatal Outcome," *American Journal of Obstetrics and Gynecology* 118 (1974), pp. 529–33; E. J. Qulligan and R. H. Paul, "Fetal Monitoring—Is It Worth It?," *Obstetrics and Gynecology* 45 (1975), pp. 96–100.
81. The first Denver study is reported in A. D. Haverkamp et al., "The Evaluation of Continuous Fetal Heart-Rate Monitoring in High Risk Pregnancy," *American Journal of Obstetrics and Gynecology* 125 (1976), pp. 310–17; the second, in A. D. Haverkamp et al., "A Controlled Trial of the Differential Effects of Intrapartum Fetal Monitoring," ibid. 134 (1979), pp. 399–408; the Melbourne one, in Renou et al., "Controlled Trial of Fetal Intensive Care," ibid. 126 (1976), pp. 470–76; the Sheffield one, in Kelso et al., (see note 74).
82. D. Banta and S. Thacker, in *Birth and the Family Journal* 6, no. 4 (1979).
83. Ibid.
84. H. L. Minkoff and R. Schwarcz, "The Rising Caesarean-Section Rate—Can It Be Safety Reversed?," *Obstetrics and Gynecology* 56 (1980), pp. 135–43; J. R. Evrad and E. M. Gold, "Caesarean Section and Maternal Mortality in Rhode Island— Incidence and Risk Factors 1965–1975," *Obstetrics and Gynecology* 50 (1977), pp. 594–97; Arthure et al. (see note 18).
85. Banta and Thacker (see note 82).

Chapter Five   The First Stage: Pain in Labor

1. C. S. McCammon, "Study of 475 Pregnancies in American-Indian Women," *American Journal of Obstetrics and Gynecology* 61 (1951), pp. 1159–60.
2. M. Richards, talk given to the Oxford Postnatal Support Group, 1977.
3. H. Read, quoted in G. Dick-Read, *Childbirth without Fear* (London: Pan Books, 1968).
4. P. Dunn, "Obstetric Delivery Today," *Lancet*, April 1976, pp. 790–93.
5. A. Rich, *Of Woman Born* (New York: W. W. Norton, 1976).
6. H. C. Hutchinson and A. Vasicka, "Uterine Contractility in a Paraplegic Patient —Report of a Case," *Obstetrics and Gynecology* 20, no. 5 (1963), p. 675.
7. Dick-Read (see note 3), pp. 62–64.
8. T. Lewis, in *Archives of Internal Medicine* 10, no. 1 (May 1932), p. 713.

9. C. Naaktgeboren, quoted in S. Arms, *Immaculate Deception* (Boston: Houghton Mifflin, 1975), pp. 130–32.

10. Dick-Read (see note 3).

11. Dunn (see note 4).

12. D. Haire, *Cultural Warping of Childbirth* (Milwaukee: International Childbirth Education Association, 1972), p. 18.

13. W. A. Brown et al., "The Relationship of Antenatal and Perinatal Psychologic Variables to the Use of Drugs in Labor," *Psychosomatic Medicine* 34 (1972), pp. 119 –27; M. Richards (see note 2).

14. Arms (see note 9), p. 126.

15. Richards (see note 2).

16. M. Shearer, paper presented at the Congress of Psychosomatic Obstetrics and Gynecology, Tel Aviv, 31 October 1974.

17. Haire (see note 12), p. 10.

18. Y. Brackbill, in *Birth and the Family Journal* 5, no. 2 (1978), p. 56.

19. L. Mackenzie, "Malpractice Hazards in Obstetrics and Gynecology," *New York State Journal of Medicine*, 1 August 1971, pp. 1877–79.

20. J. Crossland, *Lewis's Pharmacology*, 4th ed. (Edinburgh: E. & S. Livingstone, 1970), p. 599.

21. A. R. Petrie et al., "The Effect of Drugs on Uterine Activity," *Obstetrics and Gynecology* 48 (1976), pp. 431–35.

22. First trial cited by Richards (see note 2); second trial by A. M. Grant et al., in *Journal of Obstetrics and Gynaecology of the British Commonwealth* 77 (1970), pp. 824 –29.

23. A. Holdcroft and M. Morgan, in *Journal of Obstetrics and Gynaecology of the British Commonwealth* 81 (1974), pp. 603–7.

24. R. E. Kron et al., "Newborn Sucking Behavior Affected by Obstetric Sedation," *Pediatrics* 37 (1966), p. 1012; J. Dunn and M. P. M. Richards, "Observations on the Developing Relationship between Mother and Baby in the Neonatal Period," in *Studies in Mother-Infant Interaction*, ed. H. R. Schaffer (New York: Academic Press, 1977); Richards (see note 2).

25. Richards (see note 2).

26. Y. Brackbill et al., "Obstetric Premedication and Infant Outcome," *American Journal of Obstetrics and Gynecology* 118 (1974), pp. 377–84; W. A. Bowes, Y. Brackbill, E. Conway, and A. Steinschreider, eds., "The Effects of Obstetrical Medication on Fetus and Infant," *Monographs of the Society for Research in Child Development* 4 (1970), p. 137.

27. M. I. Hogg et al., "Urinary Excretion of Pethedine and Norpethedine in the Newborn," *British Journal of Anaesthesia* 49 (1976), pp. 891–99.

28. Richards (see note 2); M. K. Aleksandrowicz, "The Effects of Pain-relieving Drugs Administered in Labor and Delivery on the Behavior of the Newborn: A Review," *Merrill-Palmer Quarterly* 20 (1974), pp. 121–41.

29. Martindale, *The Extra Pharmacopeia*, 28th ed. (London: Pharmaceutical Press, 1982), pp. 1001–2, 1018–19.

30. M. Rosen, in *Benefits and Hazards of the New Obstetrics*, ed. T. Chard and M. Richards (London: Heinemann, 1977), p. 103.

31. Richards (see note 2).

32. Rosen (see note 30).

33. A. K. Brown, in *Paediatrica* 53 (May 1974), p. 816.

34. M. Rosen, in *British Medical Journal* 3 (1969), pp. 263–67; M. Rosen, "Survey of Current Methods of Pain Relief in Labour," in *The Management of Labour: Proceedings of the Third Study Group of the Royal College of Obstetricians and Gynaecologists,*

ed. R. Beard, M. Bradwell, P. Dunn, and D. Fairweather (London, 1975), pp. 140 –48.

35. V. Weiss and G. de Carlini, in *Experientia* 31 (1975), pp. 339–41; Richards (see note 2).

36. Rosen (see note 30).

37. Ibid.

38. See A. Vasicky, "Fetal Bradycardia after Paracervical Block," *American Journal of Obstetrics and Gynecology* 38 (1971), pp. 500–512; J. Rosefsky and M. Petersiel, "Perinatal Deaths Associated with Mepivocaine Paracervical Block Anesthesia in Labor," *New England Journal of Medicine* 278 (1968), pp. 530–33.

39. W. Johnson, "Regionals Can Prolong Labour," *Medical World News,* 15 October 1971.

40. Rosen (see note 30), p. 107.

41. Ibid.

42. Ibid.

43. C. F. Goodfellow, M. G. R. Hull, et al., "Oxytocin Deficiency at Delivery with Epidural Analgesia," *British Journal of Obstetrics and Gynaecology* 90 (March 1983), pp. 214–19.

44. I. J. Hoult, A. H. MacLennan, and L. E. S. Carrie, in *British Medical Journal* 1 (1977), pp. 14–16.

45. J. S. Mcdonald, L. L. Bjorkman, and E. C. Reed, "Epidural Analgesia for Obstetrics," *American Journal of Obstetrics and Gynecology* 120 (1974), p. 1055.

46. B. S. Schifrin, in *Journal of Obstetrics and Gynaecology of the British Commonwealth* 79 (1972), pp. 332–39.

47. In the first instance, see Aleksandrowicz (note 28); G. Thomas, in *British Journal of Obstetrics and Gynaecology* 82 (1975), p. 121; M. Finster and B. S. Bergersen, in *Birth and the Family Journal* 5, no. 2 (1978), p. 77. In the second instance, see Richards (note 2); Rosen (note 30), pp. 107, 112.

Chapter Six   The Second Stage: Delivery

1. W. P. Dewees, *System of Midwifery,* quoted by R. Caldeyro-Barcia, in *Birth and the Family Journal* 6, no. 1 (1979), p. 7.

2. Caldeyro-Barcia, ibid., p. 10.

3. W. T. Lusk, *The Science and Art of Midwifery* (New York: Appleton, 1894).

4. P. Dunn, "Obstetric Delivery Today," *Lancet,* 10 April 1976, pp. 790–93.

5. F. Howard, "Delivery in the Physiologic Position," *Obstetrics and Gynecology* 11, no. 3 (1958).

6. For the investigation, see F. Naroll et al., "Position of Women in Childbirth," *American Journal of Obstetrics and Gynecology* 82 (1961), pp. 943–54. On the files, see Human Relations Area Files, *Function and Scope of the Human Relations Area Files* (New Haven, 1954); Human Relations Area Files, in *Current Anthropology* 1 (1960), p. 256.

7. See Howard (note 5); M. Newton, "The Effects of Position on the Course of the Second Stage of Labour," *Surgical Forum* 7 (1957), p. 517; N. Newton and M. Newton, "The Propped Position for the Second Stage of Labor," *Obstetrics and Gynecology* 15, no. 1 (1960).

8. I. J. Hoult, A. H. MacLennan, and L. E. S. Carrie, in *British Medical Journal* 1 (1977), pp. 14–16.

9. C. Mendez-Bauer, in *Journal of Perinatal Medicine* 3 (1975), p. 89; see also F. Howard, "The Application of Certain Principles of Physics to the Physiology of Delivery," *Western Journal of Surgery* 62 (1954), p. 607.

10. A. Blankfield, "The Optimum Position for Childbirth," *Medical Journal of Australia*, 16 October 1965, pp. 666–68.

11. W. F. Mengert and D. P. Murphy, "Intra-abdominal Pressure Created by Voluntary Muscular Effort—Relation to Posture in Labour," *Surgery, Gynaecology and Obstetrics* 57 (1933), pp. 745–51.

12. Howard (see note 5).

13. On placental delivery, see D. Haire, *Cultural Warping of Childbirth* (Milwaukee: International Childbirth Education Association, 1972); M. Botha, "The Management of the Umbilical Cord in Labour," *South African Journal of Obstetrics and Gynaecology* 6, no. 2 (1968), pp. 30–33; A. Beer, "Fetal Erythrocytes in the Maternal Circulation of 155 Rh-Negative Women," *Obstetrics and Gynecology* 34 (1969), pp. 143–50.

14. Blankfield (see note 10).

15. K. O. Vaughan, *Safe Childbirth: The Three Essentials* (London: Ballière, Tindall & Cox, 1937); J. G. B. Russell, in *Journal of Obstetrics and Gynaecology of the British Commonwealth* 76 (1969), p. 817.

16. Howard (see note 5).

17. Naroll et al. (see note 6).

18. For studies on sitting, see Newton and Newton (note 7); M. Goldman et al., "Mechanical Interaction between the Diaphragm and Rib Cage," *Journal of Applied Physiology* 35 (1973), p. 197; Howard (note 5); Mengert and Murphy (note 11); Russell (note 15).

19. Newton and Newton (note 7).

20. C. Beynon, "The Normal Second Stage of Labour," *Journal of Obstetrics and Gynaecology of the British Empire* 64, no. 6 (1957), pp. 185–200.

21. S. Arms, *Immaculate Deception* (Boston: Houghton Mifflin, 1975), p. 143.

22. Blankfield (see note 10).

23. E. Noble, "Kaleidoscope of Childbearing: Preparation, Birth and Nurturing" (paper presented to the 10th Biennial Convention of the International Childbirth Education Association, Kansas City, 1978).

24. J. V. Basmajian, *Muscles Alive: Their Function Revealed by Electromyography*, 3rd ed. (Baltimore: Williams & Wilkins, 1974); E. Agostini et al., "Electromyography of the Diaphragm in Man and Transdiaphragmatic Pressure," *Journal of Applied Physiology* 15 (1960), pp. 1093–97.

25. M. Moore, "The Conduct of the Second Stage," in *Benefits and Hazards of the New Obstetrics*, ed. T. Chard and M. Richards (London: Heinemann, 1977).

26. Beynon (see note 20).

27. Ibid.

28. Caldeyro-Barcia (see note 1), pp. 17–21.

29. Ibid.

30. J. B. De Lee, *The Principles and Practice of Obstetrics* (Philadelphia: W. B. Saunders, 1913).

31. T. N. A. Jeffcoate, in *British Medical Journal* 1 (1950), p. 1361; Beynon (see note 20).

32. Goldman et al. (see note 18), p. 197; V. Derbes and A. Kerr, "Physiological Mechanisms," in *Cough Syncope* (Springfield, Ill.: Charles C Thomas, 1955).

33. See Beynon (note 20) for the study in England; N. Butler, "National Long-term

Study of Perinatal Hazards" (paper presented to the Sixth World Conference, Federation of International Gynaecology and Obstetrics, 1970); W. R. Cohen, in *Obstetrics and Gynecology* 49 (1977), pp. 266–69.

34. M. M. Pennoyer, in *Journal of Pediatrics* 49 (1956), p. 49; for other side effects listed above, see M. L. Brandt, in *American Journal of Obstetrics and Gynecology* 23 (1933), pp. 662–67; M. Myles, *Textbook for Midwives*, 7th ed. (Edinburgh and London: Churchill Livingstone, 1972), p. 297; J. Davis, in *American Journal of Surgery* 48 (1940), p. 154; J. R. Fleigner, in *Medical Journal of Australia*, 26 August 1978, p. 193; F. K. Graham et al, in *Journal of Pediatrics* 50 (1957), p. 557; B. M. Caldwell, F. K. Graham, and M. M. Pennoyer, in ibid. 50 (1957), p. 434; N. Cooperman, F. Robovits, and F. Hesser, in *American Journal of Obstetrics and Gynecology* 81, no. 2 (1961), pp. 385–92.

35. Cooperman et al. (see note 34).

36. Hoult et al. (see note 8).

37. M. Mead, in *Childbearing: Its Social and Psychological Aspects*, ed. S. A. Richardson and A. F. Guttmacher (Baltimore: Williams & Wilkins, 1967), p. 144.

38. J. Burns, *The Principles of Midwifery: Including the Diseases of Women and Children* (New York: Clafton & Van Norden, 1831).

39. S. Merriman, *A Synopsis of the Various Kinds of Difficult Parturition, with Practical Remarks on the Management of Labors* (Philadelphia: Stonehouse, 1816).

40. F. B. Nugent, in *American Journal of Obstetrics and Gynecology* 30 (1935), pp. 249–56.

41. J. Wilmott, "Too Many Episiotomies," *Midwives Chronicle and Nursing Notes*, February 1980, p. 36.

42. L. Mehl et al., "Home versus Hospital Delivery: Comparisons of Matched Populations" (paper presented to annual meeting of the American Public Health Association, Miami Beach, (20 October 1976), reported in *Place of Birth*, ed. S. Kitzinger and J. A. Davis (London: Oxford University Press, 1978), pp. 109–13; I. Chalmers et al., in *British Medical Journal* 1 (1976), pp. 735–38.

43. P. Huntingford, "Obstetric Practice: Past, Present and Future," in Kitzinger and Davis (see note 42), pp. 229–50.

44. Mead (see note 37).

45. Quoted in L. Mehl, G. Peterson, and C. Brandsel, "Episiotomy: Facts, Fictions, Figures and Alternatives," in *Compulsory Hospitalization or Freedom of Choice in Childbirth?*, ed. D. Stuart and L. Stuart (Marble Hill, Mo.: NAPSAC Publications, 1979), chap. 15.

46. Butler (see note 33).

47. For the study, see Mehl et al. (note 45); for confirmation, see M. J. House, "Episiotomy—Indications, Technique and Results," in *Midwife, Health Visitor and Community Nurse*, January 1981, pp. 6–9.

48. M. Newton, L. Mosey, G. E. Egli, W. B. Gifford, and C. T. Hull, "Blood Loss during and Immediately after Delivery," *Obstetrics and Gynecology* 17 (1961), pp. 9–18; Wilmott (see note 41).

49. S. Baker, *A Survey into Postnatal Perineal Discomfort* (London: Royal College of Midwives, 1971).

50. J. J. Nel, in E. Montgomery, *Episiotomy: Physical and Emotional Aspects* (London: National Childbirth Trust, 1972), p. 12.

51. P. C. Buchan and J. A. J. Nicholls, in *Journal of the Royal College of General Practitioners* 30 (1980), pp. 297–300.

52. S. Kitzinger, in Montgomery (see note 50).

53. J. Sleep et al., reported at British Congress of Obstetrics, Birmingham, 14 July 1983.
54. Mehl et al. (see note 42).
55. K. K. Shy and D. A. Essenbach, "Fatal Perineal Cellulitis from an Episiotomy Site," *Obstetrics and Gynecology* 54, no. 3 (1979).
56. For 1968 and 1973 figures, see E. Alberman, "Facts and Figures," in Chard and Richards (note 25); for 1977 and 1979 figures, see Wilmott (note 41).
57. Montgomery (see note 50), p. 2.
58. C. Fieldhouse, "Treatment Note: Ultrasound for Relief of Painful Episiotomy Scars," *Physiotherapy* 65, no. 7 (1979).
59. Arms (see note 21), pp. 90–91; N. W. Cohen and L. J. Estner, *Silent Knife* (South Hadley, Mass.: Bergin & Garvey, 1982); C. Brendsel et al., "Episiotomies: Facts, Fictions, Figures and Alternatives," in Stuart and Stuart (see note 45); M. Mesure et al., *Where to Go: Having a Baby in Philadelphia* (Philadelphia: CHOICE, 1982).
60. For Holland rate, see Mehl et al. (note 45); Arms (note 21), p. 83; F. M. Ettner, *Safe Alternatives in Childbirth* (Marble Hill, Mo.: NAPSAC Publications, 1975). For Reading trial, see Sleep et al. (note 53).
61. R. Caldeyro-Barcia, quoted in Arms (note 21), p. 83.
62. Blankfield (see note 10).
63. Mehl et al. (see note 45); J. Balaskas and A. Balaskas, *New Life* (London: Sidgwick & Jackson, 1979), chap. 4; A. H. Kegel, "Early Genital Relaxation," *Obstetrics and Gynecology* 8, no. 5 (1956).
64. Hoult et al. (see note 8).
65. Wilmott (see note 41).

Chapter Seven The Third Stage: After the Delivery

1. W. M. O. Moore, in *Benefits and Hazards of the New Obstetrics*, ed. T. Chard and M. Richards (London: Heinemann, 1977), p. 120.
2. M. C. Botha, "The Management of the Umbilical Cord in Labour," *South African Journal of Obstetrics and Gynaecology* 16, no. 2 (1968), pp. 30–33.
3. For the Texas figures, see C. F. Gibbs and W. E. Locke, "Maternal Deaths in Texas, 1969–73," *American Journal of Obstetrics and Gynecology* 126 (1976), p. 687; for Oklahoma, see Jimerson and Grosby, in *Oklahoma State Medical Association Journal* 71 (1978), p. 197; for England, see M. M. Garrey et al., *Obstetrics Illustrated* (Edinburgh and London: Churchill Livingstone, 1974), p. 498.
4. J. D. Paull and G. J. Ratten, in *Medical Journal of Australia* 1 (1977), p. 178.
5. Editorial, *Obstetric and Gynecological Survey* 12 (1957), p. 169; W. J. Fitzgerald, in *New York State Journal of Medicine* 58 (1958), p. 4081.
6. E. A. Cameron and E. B. French, in *British Medical Journal* 2 (1960), p. 28.
7. See J. Chassar Moir, "The Obstetrician Bids, and the Uterus Contracts," *British Medical Journal*, 24 October 1964, pp. 1025–30.
8. Ibid., Editorial: "The Relationship of the Recently Discovered Ergot Alkaloids," *British Medical Journal*, 7 December 1935, pp. 1114–16; A. C. Turnbull, in *Postgraduate Medical Journal* 5 Suppl. (1976), pp. 15–16.
9. A. Stoll and Hoffmann, in *Helvetica Chimica Acta* 26 (1943), p. 944; Fitzgerald (see note 5); F. F. Schade, in *American Journal of Obstetrics and Gynecology* 61 (1951), p. 188; R. C. Gill, in *Journal of Obstetrics and Gynaecology of the British Empire* 54 (1947), p. 482.

10. J. M. Munro Kerr and J. Chassar Moir, *Operative Obstetrics,* 5th ed. (London: Ballière, Tindall & Cox, 1949), p. 180; for 1947 view, see Gill (note 9).
11. Chassar Moir (see note 7).
12. B. Sorbe, in *Obstetrics and Gynecology* 52, no. 6 (1978).
13. J. D. Martin and J. G. Dumoulin, in *British Medical Journal* 1 (1953), p. 643; P. Spencer, in *British Medical Journal,* 23 June 1962, pp. 1728–32.
14. Chassar Moir (see note 7).
15. For textbook information, see *Williams' Obstetrics: A Textbook for the Use of Students and Practitioners,* 16th ed. (New York: Appleton, 1980), p. 429; for Philadelphia study, see M. Mesure et al., *Where to Go: Having a Baby in Philadelphia* (Philadelphia: CHOICE, 1982); S. Arms, *Immaculate Deception* (Boston: Houghton Mifflin, 1975), p. 90.
16. S. Olds, *Obstetric Nursing* (Reading, Mass.: Addison-Wesley, 1980), p. 500; N. W. Cohen and L. J. Estner, *Silent Knife* (South Hadley, Mass.: Bergin & Garvey, 1982), p. 196.
17. D. J. Browning, "Serious Side Effects of Ergometrine and Its Use in Routine Obstetric Practice," *Medical Journal of Australia* 1 (1974), pp. 957–58.
18. E. A. Friedman, in *American Journal of Obstetrics and Gynecology* 73 (1957), p. 1306.
19. J. D. Foreman and R. L. Sullivan, in *American Journal of Obstetrics and Gynecology* 63 (1952), p. 640.
20. Turnbull (see note 8); Browning (see note 17); Friedman (see note 18); Foreman and Sullivan (see note 19); C. A. D. Ringrose, in *Canadian Medical Association Journal* 87 (29 September 1962); W. F. Howard et al., in *Journal of the American Medical Association* 189, no. 6 (10 August 1964); N. F. Hacker and J. S. G. Briggs, in *British Journal of Obstetrics and Gynaecology* 86 (August 1979), p. 633.
21. Browning (see note 17); see also C. H. Hendricks and W. E. Brenner, in *American Journal of Obstetrics and Gynecology* 108 (1970), p. 751.
22. For these different studies, see Turnbull (note 8); Browning (note 11); Ringrose (note 20), D. W. J. Cullingford, Letter, *British Medical Journal,* 10 August 1963, p. 386; *Confidential Inquiry into Maternal Deaths* (London: HMSO, 1961–63).
23. P. Vardi, in *Lancet* 2 (1965), p. 12.
24. T. L. Montgomery, in *Clinical Obstetrics and Gynecology* 3 (1960), pp. 900–910.
25. J. M. Gate, Letter, *British Medical Journal* 1 (7 January 1978), p. 49.
26. L. Weinstein et al., in *Obstetrics and Gynecology* 37, no. 1 (1971); S. Z. Walsh, in *Lancet,* 11 May 1968, pp. 996–97; Botha (see note 2).
27. Sorbe (see note 12).
28. C. J. Dewhurst and W. A. W. Dutton, in *Lancet,* 19 October 1957, pp. 764–67; see also L. Snaith, in *Journal of Obstetrics and Gynaecology of the British Empire* 58 (1951), p. 633; Martin and Dumoulin (note 13); C. K. Vartan, in *British Medical Journal* 1 (1953), p. 1108.
29. J. R. Fliegner, in *Medical Journal of Australia,* 26 August 1978, pp. 190–93.
30. Howard et al. (see note 20).
31. M. Newton, L. Mosey, G. Egli, W. B. Gifford, and C. T. Hull, in *Obstetrics and Gynecology* 17 (1961), pp. 9–18.
32. Hacker and Briggs (see note 20).
33. Friedman (see note 18).
34. E. A. Friedman, in *American Journal of Obstetrics and Gynecology* 52 (1946), p. 746.
35. G. L. Clarke and C. P. Douglas, in *Journal of Obstetrics and Gynaecology of the British Commonwealth* 69 (1962), p. 404.
36. Sorbe (see note 12); U. Neiminen and P. A. Järvinen, in *Annales Chirurgiae et Gynaecologiae Fenniae* 53, no. 4 (1964), pp. 424–29.
37. E. M. Greenberg, in *American Journal of Obstetrics and Gynecology* 52 (1946), p. 746.

38. Ringrose (see note 20).

39. Moore (see note 1).

40. *Association of Radical Midwives, Minutes, meeting in Boston, 26–28 October 1979.*

41. S. Z. Walsh, in *Lancet,* 11 May 1966, pp. 996–97.

42. Howard et al. (see note 20).

43. J. H. Patterson, Letter, *British Medical Journal,* 15 October 1966; Clarke and Douglas (see note 35); Paull and Ratten (see note 4); Munro Kerr and Chassar Moir (see note 10), p. 807.

44. M. Mead and N. Newton, "Cultural Patterning of Perinatal Behavior," in *Childbearing: Its Social and Psychological Aspects,* ed. S. A. Richardson and A. F. Guttmacher (Baltimore: Williams & Wilkins, 1967); C. S. Ford, "A Comparative Study of Human Reproduction," *Yale University Publications in Anthropology,* no. 32 (New Haven: Yale University Press, 1945).

45. Mead and Newton (see note 44), p. 144.

46. A. E. B. De Courcy-Wheeler, in *British Medical Journal,* 18 August 1973.

47. Botha (see note 2).

48. C. Darwin, quoted by L. Courtney, in *British Medical Journal,* 28 July 1973, p. 236; A. F. Meadows, *Manual of Midwifery,* 4th ed. (London: Henry Renshaw, 1882), p. 192.

49. J. R. C. Burton-Brown, in *Journal of Obstetrics and Gynaecology of the British Empire* 56 (1949), pp. 847–55; M. L. Brandt, in *American Journal of Obstetrics and Gynecology* 23 (1933), pp. 662–67.

50. Györy and Damahidy, in *Mschr. Geburtsh. Gynak.* 118 (1944), p. 192.

51. Botha (see note 2).

52. Ibid.; on "fundal fiddling," see Brandt (note 49).

53. S. Z. Walsh, in *Lancet* 1 (1968), p. 996.

54. Botha (see note 2).

55. Ibid.

56. Brandt (see note 49).

57. O. A. Lapido, in *British Medical Journal* 1 (1972), pp. 721–23.

58. See P. M. Dunn, I. D. Frazer, and A. B. Raper, in *Journal of Obstetrics and Gynaecology of the British Commonwealth* 73 (1966), pp. 757–60; J. E. Doolittle and C. R. Moritz, in *Obstetrics and Gynecology* 27 (1966), p. 529, and in ibid. 22 (1963), p. 468; Lapido (note 57); D. A. Berriman, in *Midwives Chronicle and Nursing Notes,* March 1970; L. Weinstein et al., in *Obstetrics and Gynecology* 37, no. 1 (1971), pp. 70–73.

59. Berriman (see note 58); Lapido (see note 57).

60. Clarke and Douglas (see note 35).

61. Montgomery (see note 24).

62. Ibid.

63. The studies cited in this paragraph are A. J. Moss and M. Monset-Couchard, in *Pediatrics* 40, no. 1 (July 1967); A. C. Yao and J. Lind, "Placental Transfusion," *American Journal of the Diseases of Childhood* 127 (1974), pp. 128–41; J. Lind, W. Oh, and M. A. Oh, in *Acta Paediatrica Scandinavica* 56 (1966), p. 197; L. D. Courtney, Letter, *British Medical Journal,* 28 July 1973, p. 236 (reported in G. S. Dawes, *Fetal and Neonatal Physiology* [Chicago: Year Book Medical Publishers, 1968]); Vardi (see note 23); J. W. Williams, *Obstetrics,* 4th ed. (New York: Appleton, 1919), p. 298.

64. Gate (see note 25).

65. A. C. Yao and J. Lind, in *Birth and the Family Journal* 4, no. 3 (1977), p. 91.

66. Moss and Monset-Couchard (see note 63); for the other research cited above, see A. Redmond, S. Isana, and D. Ingall, in *Lancet* 1 (1965), p. 283; Courtney (note

63); A. J. Moss, E. D. Duffie, and L. M. Fagan, in *Journal of the American Medical Association* 184 (1963), p. 48.

67. R. D. Laing, quoted in Brook, *Nature Birth* (Harmondsworth, Eng.: Penguin, 1976), pp. 92–95.

68. Botha (see note 2).

69. Brandt (see note 49); for a discussion of Mauriceau's treatise, see also Botha (note 2).

70. J. H. Patterson, Letter, *British Medical Journal* 1 (1964), p. 377; J. Barnes, "Emergencies in General Practice—Postpartum Maternal Collapse," *British Medical Journal*, 28 May 1955, p. 1333.

71. Barnes (see note 70); on Crede, see also Patterson (note 70).

72. B. M. Hibbard, in *British Medical Journal* 1 (1964), p. 1485; Brandt (see note 49); I. Donald, *Practical Obstetric Problems* (London: Lloyd-Luke, 1974), p. 682; J. R. Fliegner, in *Medical Journal of Australia*, 26 August 1978, p. 193.

73. J. H. Patterson, Letter, *British Medical Journal*, 31 August 1963, p. 563. On Ahlfeld, see Patterson (note 70).

74. J. R. Fliegner and B. M. Hibbard, "The Active Management of the Third Stage of Labour," *British Medical Journal*, 10 September 1966, p. 623.

75. Brandt (see note 49).

76. J. Kemp, Letter, *British Medical Journal*, 31 August 1963, p. 563; M. R. Fell, Letter, *British Medical Journal*, 15 October 1966.

77. Fliegner and Hibbard (note 74); Fell (note 76).

78. Patterson (see note 70). For the 30-minute findings, see Fliegner and Hibbard (note 74); for the 10-minute findings, see Walsh (note 53); Botha (note 2).

79. W. M. O. Moore (see note 1).

80. A. N. Cowan, Letter, *British Medical Journal*, 10 August 1963, p. 387.

81. F. Leboyer, *Birth without Violence* (New York: Alfred A. Knopf, 1975).

82. J. M. Weekly, in *Obstetrics and Gynecology News* 1 (1 August 1975); Anon., in *Medical World News* 16, no. 10 (1975), pp. 22–30; N. Whitely, in *Journal of Nurse Midwifery* 21 (1976), pp. 27–28.

83. A. Macfarlane, *The Psychology of Childbirth* (London: Fontana/Open Books, 1977), p. 19.

84. J. Lind, "The Family in the Birth Room," *Birth and the Family Journal* 5, no. 4 (1978), p. 25. For the finding on sound above, see D. Walker et al., "Intrauterine Noise—a Component of the Fetal Environment," *American Journal of Obstetrics and Gynecology* 109 (1971), pp. 91–95.

85. N. M. Nelson et al., "A Randomized Clinical Trial of the Leboyer Approach to Childbirth," *New England Journal of Medicine* 302 (1980), pp. 655–60. On the infrared heater, see L. S. Dahm and L. S. James, "Newborn Temperature and Calculated Heat Loss in the Delivery Room," *Pediatrics* 49, no. 4 (1972), pp. 504–13.

86. D. Rappoport, in *Bulletin psychologique* 29 (1976), pp. 552–60.

87. Nelson et al. (see note 85).

88. G. Chamberlain et al., *British Births 1970*, vol. 2: *Obstetric Care* (London: Heinemann, 1978).

89. D. Garrow, cited in S. Kitzinger, *Birth at Home* (London: Oxford University Press, 1979), p. 40.

90. L. Cordero and E. Hon, "Neonatal Bradycardia Following Nasopharyngeal Stimulation," *Journal of Pediatrics* 78, no. 3 (1971), pp. 441–47.

91. M. Myles, *Textbook for Midwives*, 7th ed. (Edinburgh and London: Churchill Livingstone, 1972), p. 310.

92. See Leboyer (note 81); R. Salter, in *Medical News* 12, no. 44 (1980), p. 10.

93. C. Phillips, "Neonatal Heat Loss in Heat Cribs v. Mothers' Arms," *Journal of the Nurses Association of the American College of Obstetricians and Gynecologists* 3, no. 6 (1974); M. Cornblath and R. Schwartz, *Disorders of Carbohydrate Metabolism in Infancy* (Philadelphia: W. B. Saunders, 1966); J. M. Stephenson et al., "The Effect of Cooling on Blood Gas Tensions in Newly Born Human Infants," cited in Dahm and James (see note 85); D. A. Fisher, T. H. Oddie, and E. J. Makoski, in *Pediatrics* 37 (1966), p. 583; L. Stern et al., in ibid. 36 (1965), p. 367; D. Schiff, L. Stern, and J. Leduc, in ibid. 37 (1966), p. 577.

94. Phillips (see note 93).

95. M. Klaus and J. Kennell, "Human Maternal Behavior at First Contact with Her Young," *Pediatrics* 46, no. 2 (1970), pp. 187–92.

96. Macfarlane (see note 83), p. 51.

97. D. Hales et al., "How Early Is Early Contact? Defining the Limits of the Sensitive Period," *Pediatric Research* 10 (1977), p. 448; P. de Chateau et al., in *Birth and the Family Journal* 3 (Winter 1979), p. 149.

98. Dahm and James (see note 85).

99. A. MacLennan, personal communication (Adelaide Hospital, 1970).

100. D. C. Turk and I. A. Porter, *A Short Textbook of Medical Microbiology* (London: English Universities Press, 1969), pp. 94–95.

101. M. Myles, *Textbook for Midwives*, 8th ed. (Edinburgh and London: Churchill Livingstone, 1981), pp. 560–61.

102. H. L. Ormsby, "Ophthalmia Neonatorum," *Canadian Medical Association Journal* 72 (1955), pp. 576–80; E. B. Shaw, "Should Silver Nitrate as a Routine Be Abandoned?," *NAPSAC News* 4, no. 1 (Spring 1979), pp. 5–6; J. Gottlieb and W. Freeman, in *Maine Medical Journal* 25 (February 1934), p. 28.

103. H. Nishida and H. M. Risemberg, "Silver Nitrate Ophthalmic Solution and Chemical Conjunctivitis," *Pediatrics* 56, no. 3 (1975), pp. 368–72; E. B. Shaw, Letter, in *New England Journal of Medicine* 274, no. 13 (1966), p. 281; M. Kallings and V. Wahlberg, "Antibacterial Effects of Silver Nitrate as Used for Crede's Prophylaxis and of a Colloidal Silver Compound—Hexarginum," *Acta Paediatrica Scandinavica* Suppl. 295 (1982), pp. 37–42; S. Yasunaga and E. H. Kean, "Effects of Three Ophthalmic Solutions on Chemical Conjunctivitis in the Neonate," *American Journal of Diseases of Children* 131 (February 1977), pp. 159–61.

104. L. Lehrfeld, "Limitations of the Use of Silver Nitrate in Prevention of Ophthalmia Neonatorum," *Journal of the American Medical Association*, 27 April 1935, pp. 1468–69; H. H. Seedorff, "Is Prophylactic Treatment of the Eyes of the Newborn Infants Still Necessary?," *Danish Medical Bulletin* 7, no. 5 (1960), pp. 128–32.

105. M. Greenberg and J. E. Vandow, "Ophthalmia Neonatorum: Evaluation of Different Methods of Prophylaxis in New York City," *American Journal of Public Health* 51, no. 6 (1961), pp. 836–45. For a sampling of the inconclusive and conflicting research, see Ormsby (note 102); Seedorff (note 104); M. S. Mayan, "Observations on Ophthalmia Neonatorum" (unpublished report to the Department of Health, Province of Ontario, 1953), cited in Ormsby (note 102); Lehrfeld (note 104); H. E. Pearson, "Failure of Silver Nitrate Prophylaxis for Gonococcal Ophthalmia Neonatorum," *American Journal of Obstetrics and Gynecology* 73, no. 4 (April 1957), pp. 805–807; J. H. Armstrong, F. Zacarias, and M. F. Rein, "Ophthalmia Neonatorum: A Chart Review," *Pediatrics* 57, no. 6 (June 1976), pp. 884–92.

106. Greenberg and Vandow (see note 105).

107. Kallings and Wahlberg (see note 103).

108. Ibid.

109. Yasunaga and Kean (see note 103); H. Mallek, P. Spohn, and J. Mallek, "On the Comparative Use of Silver Nitrate and Penicillin in the Eyes of the Newborn,"

Canadian Medical Association Journal 68 (February 1953), pp. 117–19; Nishida and Risemberg (see note 103); J. R. Christian, "Comparison of Ocular Reactions with the Use of Silver Nitrate and Erythromycin Ointment in Ophthalmia Neonatorum Prophylaxis," *Journal of Pediatrics* 57, no. 1 (1960), pp. 55–60; Greenberg and Vandow (see note 105).

110. American Academy of Pediatrics, "Prophylaxis and Treatment of Neonatal Gonococcal Infections," *Pediatrics* 65, no. 5 (May 1980), pp. 1047–48. For reports on disadvantages, see also Committee for the National Prevention of Blindness, "Control of Ophthalmia Neonatorum," *Sightsaving Review* 43 (1973), pp. 11–13; D. J. Lyle, "Allergic Reaction of a Previously Sensitized Eye to Parenteral Penicillin," *American Journal of Opthalmology* 31 (1948), p. 1490; American Academy of Pediatrics, *Standards and Recommendations for Hospital Care of Newborn Infants*, 5th ed. (Evanston, Ill., 1971), pp. 103–4; J. F. Martin et al., "Comparative Study of Gonococcal Sensitivity to Penicillin in the United States, 1955–69," *Journal of Infectious Diseases* 122 (1970), p. 459; G. L. Spaeth, "Treatment of Penicillin-Resistant Gonococcal Conjunctivitis with Ampicillin," *American Journal of Ophthalmology* 66 (1968), p. 427.

111. H. H. Seedorff (see note 104); P. C. Barsam, "Specific Prophylaxis of Gonorrheal Ophthalmia Neonatorum," *New England Journal of Medicine* 274, no. 13 (1966), pp. 731–34.

112. Kalling and Wahlberg (see note 103); see also Nishida and Risemberg (note 103).

113. P. M. Butterfield, "Does the Early Application of Silver Nitrate Impair Maternal Attachment?," *Pediatrics* 67, no. 5 (May 1981), pp. 737–38.

114. V. Wahlberg, "Reconsideration of Crede's Prophylaxis," *Acta Paediatrica Scandinavica* Suppl. 295 (1982), p. 17.

115. Department of Health and Social Services, *Health and Personal Social Services Statistics for England 1977* (London: HMSO, 1977); Office of Population Censuses and Surveys, *Communicable Disease Statistics*, Series MB2, no. 4 (London: HMSO, 1982), table 1A; *Blindness and Partial Sight in England 1969–76*, Reports on Public Health and Medical Subjects, no. 129 (London: HMSO, 1979), tables 5A, 8A.

116. W. B. Boone et al., "Ophthalmia Neonatorum: Value of Prophylactic Treatment," *Minnesota Medicine* 56 (1973), pp. 940–43.

117. Wahlberg (see note 114); Greenberg and Vandow (see note 105).

118. G. J. Annas, "Legal Aspects of Homebirths and Other Child Birth Alternatives," in *Safe Alternatives in Childbirth*, ed. D. Stewart and L. Stewart (Marble Hill, Mo.: NAPSAC, 1976).

119. Cohen and Estner, (see note 16).

120. S. Kitzinger, in *Place of Birth*, ed. S. Kitzinger and J. Davis (London: Oxford University Press, 1978), p. 136.

121. S. O'Connor, K. B. Sherrod, H. M. Sandler, and P. M. Vietze, in *Birth and the Family Journal* 5, no. 4 (1978).

122. M. Klaus, in "Symposium: Parent-Infant Attachment," *Birth and the Family Journal* 5, no. 4 (1978).

123. S. Kitzinger, *Women as Mothers* (London: Fontana, 1978).

124. De Chateau et al. (see note 97).

125. T. B. Brazelton, in "Symposium: Parent-Infant Attachment," *Birth and the Family Journal* 5, no. 4 (1978); O'Connor et al. (see note 121).

126. M. Klaus, "The Biology of Parent-to-Infant Attachment," *Birth and the Family Journal* 5, no. 4 (1978), pp. 200–203.

127. A. Macfarlane (see note 83), p. 102.

128. H. Leiderman and M. Seashore, cited in ibid., p. 99.

129. M. Klaus and J. Kennell, "Maternal Attachment—Importance of the First Post-partum Days," *New England Journal of Medicine* 286 (1972), p. 460.

130. D. Harvey, in *Breastfeeding Promotion Group News* 11 (National Childbirth Trust, November 1980), p. 10.

131. P. Stanway and A. Stanway, *Breast Is Best* (London: Pan, 1978), p. 25.

132. Leboyer (see note 81).

133. C. Fisher, "Successful Breast Feeding," in *Chatelaine's 'New Mother,'* ed. M. Isatona (Toronto: MacLean & Hunter, 1980).

Chapter Eight   Alternatives and Improvements

1. J. H. Meyer (International Editor, *Journal of Nurse Midwifery,*), personal communication (1974); Report of the Work of the Central Midwives Board (1980; available from United Kingdom Central Council).

2. B. Hunter, "Midwifery in America," *Association of Radical Midwives' Newsletter* 15 (Autumn 1982), pp. 14–15.

3. E. Alberman, "Facts and Figures," in *Benefits and Hazards of the New Obstetrics,* ed. T. Chard and M. Richards (London: Heinemann, 1977).

4. P. J. Placek, S. Taffel, and M. Moien, "Cesarean Section Delivery Rates in the United States, 1981," *American Journal of Public Health* 73, no. 8, (August 1983), pp. 861–62.

5. L. E. Mehl (see note 11, Chapter One); also see "Nosocomial Infection Surveillance: 1980–1982," in Center for Disease Control, *Mortality and Morbidity Weekly Report Survey* 32, no. 4ss (November 1983) pp. 1ss–16ss; and "Summary of the Workshop on Perinatal Infections Due to Group B Streptococcus," in National Institutes of Health, *Journal of Infectious Diseases* 136 (1977) pp. 137–52.

6. G. Chamberlain et al., *British Births 1970,* vol. 2: *Obstetric Care* (London: Heinemann, 1978).

7. G. Kloosterman, in S. Arms, *Immaculate Deception* (Boston: Houghton Mifflin, 1975), p. 287; G. Chamberlain et al. (see note 6); L. E. Mehl (see note 5).

8. A. N. Bennetts and R. W. Lubic, "The Free-Standing Birth Centre," *Lancet,* February 1982, pp. 378–80.

9. F. Leboyer, *Birth without Violence* (New York: Alfred A. Knopf, 1975); M. Odent, *Birth Reborn* (New York: Pantheon Books, 1984).

10. American College of Nurse-Midwives, 1000 Vermont Avenue N. W., Washington, D.C. 20005. Two consumer-oriented information organizations are the National Association of Parents and Professionals for Safe Alternatives in Childbirth (NAP-SAC), PO Box 267, Marble Hill, Mo. 63764; and the International Childbirth Education Association (ICEA), PO Box 20852, Milwaukee, Wis. 53220.

11. P. Simkin, in *Birth* 10, no. 3 (Fall 1983), pp. 184–85.

12. M. Klein, in *Birth* 10, no. 3 (Fall 1983), p. 182; M. Klein, "Contracting for Trust in Family Practice Obstetrics," *Canadian Family Physician* 29 (1983), pp. 2225–27.

13. E. H. Shabanah, A. Toth, and G. B. Maughan, "The Role of the Autonomic Nervous System in Uterine Contractility and Blood Flow," *American Journal of Obstetrics and Gynecology* 89, no. 7 (1964), pp. 841–59.

14. J. K. Burns, "Relation between Blood Levels of Cortisol and Duration of Human Labor," *Journal of Physiology* 254 (1976), p. 12; R. P. Leiderman et al., "The Relationship of Maternal Anxiety, Plasma Catacholamines and Plasma Cortisol

to Progression in Labor," *American Journal of Obstetrics and Gynecology* 132 (1973), pp. 495–500; E. Leiderman et al., "Maternal Psychological and Physiologic Correlates of Fetal-Newborn Health Status," ibid. 139 (1981), pp. 956–58.

Appendix: *The Cascade of Intervention*

1. M. Blancow, M. N. Smith, M. Graham, and R. G. Wilson, in *Lancet* 1 (1975), p. 217.
2. I. Chalmers, H. Campbell, and A. C. Turnbull, in *British Medical Journal* 2 (1975), p. 116.
3. A. A. Calder and M. P. Embury, in *The Management of Labour: Proceedings of the Royal College of Obstetricians and Gynaecologists Third Study Group* (London, 1975), p. 64.
4. W. A. Liston and A. J. Campbell, in *British Medical Journal* 3 (1974), p. 606.
5. M. P. M. Richards, in *Early Human Development* 1 (1977) , p. 3.
6. I. Chalmers, J. G. Lawson, and A. C. Turnbull, in *British Journal of Obstetrics and Gynaecology* 83 (1976), p. 921.
7. J. Arroyo and C. J. Mendez-Bauer, in *Perinatal Medicine* 3 (1975), p. 129.
8. I. J. Hoult, A. H. MacLennan, and L. E. S. Carrie, in *British Medical Journal* 1 (1977), p. 14.
9. P. R. S. Brinsden and A. D. Clark, in *British Medical Journal* 2 (1978), pp. 855–56.
10. P. Yudkin, A. M. Frumar, A. B. M. Anderson, and A. C. Turnbull, "A Retrospective Study of Induction of Labour," *British Journal of Obstetrics and Gynaecology* 86, no. 4 (1979), pp. 257–65.
11. M. Newton, L. Mosey, G. E. Egli, W. B. Gifford, and C. T. Hull, "Blood Loss during and Immediately after Delivery," *Obstetrics and Gynecology* 17 (1961), pp. 9–18.
12. M. A. Lyon, in *Lancet* 2 (1975), p. 317.
13. E. A. Friedman, M. R. Sachtleben, and B. A. Bresky, in *American Journal of Obstetrics and Gynecology* 127 (1977), p. 779.

INDEX

About the Author

Sally Inch was trained at Oxford, and is now an advanced childbirth educator for the National Childbirth Trust in England.